LOVE THE DARK DAYS

DEDICATION

My grandparents: Shahnur Jehan Begum & Saied-Uz-Zafar Khan

father and mother: Col. Mahendra Nath Mathur & Anvar Zia
Sultana Khan-Mathur

children: Anika & Kiran
siblings: Winky & Rashmi
Anoushka, & Arun, Priyanka & Sanjana,
Khaleeq, Aialia, Nathiel

Monique Roffey
Amanda Smyth
Jeremy Poynting
Jacob Ross

beloved: Imshah

&

Derek Walcott

Several people in this book are given pseudonyms, not so much to prevent identification, but to remind the reader that these people are seen through the prism of my individual perceptions and memory, which are as truthful and fictive as perception and memory always are. Based on actual events, the scenes and dialogues make up my very particular view of what happened. I have recreated situations and conversations that are as truthful as memory allows, but this is truth to the shape of the writing process I was engaged in, not the truth of recorded and verifiable facts. There must be as many versions to this as there are people and characters inhabiting this book.

IRA MATHUR

LOVE THE DARK DAYS

PEEPAL TREE

First published in Great Britain in 2022
by Peepal Tree Press Ltd
17 King's Avenue
Leeds LS6 1QS
England

ISBN13: 97818452325352

Printed in the United Kingdom by
Severn, Gloucester,
on responsibly sourced paper

Supported using public funding by
ARTS COUNCIL
ENGLAND

PART ONE

And did you get what
you wanted from this life, even so?
I did.
And what did you want?
To call myself beloved, to feel myself
beloved on the earth.
— Late Fragment by Raymond Carver

ONE

Kelly Village, Trinidad, 2000

I would like to see a kite in the blank blue sky. This rootless place of sameness is not where she, or we, thought she would end her days.

Mummy, Daddy, Winky, Angel and I have been standing under the shed watching Burrimummy's grave being dug. She has been dead for less than twenty-four hours.

The noonday sun bounces off lumpy graves covered in thick weedy grass, off whitewashed houses on stilts, skims over the fields to the narrow river where it rests its egg-yolk reflection.

Burrimummy is inside an open wooden box on the concrete floor to our right, swaddled from head to foot like a mummy in two yards of white cotton. This is the two yards of white cotton she always talked about, carried about with her, repeatedly replaced. It is now being put to use.

Her creamy skin, of which she was so proud, is now a marmoreal jaundiced yellow, its dull shine reflecting the harsh light as if it were a crumbling bust in a museum.

The round-faced mortician with the red-hennaed beard informed us he had turned her head to the East the previous night, 'before she get too stiff.'

It is so quiet I can hear the flapping of Angel's white dupatta against her narrow shoulders.

Angel never thought Burrimummy would actually die. My first memory of Angel is of a chubby, pink-faced three-year-old, stumbling around in the many rooms of Rest House Road crying, saying that Burrimummy was 'dying of a broken heart'. Burrimummy had then appeared and asked, 'What would Angel do in this big house by herself?' The two wept, unaware of anyone else.

Angel says 'no' decidedly when the mortician says this is our last chance to touch her face. She had already had her time doing that yesterday evening when she lay down on Burrimummy's bed with her and stroked her still warm face for almost an hour until the white van came to take Burrimummy away. When the paperwork was finished and the body released from the nursing home, Angel wanted to climb in because, as she explained patiently to everyone who tried to prevent her, 'Burrimummy will be alone. She needs me.'

We held Angel back while the van raced into the dark.

If I close my eyes, I reach back to the beginning when we were young and in her care in 17 Rest House Road.

Bangalore, India, 1976

It's three in the afternoon; the end of the school day.

The nuns of the Sacred Heart Girls' High School unlock the heavy padlock and pull open the tall, black, wrought-iron gates, releasing girls in white, pleated uniforms and red ties into the bustle of Bangalore's fashionable Brigade Road.

My sister Angel and I are carried along with the flow, a jumble of elbows and legs. Angel is seven; I am ten.

I spot our ayah's enormous yellow-and-red striped umbrella before I see her. Khaja is one of Burrimummy's oldest servants; she is here to take us on the short walk home. She is a tall, lantern-jawed woman whose thin cotton sari does nothing to disguise her angular limbs. The sharp point of her umbrella is a weapon dodged by drivers, ayahs and orderlies. She looks after Angel, not me. She gives me a warning look.

Ignoring Khaja, I duck behind the other girls and shove towards the vendors' carts where flies circle sliced green mangoes and cucumbers. I push between the jumping schoolgirls waving their money and thrust a crumpled rupee note at the vendor.

I return with sour cucumber in powdered chilli pepper, wrapped in newspaper. Salty water seeps through, making my hands sticky.

Khaja holds Angel with one hand and balances the umbrella over her head.

'Baby, baby, don't eat that,' she screeches at me.

I bite into the fly-infested vegetable.

'Want some, Angel?'

'No, Baby!' Khaja cuts in sharply. 'Your grandmother will be angry. Angel baby will get sick.'

Angel lives with Burrimummy all the time.

I am sent to Burrimummy for months at a time when Mummy is tired. Mummy says army life is a strain with constant moving and all the cocktail parties.

We pass Bishop Cotton Boys', a rectangular redbrick building next to our school. Mummy can't manage Winky either because he's impossible to control. When Mummy was unpacking her china in Chandigarh, he said, 'I can jump over glass. Want to bet?' Before she could stop him, Winky took a giant leap and landed in the middle of her dinner set, sending glass everywhere and ended up with a bleeding chin. Mummy had had enough and put him on a flight to Bangalore to live with Burrimummy.

I stop to look back at the boys walking out of Bishop Cotton Boys' School dressed in white shirts, blue ties and khaki shorts, hoping Winky will be one of them. But he never is, even though at fourteen, he sometimes gets to leave the compound. Winky boards at Bishop Cottons because he was rude to Burrimummy, calling her a Pakistani spy after Burrimummy caught him shooting rubber bands at the servants' quarters from the terrace. I was standing with him when she hauled him down and booked a trunk call to Simla, bellowing at Mummy for bringing up her son like an infidel. She wouldn't keep her Hindu grandson for a moment longer under her roof. 'Do what you think is best,' Mummy told her. Burrimummy marched Winky to Bishop Cottons and admitted him as a boarder with immediate effect. I begged and begged her, but she refused to take him back.

I don't know why, but I always felt afraid I wouldn't see Winky again. I remember listening to the radio news with Mummy when we lived in Guwahati. Mummy screamed. A school bus had turned over on a slope near a tea plantation, and children may have been killed. It was always raining in Guwahati, and I climbed up on a stool watching the rain on the window and sobbed until Winky came charging in.

Winky has lived with Mummy and Daddy the longest, moving with them from Calcutta, where he was born, then Guwahati, where I was born. We got broken up when Angel was born in Sagar, and Burrimummy came to look after Mummy and took Angel away at just five days old and never gave her back. We four kept moving to Chandigarh, Bangalore, Simla, but Angel stayed in Bangalore – that's why she's a civilian, we military.

Winky and I are always last in class because of the changing languages in the different states we've moved to. Apart from English and Hindi, we need to learn Punjabi, Himalayan and Kannada. The resulting incomprehension bleeds into maths, geography and history. I feel I don't belong here or anywhere. In class I pretend I'm not me, and the not-me is not there. That's why I don't mind being short-sighted. I don't mind the foggy blackboard because it reminds me of Simla before the snowfalls.

Our teachers are Irish nuns, Anglo-Indian and South Indian women. Only two are men. The PE teacher is stern-looking with sensual lips and a moustache; the male art teacher has a pink harelip. A week ago, he drew a bird in ink and smudged it as he went along. That smudge was the only thing that made sense to me. When a teacher draws attention to one of my shortcomings – forgetting homework, not copying from the blackboard, not understanding – I imagine floating outside, feeling sunshade and breeze and hear the teacher from far away through the chattering of insects. I hear no shouting and feel no shame.

Even when Daddy was posted to Bangalore, and Winky, Mummy and

I lived together in St John's Road, near the officers' mess, Angel never came to stay, except for one night when Burrimummy, wearing a crisp white linen sari, dark glasses and her lips in a flattened red line, brought Angel from Rest House Road, looking as if she was going to a funeral. Mummy met them at the door in her dressing gown, halfway through getting ready to go out, as she and Daddy did every evening. When Burrimummy drove away out of the circular driveway, Angel strained to watch her car long after it was gone, standing on the veranda like a statue, refusing to come in. Mummy asked me to take her to the dining room where dinner was laid out, and she took my hand, but once inside Angel walked backwards until she was standing against the dining room wall and wouldn't touch her food, so before Mummy and Daddy left for a dance at the officers' mess, Mummy gave her my doll, which had blonde curly hair and was almost two-feet tall. I brought her to my bedroom and let her hold my doll in my bed.

I thought how nice it would be if she lived with us. With my arms around her, I tried to convince her St Johns Road was a place of fun, but she said it looked like school, with halls and wooden floors, so I told her of the nights Mummy and Daddy gave parties, how the floors shone, and silver gleamed like mirrors. Lots of people came; the army band played, and the grownups danced in the drawing room; wandered about in the garden and drank and swayed and kissed people who weren't married to them. Once I saw a couple near the swing under the tamarind tree; they looked as if they were wrestling, but now I knew what it was, and I told Angel I would tell her if she lived with us. I told her Mummy was always the loveliest of them all in her chiffons and neon silks; how Daddy looked like the actor Dharmendra in his dark evening suits. I told her the orderly played Snakes and Ladders with me when they went out.

Angel looked at me with large uncomforted eyes. I didn't tell her that I would often hear shouting; glass would be thrown and shattered; then they would go to bed. Desperate for her to unfreeze, sleep and not lie down like a doll with its eyes permanently open, I told her we could go outside and play Winky's grownup game. The shouts outside were him pretending to be Daddy ordering the orderlies. Winky made the servants turn off the lights, and they would walk through the dark house looking for Pakistani spies and then go into the garden with a flashlight and knife, where they would follow him around the walled house, behind the long deep shadows of the tamarind tree. Angel remained motionless. I told her how when Winky's friends came to play, he let me play *Dhakka* with them – it was like hide-and-seek except you had to hit the person who got caught hard on the back and then they were 'it'. The boys hit me hard whenever I played, and I would be 'it' for hours because I never caught them. When Angel turned away, I continued, even though I was aware I was making it worse, telling her how Winky played *kabaddi* and sometimes wrestled the boy servant right down to the ground. I told her about how the mummy rabbit ate the bunny in the hutch we kept at the bottom of the garden and we'd found the bones. When she began to cry loudly, I stopped.

Mummy had to call Burrimummy to fetch her back to Rest House Road the following day. The two of them ran to one another as if they had been holding their breaths all along and could finally breathe. After, I found my doll's legs had been wrenched out. I went wailing to Mummy saying I would thrash Angel when I saw her next. Mummy slapped me for saying such cruel thing about my little sister.

The afternoon traffic is revving – scooters, autorickshaws, cars – tooting and disappearing. Our stunted shadows are barely visible on the concrete. Khaja darts behind us to provide cover from the sun for the five-minute walk to Rest House Road. I dodge the umbrella to keep her hopping about on the pavement.

Angel walks placidly behind me under the umbrella, her hand in Khaja's while I skip around, past giant movie billboards of voluptuous actresses displaying cleavages and candy-pink-and-white made-up faces. Like Angel. And Mummy.

Angel, tucked obediently under Khaja's umbrella, says, 'Can you save some cucumber for me, Aapa?' She uses the respectful term for older sister. She has exquisite manners. 'I'll have it when Khaja isn't looking.'

Burrimummy would be furious with me if I gave Angel some. She says Angel is delicate and quickly gets infections and colds, especially from filthy outside food. I eat it all by myself, making huge licking sounds, saying, 'Khatta, khatta, nice and sour.'

I am dark and thin with wispy brown hair; Angel is fair, plump, with slanting light eyes and cupid-bow lips – so red the teacher once checked her for lipstick. That's why Burrimummy calls her Angel, after her own mother. Her thick black hair is neatly plaited and held in place with rubber bands and red ribbons. Mine won't go black or thick – even with daily applications of olive oil. Winky is dark, but Burrimummy says that's okay because he's a boy, handsome and tall.

Angel edges towards me, and I shoo her away. Sometimes, I forget I hate her for getting me into trouble, and we play as sisters. Last week we stuffed newspapers into a broken piano stool and covered it with a cloth and laughed and laughed when the Anglo-Indian piano teacher, Miss Mosquito, fell into it, her bony hip sinking deep inside the chair. When she said she wanted her money and was never coming back, Burrimummy thrashed me, breaking a slipper on my back. Angel can prevent Burrimummy from beating me with just a look – if she feels like it – but that time she put her thumb in her mouth and watched. Burrimummy never beats her.

I wanted to teach Burrimummy a lesson for that thrashing, so yesterday,

instead of coming home with Khaja after school, I asked my army friend
Saloni if I could go home with her in the army truck. I wanted Burrimummy to be worried about me. Saloni's mother believed me when I said
Burrimummy had given me permission to spend the night. She gave me a
frock to change into, made sure I ate properly at dinner, put me in Saloni's
pyjamas and tucked us into bed. After breakfast, her father took us to school
in his army uniform, making me miss Daddy more. The last time Daddy
came to Bangalore, he took me to a Laurel and Hardy movie – to watch me
watching the film to see me laugh – and then to the officers' mess where
I drank lime juice in the garden with the grownups. Everyone is always
saluting my handsome daddy.

Khaja says, 'Burrimummy is furious. Whole night she wanted to know
where you were.'

Angel says, 'Yes, Poppet Aapa, she is. Saloni's mummy phoned early this
morning, saying her driver would drop you off to school. Since then,
Burrimummy's been shouting and shouting.'

My palms are sweaty; I know I will get another thrashing today. I dawdle.
I don't want to go to 17 Rest House Road. I stop to stare at the chauffeur-
driven cars with curtains for women in purdah and jump out of the way of
sputtering lorries spilling grey fumes. Men riding scooters and cycles with
women holding on tight, their kurtas and saris flapping around them, swish
past us.

Khaja makes us cross the street to avoid Cubbon Park. Its large shadowy
grounds – laid out with shrubs and flower beds, benches and little paths –
feel dangerous. Burrimummy says the park is for low-class people.

I've been there with the servants' children in the afternoon while
Burrimummy and Angel nap. Men and women do vulgar things there,
fondling and whispering under dense trees. Flies, bees, armies of ants, and
endlessly chirping insects hover around oozing fruit on the damp ground.
As we pass, I play games with my eyes, blinking at the imprint of the green
of the park, the flash of South Indian saris, the light in the puddles of water.
Then I pretend I'm blind, put my hands out, palms up while walking. Khaja
roughly straightens me when I collide with a beggar.

'If you behave like this,' she tells me, 'Burrimummy will write to your
Mummy.'

I haven't seen Mummy in months.

The last time she flew to Bangalore, she had to come from Simla to see
me. Mummy said she dreamt I was wearing a white dress, floating towards
her, asking for her. She missed me so much she came to the school straight
from the airport. With her peach lipstick, shades and a chiffon sari, she
caused a sensation among the dark South Indian girls. She took me, but not
Angel, out of school for the day.

We sped out of the school in the army jeep to the silk sari shop, where we spent the morning. Two male attendants leapt about, throwing open bolts of silks, chiffons and georgettes. She examined borders, patterns and materials and waved most of them away. 'Gaudy', she would say, or 'terrible', or 'absolutely frightful'.

Eager to please her, the attendants threw them aside and unfolded yards of material to show her different ones, creating heaps of crumpled silk on a white sheet. They served her cup after cup of hot tea. I sat quietly and watched, drinking Coca-Cola. They stared at her throughout.

She picked out a dozen saris – some from the heap, some from the neatly folded stacks. She chose French chiffons in colours Burrimummy taught us: Mountbatten pink, aureolin, amaranth, cerulean, or heavy silks in jewel shades with broad contrast borders.

Afterwards, she took me into a crowded bakery – Koshi's, Bangalore's most famous – and treated me to dosas, pancakes filled with spicy potatoes, and mango lassi. While we waited, she drew me to her and kissed me. 'My quarter pint, what tiny hands you have, pet. Is anyone unkind to you?' Before I could answer, she saw a friend, and they began talking and admiring one another. She dropped me at 17 Rest House Road, saying she was late for dinner with friends at the Bangalore Club and she didn't want to be late back to the officers' mess where she was staying. I hadn't seen her since.

I want to turn around, go back to Saloni's house. I felt safer there, with an army family, safe from the thrashing I know is coming, but there is nowhere to hide.

17 Rest House Road has a red postbox marked BAIG in uneven white paint at the gate. The high walls with their yellowing decay and missing chunks of plaster make the house look sad. They are partially covered in jasmine, tiny crimson and green parasitic creepers and wood roses painted in dull silver. For years I thought they grew like that until I saw the painter on a ladder in the garage, colouring them in.

Burrimummy's shouting never stops the dark, dirty, semi-naked servants' children appearing from their quarters, where I often run off to play. These are five tiny, dark, airless concrete structures at the back of the house where the ayahs' families sleep, cook and eat. The women crouch over smoky stone stoves built with sticks and newspaper; thin children in rags, who never go to school, play cricket with sticks and chase bony dogs. Some afternoons, while Angel and Burrimummy sleep, I go to their quarters and eat rice and dal smelling of ghee and firewood off a plastic plate from Burrimummy's kitchen. I enjoy myself while they sit around me as if I am doing them a favour, and then we play.

The ayahs' 'men' – as Burrimummy insists on calling them, even though they may be married to the ayahs – are rarely visible. They are not encouraged to hang around the house. They disappear swiftly, either into the rooms or out of the compound.

A nine-year-old girl comes running towards us to meet us at the gate. She is Mary, the cook's daughter. She is followed by a boy of the same size with snot running down his nose. Mary looks at me and asks if I'm coming to play. I give her what I hope is Burrimummy's withering look. Light streams behind Mary's sun-bleached, matted hair, turning it ashen; briefly, she is a haloed angel. Close up, her skin, patchy with white spots, and her protruding stomach makes her look diseased. She races back to the servants' quarters while the boy stares at us defiantly, one hand sweeping the snot upwards around his face.

We pass the three steps to the front door and go through the green gates at the side of the house, along a path to the kitchen, past the Millingtonia tree with its fragrant long white leaves and the lime tree. Under the mango tree in the courtyard, Ansia, Burrimummy's youngest ayah, is pounding fresh masala paste with a large mortar, hammering away so the smell of crushed garlic, ginger, mint and green chillies overpower the nearby roses and lime tree.

We walk into the kitchen to the smells of cooked golden onions and butter. Three table settings have been laid on a gingham tablecloth.

Margaret, Burrimummy's cook, looks like all the other ayahs – dark and tiny and beaten up, with a brood of small, undernourished children. Burrimummy says there is not a drop of Anglo blood in her, even though she says her great grandfather was British, and she goes to church to prove it. Even if she had Anglo blood, Burrimummy tells Margaret, it's worse than being Hindu, since she's neither here nor there.

We hear the jangle of keys on Burrimummy's dressing gown before we see her and when she comes towards us, Angel bows her head and curves her right hand to her forehead, saying 'Salaam, Burrimummy', after which Burrimummy engulfs Angel in her arms. 'You've come. You've come. Sweetheart. The child of my life, my *chand ka baccha*, my moonchild, my darling child, is here. May you live long, my belovedest.'

I'm hiding behind Khaja and I am looking at both Burrimummy and a large black and white portrait of her on the wall – her eighteen-year-old self: wide eyes on a broad, pale face; full, painted lips; pearls, a diamond in her crimped hair – a remote actress on a billboard. At sixty, Burrimummy is a hard beauty – tall, boxy, muscular, broad-faced with deeply-set eyes, and a tight, thinly curvaceous mouth stained with tobacco and betel nut. Her stomach is round but firm, with little fat on her, which is strange because we never see her exercise. She doesn't look at me. I touch her arm. She brushes me off, draws Angel closer and shouts for Khaja.

'Angel, your face is so hot. Khaja, Khaja, you *haramzadi*, daughter of a pig, where are you, you black Tamilian? Ooh God, she's gone to the servants' quarters again.' She slaps her forehead hard as if the only way to get anything done is to maim herself. 'Ansia, quickly, fetch lime juice for baby.'

She holds Angel's head. 'My baby is getting a fever in this heat.'

Ansia appears. 'Yes, Maa, yes, Maa.'

Burrimummy towers over Ansia, her face and torso like a marble bust in the museum. When she is angry like this, I don't know what to feel. I hate it when she thrashes me but am sadder when she doesn't notice me at all.

I get tired of hearing Angel's name. I long for the moments when Burrimummy puts her large arms around me and says Angel and me are her two eyes, that without us she is blind, and tells me I possess the dark olive colouring of the Prophet Mohammed himself. I'm purposefully naughty just so she can say 'Poppet this' and 'Poppet that'.

'Bring the lime juice. Bring ice. Where is that woman whose teeth stick out? Khajaaaaa! She was just here. Call her. Khaja of the unlucky face. Every time I turn my back, you run off like a whore to the servants' quarters. Take off Angel Baby's socks and shoes. Wash her hands and face. Quickly. My bacchas are hungry, you haramzadi.'

The servants, sensing my lower status, are careless with me. I like their food but hate their hands on me, bony fingers smelling of cheap soap and the smells of poverty that can never be scrubbed out.

Finally, Burrimummy stands over me. My uniform is a dirty white, stained with dust and food from yesterday.

'Mrs Bhaveja called me this morning, you know.' Burrimummy sounds dangerously calm. 'You wicked child.'

'I wanted to be with army people,' I say, sticking my chin out. 'Her mummy and daddy are in the army.'

'And what if you'd been run over, stolen, taken by beggars? What would I say to your parents then?'

'Oh, you get your money from Daddy for keeping me, don't you? Why do you care where I go?'

She picks me up as if I am a stick and turns me on my stomach. I can feel her knees. She hits me with the flat of her hand on my skinny bum, striking bone. I'm not here. I'm with Mummy and Daddy in Simla in the Officers' Club. Daddy is in uniform and playing bridge. I'm sheltering behind Mummy's billowing sari on the terrace, looking at mountains with snow.

'Are you truly repentant?'

I say nothing.

I feel pain in my arm, where Burrimummy grasps me with one hand. She uses the other to strike me in tapping movements as if she was playing the piano. She wasn't sad that I was gone. I don't care that she wants to hurt me. She regards me as if, like Daddy, I'm a Hindu outsider. I am a constant reminder of Mummy's defection from Islam and towards lowly, dark-skinned Hindu blood. Well, then, I am Hindu, like Daddy, who loves me best.

'Your damned father would have torn me to pieces if something terrible had happened to you.' She hits me until her hands are bright red; I let out a cry, and then she lets me go abruptly as if disgusted with my tears.

Angel tugs her. 'Burrimummy, I'm hungry.' She holds out her little hand to me. 'Poppet Aapa must also have lunch.'

Burrimummy promptly softens. 'Wash your face, Poppet darling. Khaja, take Poppet to the bathroom.' She switches like this. I never know how she's going to be.

In the bathroom, Khaja splashes water on my face, takes my hands and washes them, then wipes me dry. I'm not grateful to Angel. She shouldn't decide whether I'm thrashed.

When I return, Ansia has served up the soup. She is barely fifteen, dressed in a petticoat and old dupatta, still not old enough for a sari, but she seems so much older than my ten. Burrimummy turns to Ansia. Her hand is chalky against Ansia's chocolate face.

'Ansia, haramzadi, you bastard's child, the fork is not laid on this side. It's on this side. How many times am I to tell you, you silly girl?'

'Put faark on this side, Maa?'

'Yes, put the faark on this side.'

After the forks are laid on the right side of the table, she points, plump white fingers upwards, blowing paan, spit and obscenities into the ayahs' gaunt, dark faces.

'Bring cold water. Put ice. Put more ice. Bring limes. Cut them in four. Give to Baby. Not with your filthy hands. Let me do it. Bring chillies.'

'Saarlt, Maa?'

'Bring. Take back the soup.'

'Courld, Maa?'

'Yes, cold, Maa. Don't you know soup is meant to be hot, you daughter of a donkey? Oooh God.'

Margaret hovers near the stove and helps Ansia.

Ansia brings the hundi – the steel pot with no handles – back to the table. We all pour our soup back in the pot.

It comes back spouting steam. Ansia scalds her fingers while pouring soup back into our bowls. Burrimummy shouts. 'What will I do if you get burnt? Your drunken men will be after me. Now go wash your hands in cold water.'

The girl doesn't bother to wipe away the tears sliding down her face. Burrimummy's voice is suddenly gentle, caressing. 'After you wash your hands, go and wash your entire body.'

Ansia nods and runs out.

Burrimummy is continually frustrated in her attempts to force her bewildered, shrunken, Tamil-speaking Bangalore ayahs to recreate her exquisite, courtly Mughal food, to cultivate the mannered household of her Hyderabadi ancestors in that long dark kitchen. Inevitably, it's a failure since Burrimummy's explosive obscenities destroy the thing that she tries to recreate.

The roast is well done, surrounded by spicy, plump red chillies. Vegetables rarely make an appearance in our diet unless they are heavily disguised or dissolved in meat.

As we eat, Burrimummy's mood improves. She smiles at us.

Everyone brightens and relaxes.

'Go now, Maa?' Ansia says.

'Yes, Ansia, you can go. Be back by three sharp.'

'Yes, Maa.'

Now Margaret is in her line of attack.

'Fetch the bread-and-butter pudding. Bring cream. Bring coffee. More water for Small Baby. Don't put your filthy hands in the glass, you ignorant gavaar woman of the streets. Now, come on, Angel, finish up.'

We can all tell by her tone she is no longer furious.

After a second helping of pudding, I want to bury myself in her warmth, her pale hugeness. I want her to love me properly. Without looking at them, she tells Margaret and Khaja, hovering now in corners of the kitchen, 'Clear the table. Take it away.'

The table is cleared. After Margaret hands her a cup of strong black coffee, Burrimummy sends her away, too. 'Go, eat your lunch. Be back at five o'clock SHARP for tea. No lolling. Tell Ansia to come back.'

Khaja, Angel and I follow Burrimummy into the spacious bedroom, with a big bed specially made for three. It's time for our afternoon nap.

Angel is whisked under Burrimummy's arms with a stream of endearments. 'Come, my child of the moon, my liver, my life, let's lie down.'

I lie down next to Angel. The sheets are fresh and soft.

We hear the horns of the traffic on the main road and, closer, the sharp rustle of monkeys jumping on the mango tree outside. The tree is so tall that we can reach out and pick mangoes from the terrace.

A hawker on the street below shouts, as if reciting a poem; curtains lift in the breeze and bring us glimpses of Burrimummy's tea roses, miniature and fragile. The wind goes wild briefly, parting the branches of the mango tree; a monkey leaps; sunlight slants through closed curtains; light moves in squares on terracotta tiles.

Wanting to please Burrimummy, I say, 'Please, can we see the photograph of your great-grandfather, Sir Afsar, who was appointed the general of the army of the Nizam of Hyderabad?'

'Go fetch it, darling.'

I run to the drawing room, take it off the wall and fetch it for her, as if transporting a treasure. Burrimummy shifts to the centre of the bed. Angel and I curve into either side of her as if concentrating for an exam. I know it well, this photograph of a trim, old, European-looking man in uniform with a curly moustache and a tiny woman with her *sari pallu* pulled over her head, surrounded by many people: young men in high-collared shirts, ties and pin-striped, three-piece suits. The women are like dark-haired Europeans, pouty, dressed in fine gauze. What Burrimummy tells us is dull gold shows through a photograph that's almost a century old. The impression is of the sulking ease of the privileged who are rarely pleased.

I am acutely aware, as I place my hand on her arm – as tiny and brown as that of the servants' children – that I would never be one of them. I'm too dark, too rebellious. My father doesn't send me enough money to dress like Angel. Maybe by showing an interest in Burrimummy's people, I could claim them too. Angel doesn't need to do anything to belong.

Burrimummy points at the man. 'Here is Sir Afsar. My great-grandfather and your great-great-great-grandfather.'

Angel says, 'Great great great great.'

Burrimummy puts her finger on Angel's mouth.

'Afsar was only three when he accompanied his parents from Uzbekistan to India. The British offered Afsar's father, Balath, money to fight against the Indians in the mutiny of 1857. He was a poor man, so naturally, he agreed. Balath, my great-great grandfather, came down with dysentery because of the faeces and rubbish in the filthy water in Delhi, Agra, Kanpur and Allahabad, where the fighting took place. He was brought back to Hyderabad half-dead and between sleep and wake kept asking Allah for forgiveness for what he'd done in Allahabad, where he had to stand over Indian soldiers – fellow Muslims and Hindus – with a whip, while they were force-fed pork and made to lick the blood off the floor of the British women and children slaughtered by Nana Sahib. Then they were hanged while British soldiers jeered. After Balath died, a young British officer, Sir Charles, who had just lost his own wife in childbirth, adopted Balath's son, Afsar, when he was just eight, and when Afsar was sixteen, enrolled him with the Gurkhas in the British army, sending him to fight for them in Afghanistan and China before he became the general of the army of the Nizam of Hyderabad.'

The ceiling fan goes a creaky flap flap over our heads, above the mosquito curtain in the room.

Burrimummy shuts out the Bangalore of temple dances, Kannada songs, *kanjivarum* gold-bordered saris, spicy vegetarian food, Gods and garlands displayed on autorickshaws, homes and temples, cinema posters of dusky voluptuous Tamil actresses that take up entire walls, and hawkers selling garlands of jasmine flowers for the oiled black hair of chocolate-skinned women.

Burrimummy reads the caption under the photograph: *General Nawab Sir Afsar-ul-Mulk Bahadur, KCSI SCIE MVO ADC. 1852-1930. 1877: On his first visit to India, the Prince of Wales conferred the title of the Order of the Star of India to Sir Afsar.*

Angel says into Burrimummy's ears, 'abcdefg...'

I shove Angel. 'Don't be so silly,' I say.

'Poppet, don't hurt Angel.' Burrimummy's voice is cold.

Burrimummy turns to the darker lady at Sir Afsar's side, with none of the glamour of her ten children, and dismisses her by saying she was a good woman, a child bride from Arabia who could not speak English and lived in purdah all her life.

'Sir Afsar loved position and titles. He forced ALL his daughters to marry men they hated because they were powerful landowners.'

'All of them were miserable, Burrimummy?' I look at the six beautiful girls: my great-great-grandmother and her sisters.

'Not all. One ran away and married a common man, and Sir Afsar never spoke to her again.'

'Soo soo,' says Angel, and Ansia takes Angel to the bathroom. I have Burrimummy to myself.

'This is your great-great-grandmother, Sadrunissa, Sir Afsar's eldest child.' Burrimummy is pointing to a sharp-featured woman. She is captured off-guard by the camera while adjusting something gauzy over her head, a gesture beautiful women in India use to bring attention to themselves. 'Sir Afsar made her marry Mumtaz Yar Jung, just because he was a companion to the Mir Osman Ali Khan, the VIIth Nizam of Hyderabad. Mumtaz was old enough to be her father, married with two grown daughters the same age as Sadrunissa. Unhappy all her life. My grandfather tried to impress his second wife with his close relationship with the Nizam, walking her through the Nizam's terraces where mountains of pearls were washed and laid out in the sun to dry, and keeping her in a grand house with a zenana, even driving her in the Nizam's Rolls Royce Silver Ghost Throne car. None of that grandeur meant anything to my grandmother because she could never get him to divorce his first wife.'

'This is Mumma, my mother and your great-grandmother. Shortly after this photo was taken, her grandfather, Sir Afsar, got wind of a plan by the Nizam to abduct her for his harem and so he married her off in a proxy ceremony.' She was a teenager in the photo in a cream, puffed-sleeve Victorian dress, her hair wild and wavy, sulking as if she'd rather be elsewhere. 'The grand Begum of Savanur. She was sulking because Sir Afsar brought her back from boarding school in England on her sixteenth birthday.'

I can't connect this with Mumma – obese, without teeth in my great-uncle's home in Bangalore's old city.

'She was brilliant, too, you know, Poppet, and athletic – fenced, rode, played tennis. She was the first Indian woman to be sent to boarding school in England. She felt duped by that proxy marriage because they let her think she was marrying the richest man in the world, the Nizam, but when she was asked to sign her acceptance, she saw my father's name. She'd never heard of this minor state and kicked up a fuss. She refused to sign, so Sir Afsar signed on her behalf. Sir Afsar married her to the Nawab of Savanur. She was forced.'

'So much forcing,' I say.

Sir Afsar looks thin and mean. I don't like him. I don't say that he makes me think of Burrimummy, the way she is constantly forcing the servants to do things, forcing me not to fidget, forcing me to be helpful to Angel.

'Mumma's the real Angel,' I say, as she returns from the bathroom.

Angel makes a crying face.

Burrimummy's eyes narrow with a look that makes my heart race.

'Poppet, stop talking rot.'

She shifts to the edge of the bed, gathering Angel into her.

I tell Angel it is my turn to sleep next to Burrimummy.

'You lost your turn when you didn't come home last night,' Burrimummy replies.

Angel lies between us, like an ocean I can't cross.

'Where did I come from, Burrimummy?' Angel asks.

A muscular chalky arm encircles her.

'My baby, my Angel, six farishtas, brought you from heaven on a gold chariot on their wings. They put you in my arms. You had skin like milk, so I called you Angel after my own mother. I called you Sadrunissa after my grandmother. I called you Puppa after Father. I asked Allah for you, and that's how He sent you, my tiny mite.'

Angel sleeps in the crook of Burrimummy's arm while I lie alert. She changes her tone when she speaks to me. 'DON'T fidget, Poppet. Go to sleep. You'll be ill if you don't rest in the afternoons, and your mother will be at my throat.'

I touch her face. Soft as roses. I want her to love me.

Burrimummy is now reading Georgette Heyer, and I ask her how I was born. She looks outside at the monkeys around the mango tree.

'You've seen how baby monkeys are born, haven't you? From the mother's gaaf.'

I feel ashamed, not knowing what I'd done wrong.

TWO

St. Lucia, 2016

In the air, through thick clouds on the rocking plane to St Lucia, I feel like a late guest at a party. The Nobel Laureate had invited me to see him for the weekend about my writing. I wonder whether he was just in need of an acolyte to buoy him up. Perhaps I'm good at the trope: woman, a worshipper of language, sensitive to rejection.

The invitation followed an interview I did with him when the university at St Augustine honoured him. I was in the audience, craning my neck to see him, eager to hear him read from his latest work, as if he had answers to all things.

Walcott didn't fuck up the audience or professors as V.S. Naipaul had done, in this same hall, with his supercilious, truncated, pained answers. He hadn't, like Naipaul, sneered at questions from students. 'I don't understand', or said, 'Schoolchildren shouldn't study Literature.' No, he was all theatre, with his solid build, the leathery, slashed skin of a seafarer, the darting green eyes of a sunning iguana. He held back from being intimidating by being alert, alternately jokey and silent.

Amidst knowing literary laughter (and the academics collectively holding their breath when a student got something wrong), he grinningly skirted peccadilloes, turned the audience into his private performance, and said the things he always did: 'The English language is nobody's special property. It is the property of the imagination: it is the property of the language itself' and, 'The Caribbean is full of visual surprise.' He took his time, comfortable with saying nothing we had not heard before.

Afterwards, he patiently signed old books and new copies of his latest volume, unlike Naipaul, whose wife Nadira, in the same venue last year, shrieked, 'No old books, only new books', like a hawker in a bazaar in Bombay.

I sat in the second row and sent a message to his daughter, Anna. Trinidad being a small place, our social circles overlap; our children go to the same school.

'Will your dad grant me a brief interview?'

During a break, Anna said, 'Dad wants to see you.'

He gestured towards a chair next to him, still signing books, seeming not to notice that I was sitting at the head table facing an audience and flanked by him and the Dean of the University. I couldn't look ahead at the audience, nor could I be seen staring at Derek.

I still have those photos of me wearing a baby-blue cotton dress, showing an abundance of cleavage. It wasn't intentional. Squirming like a trapped insect on the stage, unable to explain my presence there, I touched Derek lightly on his back.

'I'm sorry, I have to go.'

'Go away and have a sandwich while I decide what to do with you,' he said. Off I trotted, obediently.

He still hadn't learned how to speak to women, despite the damning book in which allegations had been made against him – an extract from which had damaged his reputation in England when he was a candidate for the Oxford professorship of poetry in 2009. In the book, called *The Lecherous Professor*, published in 1984, Walcott had featured in four pages of a general account of sexual harassment on American campuses. He had allegedly taken a student from his poetry class to coffee and asked her how she made love with her boyfriend. She had reportedly said, 'Why should I tell you? It's none of your business.'

He allegedly persisted. After all, he was the professor and the gatekeeper of poetry. Did he imagine this was his due as man and poet? 'Would you make love with me if I asked you?'

'No,' had insisted. 'No way. You're married. Don't you love your wife?'

Walcott, thrice-married, had reportedly replied, 'Love has nothing to do with lust.'

There was a complaint to the Dean. How this was settled was not revealed.

I knew I should leave, but I stayed, as I always do, having learned from Burrimummy that patience yields approbation and sat down on the stairs in the Faculty of Literature, watching students go by.

I wasn't sure why I asked for the interview, let alone why I waited, wondering if it had anything to do with standing by while someone else interviewed Walcott years before, or if I had begun the wrenching process of wondering why I only cared about the people who withheld their approval.

What unsaid thing could I ask him about his Nobel Prize for Literature, (and every literary prize worth having), his magnum opus, *Omeros,* twenty-four collections of poetry, twenty-two plays, seven books, his watercolours, essays? Faltering, I began walking towards the car park when I heard a tall black girl, with hair in cane rows, say, 'How this man rewrite Homer's *Odyssey*, for God's sake?' The boy she was with shrugged, replying, 'He reach.' The graceful girl said, 'I just want to sit at the feet of that man on a strip of sand while he paints or writes.' They wanted to absorb him as one would absorb sunlight. That's why he could just sit there without saying a word.

I waited to hear from Anna in my car, parked under the scant shade of a poui tree. I put the car windows down watched the breeze sweep yellow blossoms across the path to the Faculty of Engineering.

I'd bumped into Derek Walcott in 1992 when the news was full of his triumphant return with the Nobel Prize. I had been threading my way through the Carnival Sunday crowd across the Queen's Park Savannah at dusk, its chaotic din made worse by dust kicked up by the crowds pounding the earth in time to the music and trucks carrying the steel pans from the competition stands back to the pan yards. The traffic fumes mingled with perfume from the cannonball tree, a vine with rosebud-shaped flowers throwing out the combined scents of lilies, ylang ylang, freesia, jasmines – so extravagant it could have emanated from a maharaja's wedding chamber.

I nearly tripped and fell over the roots of the cannonball tree, spreading out beneath the cracked pavement, when a large, veiny man's hand firmly grasped my arm. It was Derek Walcott.

'If you're not red, you're dead,' they say on these islands, meaning that men like him outstrip all other men, in appeal, in imagined sexual prowess. Men like him – with that mix of European and African blood – have the reputation of getting any woman they want. A moment with him had been enough to confirm this. He was all charge, all force, deep voice, well built, skin like molasses in milk. I thought of his poem 'The Schooner *Flight*', where his poetic alter ego, Shabine, claimed it all. ('I have Dutch, nigger and English in me, / and either I'm nobody, or I'm a nation.')

'Derek Walcott?'

My question didn't warrant an answer.

'Who are you?' he asked. 'That is, apart from someone who's not looking where she's going.'

'Freelance journalist. The *Trinidad Guardian*. Congratulations on the Nobel.'

'I once wrote for that paper,' he said.

I knew that. As did V.S. Naipaul. As did Naipaul's father.

'Where are you from?'

'Tobago.'

He laughed. 'With that accent? What is it, continental? Indian English?'

Across the road, two ghostly shapes among the magnificent seven colonial mansions stood sentry over the Savannah – which some call the most giant roundabout in the world: Whitehall, with coral stone from Barbados, built in the style of a Venetian Palazzo by a cocoa planter in 1904 and home to the prime minister's office; and next to it Stollmeyer's Castle with its turrets modelled on Balmoral Castle. He was waiting to hear what I would say next.

'I'm doing freelance work, covering the Steelband competition in the Savannah for the Government Information Unit.'

He pounced quicker than light with a question: 'Information expert? Well then, can you multiply 25,435 by 234?' He'd laughed uproariously and disappeared into the dust. A full twenty-four years ago, this vanishing left me unsettled, longing to hold onto that vast ebullience bubbling from his Himalayan brain, erupting into its full laugh so much like my grandmother's it gave me a jolt. It was a depressing thought that so much time had passed. Twenty-four years, and, in some ways, nothing had changed for me.

My mobile phone rang. Anna said the interview was in an hour. I dawdled some more, looking at the students wandering the campus without seeing them, watching the dry leaves as if they could mop up something in me, and eventually drove down the highway, past cane fields, factories, and the hills where gangs warred for guns and drugs, to the Hyatt in Port of Spain where Derek was staying. It was close to the cruise ship arena where tourists gingerly stepped out for a few hours, rifling through the vendors' goods: beads, T-shirts, stewed mangoes. The five-star hotel, with its pool on the thirteenth floor seemingly dropping into the sea, water on water, was the conceit of a former prime minister.

Sigrid, his partner, ushered me into his suite, gave me her hand briefly, then dashed away, the way women do when their children are occupied, to complete necessary tasks.

Close up, without the prop of the wheelchair, slumped on the sofa the way Burrimummy used to be in the nursing home, squinting with one eye, made him look sneaky rather than imposing; he was not the same man I'd met on the Savannah. There were sagging hollows under his eyes, his face was streaked, the very flesh on his face seemed folded. I didn't want to look down at his legs in the wheelchair.

I wondered if I'd embellished the details of that first meeting. Now, twenty-four years later, there was a quiet in him I hadn't seen before, even something tremulous – the tremulousness of a majestic creature in fall. All this was reflected in his latest volume of poetry, *White Egrets*.

I sat down on the plush hotel couch, and he said, 'I don't know what you want, but it better be short.' With an unexpected familiarity and a hint of apology, he said, 'I'm diabetic.' I could see it. He would rest his head on his hand, as if falling asleep, like Burrimummy. He had death on his mind.

'My sister died last week – my twin brother last year. Friends are dying. I might be next.'

Still, I went in for the kill: the persistent bitter aftertaste of having to withdraw from standing for Oxford's Professorship of Poetry in 2009, after the resurrection of old charges of sexual harassment. He looked blank.

In the anonymous smear campaign against Walcott, up to a hundred

Oxford academics were sent photocopied pages from the book which included the sexual harassment claim made against him by a student at Harvard in 1982. Widely felt to be the favoured candidate of the Oxford English faculty, he'd resigned from the race on 12th May 2009. There was outrage amongst the black intelligentsia in Trinidad. People said Ted Hughes got away with pushing women to kill themselves with his infractions; that white professors had been getting away with far worse allegations of actual misconduct.

Did he feel he was attacked because he was mixed-race? I knew he never thought of himself as black. He prided himself on being an amalgam of continents, but he didn't escape the label in the west.

He behaved as if he hadn't heard any of that question.

Instead, he said, gazing out at the ocean, 'This is the first time I've had this view, watching the ferry coming in. It's beautiful. The sea, the sunset, the docks. These are "touristy" things, but, to me, these are beautiful experiences. The ocean, the street, the shore, and the scenes below us have the ebullience of life that Paris lacks. All these people from everywhere in the world, the Lebanese, Chinese, Indian, African, in this tiny city. Something is bound to ferment. For me, it's elation.'

I thought that at least he was not fucking with my head as he did in 1992. I saw a poet who was satisfied he had achieved immortality. But as a man, afraid of his failing body, fearful of dying. I felt our conversation was more about his wanting a witness than about poetry.

He handed me an early copy of his book *White Egrets*, with its milky-grey cover. In the heartbreaking crack in his voice, in that weathered face, I scented fear. I knew from experience he could be as dismissive and intimidating as Naipaul, even more commanding, but by the end of the interview, he had shed his crustacean exterior.

He watched me speculatively. I knew I should baulk, but I didn't. I'd seen his poetry and wanted to see the dirt – how he approached the struggle of being human among the scattered bones, excrement, selfishness and sordidness and violence of life, and how he reconciled this with his constant search for light in words, in the landscape, in faces.

Not long after, he called me.

'It's me, Derek. I'm in Trinidad still. In my daughter's home in Petit Valley.'

'Derek. Gosh. It's you. How are you?'

'The interview was okay.'

'Thank you.'

'I didn't say it was terrific.'

He must have relished my discomfort and the brief ensuing silence that would have unnerved me had I been younger. But, by now, embarrassment has become a dull instrument.

'What else do you write?'

'I'm writing about my grandmother,' I said.

'What about her?'

'She lived in the embers of the Raj in India and died in Trinidad. As a child, I subsumed myself in her and needed to push her out onto paper. I thought it a way of finding or freeing myself. You know what Naipaul said about going back and back and back.'

'Is it done?'

'Maybe,' I said miserably. 'I've got some chapters.'

'Send me them. No, bring it to the opening night of my play.'

The following night, my husband Sadiq and I arrived in the amphitheatre, the crowd buzzing around Derek in anticipation of a revival of his play, *Dream on Monkey Mountain*.

Shaved, groomed, and dressed in a crisp shirt, in his wheelchair, Derek appeared like a child being taken on an outing. He laughed the hardest at the typically West Indian bon mots, quips, fuck-ups. How he loved these islands.

He gave me a sour, side-look but didn't speak to me. I applauded and laughed hard to show my appreciation. I was anxious; had I done something wrong?

Afterwards, in the foyer, I thanked him. He took the envelope with the first three chapters with a blank look, which I suspect he had mastered to punish people, wanting his acolytes to beg for a bone. He pointedly ignored my husband's outstretched hand. We slunk away.

A week later, the phone rang.

'Come to St Lucia for the weekend.'

★

On the approach to St Lucia, the small plane swoops, drops, quivers, and the seatbelt light comes on. I close my eyes to the seraphs of blue Caribbean clouds, its phosphenes and clutch the seat even while wanting the plane to rock harder. Take me away from myself. Take me back.

THREE

Saturday. My birthday. I watch through the open window to see Angel in the garden holding a basket as Burrimummy clips roses with her scissors. Pale sunshine and a dewy rainfall keep them blooming year-round.

I'm ten today. Burrimummy got me out of bed with a kiss on my forehead. 'May Allah and his Prophet bless you. Come, I have something to show you.'

I had rushed ahead of her to the kitchen. On the table, covered in cheesecloth, was a cake in the shape of a doll wearing a pink rounded ball-gown covered in sugary, silver dots. You had to turn it around to read 'Happy Birthday, Poppet Darling'. I stared at that cake throughout breakfast, too excited for toast and even Angel couldn't resist touching it.

I only noticed I didn't get a present when Burrimummy said, 'I'm sorry, Poppet darling, but your father didn't send me any money for a present for you. Your mother is expected.' I am sure Mummy will bring presents. Will it be a dress, a doll, or an outing at Koshi's, where we'll have ice cream together?

When Burrimummy and Angel are back from the garden, we are summoned to our bath.

The ayahs fill the boiler with water, prepare the bathroom, and lay out towels. We are allotted three towels each: one for the face, one for the hair and one for the body. If they touch one another, there is the danger of transferring germs. The full bath that we have once a week will take all morning. Khaja oils my hair. Burrimummy oils Angel's hair. I feel the oil running down my scalp and to the sides of my ears, Khaja's skinny hands in my hair.

I gaze at the four of us in the triple dressing-table mirror in an enclave of Burrimummy's bedroom. It is flooded with light from the white walls of the stairs leading to the terrace. Angel's eyes are closed, her thick glossy head moving with Burrimummy's massage. Burrimummy says, while plaiting Angel's hair in two French braids, that the one thing she's learnt from South Indians is that coconut oil keeps the hair black, soft and thick. I am ashamed my plait is thin compared to Angel's.

'Put on more oil, Khaja,' I hiss. 'More.' I'm hoping, as it trickles down my neck, that it might make my brown hair black like Angel's.

After giving Angel her bath, Burrimummy sends her to stand outside to dry her hair.

The water from the boiler tap is again close to boiling point.

It's my turn. We are in a dark bathroom.

I am guided onto the low wooden stool in the bath. Two buckets, thoroughly disinfected with Dettol, one with cold water, the other with hot, are placed next to the wooden stool. Khaja fills a silver jug with water. Burrimummy says pour, and Khaja pours warm water over me. The ayah passes shampoo to Burrimummy. As Burrimummy tips my head back and rubs her strong hands into my scalp, I feel the warm soapy water on my face. The room steams up. She kneads my back as if my body is covered in rubber, showing me specks of old skin.

'Khaja, aur pani,' she orders.

Warm water glides over my back.

When Burrimummy kneads her own skin, she resembles a Rubenesque figure, her white skin coming up in stripes of bright pink. Mine goes a dark berry-brown.

I close my eyes, feeling like liquid gold at Burrimummy's touch, when Angel howls from the garden, 'Red ants, red ants!'

Burrimummy rushes out. Khaja follows. I sit on the stool, waiting, soap from my hair running down my face. Angel stops crying. I see Burrimummy holding Angel up, Khaja bending down, wiping ants from her feet, Angel burying her head in Burrimummy.

I play my blinking game, focusing on the flicker of green leaves, buds and sunlight through the latticed walls. Closing my eyes, opening them again to see a technicolour version of the same thing waving in the sunshine and shadow, weaving in and out of sight. The room gets hotter. I feel a warm, prickly bead of sweat drop to my face. The half-light gets dimmer. I dream I'm four, playing in a field surrounded by buildings occupied by army officers. I stand over a puddle of rainwater, looking at the rainbow reflected in it. Winky is with a group of boys who are poking at a puppy. The puppy collapses. They come at me, Winky leading the way. Winky pushes me. A boy hits me with a stick. Winky says, 'More, more, hit her more.' Another boy hits my head with a stone. Drops of blood fall into the rainbow puddle. They run away.

I wake with a start, my heart pounding, feeling cold water on my face. I am lying on the bathroom floor, near the bucket.

Burrimummy is wiping my face gently. Khaja is on the other side of me. 'Why did you leave her, you foolish woman? If her father hears of this, I will get hell.'

Burrimummy wraps a towel around my head like a bandage. The doctor is summoned. I am put to bed, feel a warm hairdryer on my scalp, Khaja brings me a tray of chicken soup and milk with brandy and I am safe.

Burrimummy is telling Angel to come in from the sun; she is sitting on a step by the big jar of lime pickle and the bitter gourd, which Burrimummy will grind into a paste to have for breakfast. When Angel is inside, I look out and notice the roses are gone.

'Burrimummy, what did you do with the roses?'

'Nothing, darling.' Burrimummy turns away.

'Khaja put them in my bathwater,' says Angel, as if she knows she has won again at a game I was unaware I was playing. No matter what I do, Angel and Burrimummy are a step ahead.

It's two in the afternoon – the doorbell. I start. Sit up. Mummy. But it's only the voices of Asmath and Tahira, Burrimummy's companions; they always pitch up to help Burrimummy with a party.

I wake to wafts of smells. The jasmine from the spreading bush on the walls will be woven through my hair. The lime pickle on the patio, ripening into a succulent gold from the day's sun, will be served at dinner. I hope Mummy will stay for dinner. She might even spend the night.

Burrimummy is standing in front of the tall steel cupboards, her back ramrod straight, wavy dark hair with strands of hennaed red coiled into a ropey bun on her pale neck. She takes a bunch of keys tucked into her dressing gown; deft fingers with square, squat nails grip one key amongst a colossal bunch held together by a silver clip – keys of all sizes and shapes for the tenants' houses, the fridge, the store cupboard, her writing desk, the piano, the china cupboard, her bank locker, her car, her dressing table drawers, bedroom cabinets, four steel cupboards and four steel trunks. This one key outweighs all the others.

The cupboard opens with a whine. Burrimummy is unravelling yards of uncut white cotton, saying, 'This is what you must wrap me in when I'm dead.'

'Don't, Begum,' say Asmath and Tahira in Urdu. They are her regular companions, but we are uncertain if they are servants or guests. They are allowed in her bedroom and around her kitchen table, but not in the drawing room.

Asmath, spindly, with a thin face, a sharp triangle of a nose, glasses, a timorous voice, a faded sari, short-sighted from hours of sewing for her living, is watchful and seems more intelligent than the servants. Fat, burqa-clad Tahira, who emanates waves of sickly-sweet sweat from her jiggling folds, is good-humoured.

Burrimummy gives them clothes, food and cash. In return, they act as her handmaids, useful women who accompany her to places, carry her bags, press her legs, heat up milk, listen to her speak of the Quran, supervise the servants, pray with her, fast with her, listen to her stories, cook for and with her, provide her with a captive audience.

They are courtiers, witnesses to her suffering. The burial cloth has been offered to a stream of people – her doctor, the nurse, her bridge friends, all

more Islamic and worthier than her daughter Nur in the eyes of God and
her own. No matter who her audience is – and she opens that cupboard
often – the reactions are all the same: horror, protestations that she will live
for a hundred years. Tahira says, as she always does, 'No, no.' That she
cannot die. This reassures her and us of her immortality.

Burrimummy now says, addressing their vigorously nodding faces,
though they don't speak English, 'I will NOT show or entrust my burial
cloth to Nur, whom I should have been able to charge the responsibility of
a decent Muslim burial, the person I once loved more than life, my only
daughter, Nur. She broke my heart.'

She is not looking at me, but I know she intends this will get back to
Mummy. I don't know what to say. I keep switching sides, depending on
how they treat me. I decide not to tell Mummy this.

As she shuts the cupboard, the doorbell trills.

'My The,' Mummy shouts from the drawing room, with her pun on
mother. Khaja has let her in.

Heart hammering, I race ahead of Burrimummy. An army driver is
carrying several shopping bags and piling them up in the piano room.
Mummy is flushed, artfully dishevelled.

'My quarter pint,' she says, hugging me absent-mindedly. 'Salaam,
Mother,' she says to Burrimummy. Angel sucks her thumb.

'I'm staying,' Mummy says. 'Ved is coming tomorrow with some news.'

'Mummy, is Daddy coming?'

Mummy adjusts the summery chiffon sari wrapped around her slim,
pronounced curves, looks at me and says, 'Yes, dear.'

Burrimummy looks resigned. She tells Khaja to change the sheets in the
spare room.

Apart from their colouring, oversized frames and above-average height
for Indian women, Burrimummy and Mummy bear no resemblance to
each other. Burrimummy is hard. Mummy is soft, loved, looked after and
beautiful, so she's allowed to be careless. Burrimummy is old and cares for
herself, for us, about everything.

Mummy ignores Asmath and Tahira, who are endeavouring a mixture
between a salaam and a curtsey.

'I see your chamchas are here? What people won't do for a few rupees,'
she says, looking them up and down coolly. 'Have you given them any more
shares, Mother?'

Asmath and Tahira look alarmed, their obsequiousness temporarily
suppressed. Mummy's air of fragility is a weapon of ambush, which never
fails to take its victim by surprise.

Burrimummy comes to their defence. She starts to tell Mummy of their
usefulness. 'They make parathas for me, massage my legs.'

Mummy smooths her silky-brown hair, long and straight like a schoolgirl's, behind her ears. Her earrings, bold hoops set with pearly drops, shimmer as she moves, framing her lovely buttery face. She interrupts. 'I don't know how you can bear to be around them. Tahira stinks of cheap incense. Asmath's breath smells.' She laughs.

Burrimummy's jaw locks. Her small eyes turn to slits. We wait, terrified and expectant. The ayahs look grateful they aren't on the receiving end of what they and we all know is coming. Khaja smirks, loving this.

Teeth clenched, Burrimummy jabs her outstretched hands – palms upwards – towards Mummy's eyes, her nails almost touching them. She is spraying blood-red paan liquid and semi-chewed betel nut at Mummy's face as she shouts:

'They may be in reduced circumstances, but they, unlike you, are Muslims, you know, Mrs Nath. Your beauty means nothing in the eyes of God. The day you married Nath, you became a kafir, a nonbeliever, breaking our lineage to the Holy Prophet, Peace Be Upon Him. You can call yourself a Muslim a million times, but you can't fool God, and you can't fool his Prophet, Peace Be Upon Him.'

Mummy laughs, flicking the spittle away with her hand. 'Muslim like these women? They're positively frightening. You think they are here because they like you? Tahira, what did you get today? Shares? Jewellery? Take it. It's my right and my charity. I don't give a damn for it.' Carelessness is another weapon.

Burrimummy's face changes colour to a jaundiced yellow, and the venom she can't contain is in her eyes. I know the look. 'Why do you talk about it all the time, then, if you don't care what I took from you, how I want to deny you your inheritance?'

Asmath and Tahira look away.

Mummy's beauty smothers the effect of her rage, so we all – the hangers-on, the servants, Angel and I – stop listening, transfixed by the movement of her full, lipsticked mouth.

She walks away, turns around and says, as an afterthought, 'Who gives you the right to say who is a Muslim and who isn't, anyway? Only Allah decides that, and you can rob me of everything but not my faith.'

'You are not Anvar Nur Sultana anymore. You are nothing to me. I will not put up with your rudeness in my house, Mrs NATH.'

'Really? Well, Mrs Nath would like her daughter back.'

Mummy catches hold of Angel, who is standing behind Burrimummy. 'Come on, Angel. Let's go to your father.'

'Can I come?' I ask.

Angel and Burrimummy lunge towards one another. Mummy grabs Angel back. Holds her soft fat arm firmly.

'What more do you want, Mother? You took Angel away from me when she was five days old, and I never hear the end of it from Ved.'

'You were sick; you had a migraine. You couldn't look after both children. Now you're a busy memsaab. You can't even look after Poppet!'

'You know damn well I let you take Angel so you could get off my back about marrying a Hindu.'

Angel is whimpering, tugging away from Mummy, her body in her frilly cotton dress outstretched for Burrimummy.

Burrimummy's face caves in. 'Please, Nur. I loved you, you know.'

This Burrimummy makes the world crumble.

Mummy flinches, finally stung.

'Maybe once. You took me away from everyone I loved – my father, then Puppa and Mumma from Savanur, the only people who looked after me.'

'I loved you; I always looked after you.' Burrimummy crumples; this frightens me. I'm looking from one to the other. They do this every time Mummy comes to 17 Rest House Road: fight for Angel.

'Rubbish. You left me in hotel rooms and in boarding school and went off with Baig, that cousin of yours. You took everything from me. Where are all your fabulous jewels, the ones you didn't want me to have? You sent them to him, but he didn't want you back, did he?'

Burrimummy inflates, her stomach rising, her face filling out.

'After everything I did for you, scholars from Pakistan to teach you Arabic, tennis, piano lessons. No matter what I did, you couldn't be bothered. You gave up being a Muslim. You left.'

Mummy thrusts out her arms, and Angel runs back to Burrimummy. Mummy snatches her back.

'My arms are bare. You took every gold bangle. You made me sign away this house. You call me a nonbeliever. Then you have the gall to hang on to my daughter. She's coming with me to the officers' mess.'

Angel's face is turning red. She is twisting to get away from Mummy's grip, making little noises of distress.

'Nur, don't hurt Angel.'

'That's rich. Why do you think I left you? Blows to the head. Strikes like a dozen hammers. That's when my dreadful migraines started.' Mummy's voice breaks.

'I loved you, Nur,' Burrimummy repeats in her lover's voice, the one she uses when she sings.

Burrimummy is pleading in a voice that makes me fearful. The world is sinking. 'Please, darling, please.' Her voice rises. 'If you do this, by Allah and His Prophet, I will KILL myself.'

Mummy takes a compact out of her purse and carefully covers her mouth with lipstick. 'Oh, God, Mother, don't be so dramatic.'

Mummy lets go of Angel abruptly. Angel rushes to Burrimummy and buries her head in her belly.

Burrimummy is relieved, hastening the moment of resolution, speaking in her lover's voice, rich and warm. 'Nur, darling, Margaret made potted meat and cucumber sandwiches. The good crockery has been washed. I've invited some of your friends, some of mine. It's Poppet's birthday, Nur. Surely you can't take Angel back today?'

I look at Mummy's shopping bags expectantly, but she tells the ayah to put them on the chair, carefully. 'It's not easy to get good silk in the north.'

Maybe she's going to take me out.

'All right then.' Mummy acts like the quarrel is over, that nothing has happened. 'In any event, I asked Buddy and Charlie to visit me.'

They are her two childhood friends, women from wealthy families, both doctors. Both with long South Indian names that I couldn't pronounce.

Burrimummy shrugs, back in her power. 'Do whatever you want.' She's won. She takes Angel to the bedroom for her afternoon nap.

I follow Mummy into the kitchen, where she asks Margaret for a cup of tea and a sandwich, which she then eats, her mind somewhere else. I sit next to her, waiting for her to remember properly about my birthday.

She gets up, heads to the dressing table in the guest room. I follow her. She doesn't seem to mind, hardly notices. I scrutinise her as she applies a peachy lipstick, opening her mouth to make sure it gets in the corners, wholly absorbed in her own image.

'Mummy, can I brush your hair?'

'Okay, since it's your birthday.' So she hasn't forgotten. She crouches and throws her head back and I brush her hair gently, careful not to pull it, noting how different we look. Me small and dark; she fair and tall. She smiles and pinches my cheeks saying, 'How dainty you are pet, no let's call you Dait-ny not dainty.' My heart swells with happiness.

The doorbell. Mummy's friends rush in, all short hair, dark lipstick and wild printed chiffon saris and pearls. Mummy greets them with a school-girl's delight, yelling at Khaja to tell Margaret to 'bring drinks, bring sandwiches'.

'No, no, no,' they say politely, digging into my birthday sandwiches.

'Bring more, bring more,' Mummy says. 'And what's for pudding?'

Margaret says, 'Cake, mam.'

'Bring it.'

I watch fearfully as Margaret brings in my birthday doll-cake.

Mummy cuts a large slice and puts it on a plate for Buddy, then another for Charlie. I look on in disbelief as my cake elegantly enters their mouths.

'Lovely.' Buddy leans back dabbing her mouth delicately with a napkin. 'Time for a cigarette.'

I go to the piano and start banging on it.

'Stop that terrible racket, Poppet,' Mummy says. 'Come, pet, sit next to me.' I stop.

'She's almost as bad as I was at that thing.' Buddy looks at me as if she'd like me to go away.

'Nur, didn't you meet Ved at that piano teacher… Anglo-Indian Mrs Hunt's place, no?'

'God, yes, at Mrs Hunt's. She was at least ninety, blind as a bat. We met properly when her dog began viciously snapping at me as I arrived for my lesson.'

Charlie nods. 'Oh God, I know you're terrified of dogs. I don't remember that bit.'

Mummy nods. 'Well, I still have scars on my stomach from those damn injections I needed after my grandfather's Alsatians bit me. Mrs Hunt's dog had the end of my sari in its mouth just as Ved arrived at the gate. I was crying and shaking. He flew into action like a hero, chasing the damned dog away. It started chasing him, and he was running around in circles with it.'

Tinkling laughter.

'You know how handsome he is, especially in uniform, chivalrous and awfully charming. We sat and had tea and biscuits with Mrs Hunt in her drawing room amidst all that dreadful Victorian furniture, with chintz curtains perpetually drawn to keep the Indian sun out.'

'Poor old bat.'

'He said he was Hindu, but it barely registered; his Urdu was so good, and he went to Aligarh Muslim University.'

The women cross and uncross their legs, enjoying Mummy's story. I can't stop listening.

'That's when he told me he was an engineer, a captain in the Indian army based in Bangalore. I felt I had known him all my life; he was everything I'd longed for.'

'Howwww romantic, Nur. He fell for you, na?' says Charlie, flicking ash at Burrimummy's shoe-shaped ashtray.

'I told him that if he didn't play the piano for me that day, I would never play again. He did, terribly.'

More laughter.

'Goodness, I've been babbling. Your cup is empty, Charlie.'

'Don't worry,' Charlie says. 'Carry on. Didn't he do something, rush over from somewhere?'

Now Mummy will tell them the biscuit story.

'Yes. Ved was at some army headquarters miles away, and he rode all night on a motorbike to be with me on the day. He couldn't find a cake at that late hour, so you know what he did? He got twenty-two biscuits, arranged them on a plate, and put candles all around it.'

'Too much,' Charlie says, gazing at Mummy with admiration.

'Your plates are empty. You both must have more.' Mummy cuts a slice across my name. Now I can only read 'POP'. The rest of the letters are gone. Her knife is at an angle, cutting at the cake beneath the doll. Slowly the doll in the ball-gown collapses to one side.

I try to pretend I am someone else and fail.

Buddy plunges her fork once more into my cake and says with her mouth half-full: 'You were naughty, Nur. The way you would pretend he was me when you spoke to Ved on the phone when your mother was around.'

The three women giggle like schoolgirls. Mummy pours more tea, her pearls catching the light, her face smooth and bright like the cream on the cake. She beckons me. Charlie lights another cigarette for herself, then one for Buddy. Mummy takes one too. I see them through spirals of smoke, a blur of lipsticks and teeth.

'I told you to come here, Poppet,' Mummy says kindly. I go to her.

'Stand here. Put your hands together. Now sing. Sing the Robin song.'

I sing 'Robin Sang Sweetly on a Summer's Day'.

'Is Poppet saying Robin thang sweetly on a THUMMA day?' Mummy's voice is full of mirth.

She's holding on to Charlie's arm, nearly knocking her cigarette out of her hand. 'Poppet, tell the aunties how old you are. No, don't say ten, say six.'

'Six,' I say, with my usual lisp.

'And if you're six, how old will you be next year?'

'Seven,' I say, even more sibilant.

The women are holding their stomachs in hilarity. There are tears in Buddy's eyes. They don't care how old I am; that today I am ten. Mummy is laughing, her teeth as white as her pearls.

'This child of yours, she's too much. She's a real little monkey.' Buddy is looking at me as if I am an oddity.

'Nothing like you. So dark.'

'Yes,' says Mummy. 'It can't be helped. She got that from her father's family.'

I can no longer pretend I'm not myself. I am shouting. My voice is reedy and querulous.

'I hate you, Mummy. I wish Burrimummy were my mummy. You don't give a damn about anyone but yourself. You just can't be bothered, can you?'

'How dare you?' Mummy is speaking to me as if I am an adult, like Buddy or Charlie. 'You want a woman who hates me to be your mother?' She flings back her sari pullo. Her cup clatters. Warm liquid covers my face. I don't know if it's deliberate.

'I hate you, munafiq, nonbeliever!' I shout, wiping tears and tea off my face.

Buddy and Charlie rise, fiddling with their handbags. Khaja appears in the room.

I go weeping to Burrimummy, holding Khaja's hand.

'Mummy served my cake at tea. There's no birthday cake left. She threw hot tea at me.' I cry loudly.

Burrimummy rushes out, wiping her face with her sari. Charlie and Buddy have left. Mummy is calmly pouring herself another cup of tea. 'Poppet, that's a bloody lie. It was a mistake.'

'Nur, aren't you ashamed of yourself? It's the child's birthday. You really don't give a damn, do you?'

'It's only a bloody cake, Mother.'

'It's everything to Poppet.'

'Khaja, bring Angel here,' commands Mummy.

Burrimummy stands taller. 'If you take Angel, you will not see me alive again.'

They've done this many times.

'All right, I won't take Angel. No need to kill yourself. You must keep Poppet. I will send for her when I have time. But let me tell you, Ved is terribly angry, and you will have to return Angel to us sooner than you think.'

I stand there, looking from one to the other. Burrimummy and Mummy have just bounced me back and forth as if I wasn't there.

If this ends the way it usually does, she will depart without saying goodbye to us, maybe to go to the officers' mess to join our father or to the Bangalore Club to play cards with her friends, or to the airport, the pallu of her sari streaming behind her in the autorickshaw, shimmering in the ugly splutter of grey fumes. We won't see her for months.

Now Mummy is shouting at Burrimummy's servant Moses to get her an autorickshaw at once, and at Khaja to fetch her bags because she wasn't going to stay to be abused one minute longer.

'I'm off to the mess. I'll be back tomorrow with Ved for my things. We have some news for you. Angel's days in Rest House Road are numbered.'

FOUR

Leaving India

Mummy returns to Rest House Road as promised. I hear the doorbell, then voices. Daddy. I run to the veranda to greet them. Daddy looks drawn and tight-lipped as he pays the taxi. I wonder why they haven't come in an army jeep; why he isn't in uniform. Daddy smiles tenderly at Angel who accepts a kiss on her upturned cheek. When he turns to me, he says, 'Poppet Polly Pudding and Pie.' I fling my arms around him, breathe in his aftershave, feel the roughness of his face.

I don't let go of Daddy's hand while he greets Burrimummy.

Mummy greets Burrimummy, saying 'My The', her fond, singsong way of saying Mother and kisses Angel on both cheeks. We follow the adults into the drawing room. I keep my distance from Mummy, but the minute we are in the drawing room, she bends down in front of me and pulls my resistant body towards her, covering me with kisses. 'My little quarter pint, I missed you so', she says, as if nothing happened.

Burrimummy and Mummy sit opposite one another on the chairs with the claws at the end of their legs. Angel is on Burrimummy's lap, her thumb in her mouth.

I sit down next to Daddy on the sofa; my mouth is suddenly dry at the sight of silver in his hair.

The curtains are drawn, letting in a sliver of dim light that picks up the ghostly outlines of family photographs, Burrimummy's pearls, her crisp mint-cotton sari and Daddy's white shirt. Burrimummy has prepared for this visit. Khaja brings out little kebabs and chutney and sherbet.

Daddy draws a deep breath and says, 'We won't stay to dinner. We're overnighting at the officers' mess, leave for Delhi in the morning and tomorrow at sixteen hundred hours, we fly to London. Winky flies with us. He's packed and at the mess.'

'The army is sending you to London?' Burrimummy looks puzzled.

I hold on tighter to Daddy's hand as he speaks.

'I've resigned. I've been hired to construct a highway on an island in the West Indies. We've got a connecting flight from Heathrow.'

'Why are you leaving the army?' Burrimummy's voice rises one octave.

'We didn't want to worry you,' Mummy says placidly. 'After his heart attack, he decided there is no future in the army for him.'

I can't work out if she hasn't thought about the impact of their decision on Burrimummy or if she's enjoying hijacking her like this.

I feel my heart stop. My daddy had an attack. I know what it means. I've seen one of Burrimummy's Sikh friends, Mr. Talwar, who lived two doors down, laid out in the drawing room with garlands around his neck, his turban intact. Dead.

'Are you sure you're fit to travel?' Burrimummy asks. 'Don't you want to wait a bit?' She's known about the heart attack all along.

'It's not the heart attack. It was mild; I can stay in the army if I wish. I won't be promoted beyond a Colonel, so that career feels over. And I can't serve a prime minister whose policies are abhorrent to me. Elections are suspended, civil liberties disregarded, her political opponents persecuted and imprisoned. The press is censored. As an army man, I don't agree with the mass sterilisation enforced by her son. I've risked my life enough in the trenches. It's been three wars too many.' Daddy's lips are a straight-set line.

Burrimummy looks worried, tries to sound ingratiating but sounds furious. 'I don't know why the world salutes bloody Indira Gandhi. She's as bad as her father with this emergency. Calling India a democracy and here we are practically a socialist country. That bitch won't even allow people to take ten pounds out of here.'

Burrimummy leans forward in terror, and puts a palm on his face, her hand big and white.

'Baba, Ved, is leaving the answer?'

He draws back, so her hand falls away.

I touch Daddy where Burrimummy's hand has been. He smiles, showing his Bollywood teeth.

'Are you all right, Daddy?'

'Yes, my Poppet.'

'Daddy, I want to come with you.'

'Poppet, you're coming to join me soon.'

'Will Angel and Burrimummy come too?'

Burrimummy lets out a cry of alarm. 'Nur, Ved, surely you're not thinking of taking Angel? Why am I only just hearing of all this?'

Mummy says casually, 'I tried, but your sycophants were in the house with you the last time I visited, remember? Anyway, I wanted Ved to tell you himself. Naturally, you are invited to join us.'

Burrimummy places her palms forward as she does in prayer.

'Baba, you're serious. This is not a joke?'

A look of terror crosses Angel's face. She pulls at Burrimummy's neck, wants to be lifted. Burrimummy picks her up and puts her over her shoulder. Her pink legs hang over Burrimummy's torso, the socks pink, frilled.

Excited, I imagine climbing up a coconut tree, like Mowgli, for water and food.

'Daddy, do they have electricity on the island? Will we swim in the sea?'
Daddy's voice grows harsh in a way I've never heard before.

'Don't be ridiculous, Poppet. Of course there are lights and electricity in Tobago.'

Mummy says, 'Really, Mother, it's not as if Angel doesn't have parents.'

'Where is it, Ved?' Burrimummy's wipes the corners of her mouth, stained orange from the paan.

'A tiny island in the Caribbean, south of Miami, a former British colony, like ours.'

Burrimummy stands up; Angel does too. 'That's no place for a child, Ved.'

'Their prime minister, Eric Williams, is an Oxford man. They have oil. They're commissioning a highway. They can't be barbaric.' Daddy sounds amused.

Mummy shouts for Khaja. 'I'm exhausted. Bring me a cup of tea. Make sure to heat the milk.'

Daddy looks at Burrimummy. 'I have booked you, Angel and Poppet on a flight in a month from now. If you can't come, Nur will stay back and bring Poppet and Angel.'

Burrimummy goes towards Daddy, bends down and puts both her hands on his shoulders like a tearful lover pleading for consolation. 'I just can't leave my home, my country, just like that, and go off and live on an island, Ved. Please think it over. Mrs. Gandhi is a shit, but surely you can manage until the children are older?'

Angel has her arms around Burrimummy's legs, making her sari ride up.

'I'm sorry. I've signed a three-year contract to construct a highway in Tobago. It's a new life for us all.'

Burrimummy puts her hands out, palms up, in supplication. 'Look, it's kind of you to think of me, but Angel is a sickly child, not like Poppet who is used to moving about. Take Poppet. You go, all of you. I promise I will bring Angel after you've settled down, after her tenth standard, in a few years. She will write to you every week. Won't you, Angel?'

Angel sticks her thumb in her mouth and snuggles into Burrimummy's starched sari.

'I'm sorry. It's final. It's time we had our daughter back.' Daddy stands up abruptly. 'Nur, we must go.'

Mummy absently kisses Angel and me. 'They are having a little party for him. The officers. Their wives. Goodbye, My The.'

Burrimummy stays rooted to her chair, looking stricken.

Mummy bends down and kisses her, saying pleasantly, 'Khuda Hafiz, God speed, Mother.'

Khaja shows them out.

Burrimummy stays on the chair until it is dark, and I feel responsible for

Angel and ask Khaja to please get her ready for bed. I whisper to Angel, 'It's a special night. We get to tell the ayahs what to do! Bring water!'

I read to her from *The Thousand and One Nights*, and Angel is fast asleep when Burrimummy finally comes in. With her arm around Angel, she weeps soundlessly, her body shaking, while I lie straight in the bed, eyes wide open.

I am still awake when Burrimummy gets out of the bed to the sounds of running water, revving of cars, shouts, and a chorus of frogs, crickets and birds. A rustle and she is dressed and on the raised prayer platform overlooking her rose garden. No human images are allowed. In one fluid movement, her large hand wraps the white cloth around her face and over her shoulders. All is quiet.

The servants are still. Ansia freezes, squatting on her haunches in dirty white pyjamas, holding the hairbrush she has been cleaning with a comb; her face is blurred in the darkened room. Khaja, her hair so oily it makes a wet patch where it touches the floor, pauses while folding clothes. Inside we are all silent.

Burrimummy's hands are folded, right on the left, then they rise to either side of her head.

'*Bismillah ar Rahman ar Raheem.*' Her voice is musical, pleading as if to a beloved.

I lie quiet, barely daring to breathe during her namaaz.

Her hands are now by her side. '*Allah hu Akbar.*' She is bowing, standing straight, bowing, going down on her knees, her head on the ground in sajdah, her big hands flat down on the floor, coming up again, standing, bowing. '*ALLAH Hu Akbar.*' She is sitting now, her head moving from left to right. '*Assallamwailaikum ya Rasoolullah.*' She unwraps the Quran – as it is unwrapped five times daily – from its green and crimson velvet covers shot in silver. Burrimummy turns the pages. As she reads the Arabic suras, we hear the Anglo-Indian tenants at their piano, the distant revving of scooters and autorickshaws. She rises, comes across to us, and blows on our foreheads as if to pass on the benediction. Her breath is fresh, minty.

At that, Angel wakes, sits up anxiously in bed, her white nightie flaring about her.

'You know, darling, the prayers of grownups are sullied with sin, but the prayers of innocent children go straight to God.'

'Dear Allah,' Angel says, 'please don't let Burrimummy ever, ever die. Ameen.'

I say nothing. I don't feel like an innocent child.

Burrimummy then joins us on the bed and reaches for a book of the sayings of the Holy Prophet she has copied in Urdu in pencil, in calligraphy as indecipherable and magical as the music she composes. A black and white photograph of a man drops out of it. He is looking straight at the camera, a handsome, tall man in a suit with a self-indulgent square face, leaning on a barrier at a racecourse. I pick it up and give it to her.

I can't imagine him as a father or a grandfather. Burrimummy picks up the photograph and looks at it. She lets it fall, slaps her forehead, closes her eyes and furrows her brows as if to stop the pain, and reads the caption.

'*Lieutenant-Colonel Fakhr ul-Mulk, Nawabzada Muhammad Saied-uz-Zafar Khan Bahadur, born at Jahan Numa Palace, Bhopal. Born 17th January 1907. He was seven years older than me.*'

'I say, obediently. 'You were born on the 4th of October 1914, Burri.'

'Yes. People in our circle arranged marriages with an exchange of photographs. Puppa sent him a picture of me. Saied was very insistent. He said, "I must see the girl".'

'What happened, Burrimummy?' I know the story well, but I still like to hear it.

'Puppa didn't want to put me on show, like cattle, so he dressed up somebody else, a middle-aged grandmother, a friend of his who was up for a joke, and said, "Come and see your future wife." When Saied lifted her pallo, Puppa laughed his head off. Saied said, "Never mind, very funny. But I've seen your daughter's picture. She's beautiful. I want to marry her."'

Burrimummy interrupts her story to swallow little blue pills from her bedside table. She tells us they got married without seeing each other in person before the wedding, in Bombay, on 23rd May 1936. The wedding was lavish but private, as she was his second wife. He asked her to play the piano at the Taj; they had the reception at the Willingdon Sports Club, and after that, he went out and ordered four pianos for her.

She takes out another photograph of herself, dressed in a bold leopard-print chiffon sari, leaning against him in front of an ornate marble table.

'This is us, on the day we went to a cocktail party where we saw that bloody Mrs Simpson in Vienna.'

Then, 'This is us on our honeymoon in Schönbrunn Palace in Austria.'

She shows me another of her in an Austrian dress, as European as Maria in *The Sound of Music*, and him in a suit and bowler hat with the mountains behind them. 'He made me wear this on the day he took me to Schönbrunn Palace, looking at the Imperial furniture collection, the apartments and the silver in the Hofburg. He fixed his attention on me, made me do the same with him. He taught me how to play chess until I beat him in four moves. Then, just like that, when my life was nothing but him, he got bored.'

She gently extricates her arm from under Angel's body.

'His eyes wandered. He gambled for hours. When the ship docked in Egypt, I visited the pyramids alone with his secretary. In Vienna, he produced tickets for a concert at the Wiener Musikverein, but in the evening he said he had to go elsewhere. I went with his secretary to hear

Brahms' Symphony No. 4 at the Brahms-Saal, a chamber music hall as ornate as the Nizam's Masjid, with green walls, red columns, gold trim. My heart soared and then sank in that hall where my piano teacher thought I would perform one day. I had given up a career as a concert pianist for a man who lost interest in me during our honeymoon, and it was already too late for me because I loved him. The following day he took me to a British embassy party where I saw that damn Mrs. Simpson and her husband, but my heart had already broken, and I was in a fog.'

Burrimummy rests her face on her right palm as if posing for another painting.

I knew the rest. In Switzerland, her indolent, handsome husband checked himself into a sanatorium. He lay in bed all day while Burrimummy wandered with his aide-de-camp on her honeymoon. She caught him kissing a nurse on his bed, in his pyjamas. 'Oh, darling,' he said, 'it's nothing. Why must you be so serious?' Then he gave her his lopsided smile, put his hand in hers. It was as if he had never hurt her, and she was the happiest girl in the world.

Burrimummy adds, 'It was over by the time we came back from our honeymoon. When we got to Bombay, he put me on a train to Bhopal. He stayed on in his flat in Bombay. I saw pictures of him in the society columns with women: Parsees, actresses… at the races, at parties. He was mad about horses, always rushing off to Europe to add to his stud farm, going to the races. He had advisers from everywhere, tempting him with this deal and that, and he fell for everything. He was a reckless man, gambling on anything – stocks, shares, races, horses, people, women, life, everything. Saied-uz-Zafar Khan. Nur's father. The only man I loved.'

The musky sandalwood smells from her elevated prayer area mingles with rained-on earth.

Angel says, 'I want to go to *soo-soo*.'

Burrimummy takes her to the bathroom. Once they are back in bed, Angel puts her small hands on Burrimummy's face and says, 'When will you play the piano?' She knows it takes away Burrimummy's sadness.

'Now,' Burrimummy replies.

She heads for the piano room. I follow her out of the bedroom, through the darkened house, across the drawing room to the book-lined music room. She sits, her back straight, her dressing gown tied around her sturdy frame, working with a pencil on the sheet music, writing on the neat lines she has drawn with her ruler. She turns to the piano. Head and shoulders rolling over a steel-straight spine, eyes closed, Burrimummy thrashes at the piano, her fingers raging across the keys. The avalanche of music summons Angel, who watches with stricken, wide-open eyes.

Burrimummy turns the pages of the scores in a gesture as unconscious as her breath. Bach, Mozart, Beethoven form part of a mysterious, awe-inspiring world of music which we could only gape at in wonder.

After a thunderous finale, Burrimummy shifts scores. She launches into a ditty that must have been bawdy in her mother's time when the Victorians ruled India.

> *'So, Molly dined with the Marquis, what a thing to do,*
> *She found it so nice that she asked for twi-ice,*
> *The whole of the dinner through,*
> *She TOOK champagne in a tumbler,*
> *And thought it a great success,*
> *With smiles growing wider,*
> *"Tis jolly good cider," said Molly the Marchioness.'*

'More, Burri, more,' we shout.

> *'Molly decided to go to court, WHAT a thing to do,*
> *Her neck and her sleeves were rather low,*
> *The train was a twenty YAAA-DAAAR.'*

'Again, Burri, again,' we scream, jumping up and down in our white muslin nighties.

But she abruptly changes tune, and we join in, stumbling through another song, our reedy, childish voices ineffectual beside her molten lava voice, which spills into the early morning, into the tenants' rooms, the servants' quarters, over the unending horns of the traffic across the road to Cubbon Park, where lovers skulk behind bushes.

The music goes straight into our hearts and pours out of our seven and ten-year-old eyes. Burrimummy looks at our teary faces; she keeps them wet with 'Sweet Molly Malone'. Angel and I cover our ears when Molly Malone's ghost is about to wheel her wheelbarrow through streets broad and narrow.

I sense that something in her is lost forever. I make little choking noises.

'I'm coming, I'm coming,' she wails, *'for my head is bending low, I hear their gentle voices calling poor Black Joe.'*

We join in, but Burrimummy carries the music and the momentum. She sings, *'Darling, I am growing ooold, silver thread among the gold,'* with her lover's voice, which seems to come from deep inside her stomach.

Dr Zhivago. She always ends with this. *'Somewhere, my love, there will be songs to sing.'* She stops playing and singing, and suddenly remembers us. 'What will the pieces of my liver, my two eyes, my children of the moon, who came from my own stomach, do alone in this big house all by yourselves if I die?'

Angel and I pluck at her blouse, not rivals, not separate now. We pull at her dressing gown, put our arms around her.

'No, Burri, you will NEVER, EVER die. We WON'T let you. We'd rather die ourselves. You KNOW we love you.' We don't sound like children now, but grownup, thwarted lovers.

'Not long after I left him, he died, you know. He was not yet forty. He went to a party at the palace, had a cup of coffee and died. They laid him out on a marble slab and buried him within twenty-four hours.'

Angel sits on a chair, exhausted, and shuts her eyes, copying Burrimummy's gesture. She will be too tired to go to school today. I let big fat tears pour down my cheeks as if to let her know that, one day, I will remember this and find it sad. We go to sleep grieving for people we will never meet.

FIVE

Bangalore, 1976

Angel and I climb into Burrimummy's black Deccan Herald to see our great-grandmother, the original Angel. 'I must see Mother; tell her we are going away,' she'd said earlier, putting on a crisp sari and pearls. In the car, Burrimummy's feet move as if she is navigating the pedals of a piano. Angel is in the front and I'm in the back with the windows down.

We move along Cubbon Park's leafy boulevards, sun filtering between branches, breeze rustling, a sudden shower carrying the fragrance of wet earth and tangy fruit. Burrimummy says, on cue, 'Darling, we live in the garden city of India. That's why it's so cool all year round.' We drive past Bangalore Palace's turrets and towers, past Alsur Lake, past St Johns Road, past the long, nugget-shaped Vidhan Soudha, a palatial government building glowing gold from inside, reflecting light on its vast formal gardens, and past the brick-red State High Court.

Burrimummy is the eldest of Mumma's five children. The eldest son, Rasheed, is now the Nawab of Savanur and lives in another part of Bangalore in a bungalow known as Savanur House, the only visible remnant of the princely state of Savanur gifted to their ancestor in 1672 by Aurangzeb.

On the way, we continue to hear the usual complaints, how she, Burrimummy, who had done the most for her ungrateful mother, got so little and the others, who didn't give a damn, got so much. Burrimummy and Wahid resent Rasheed, who inherited the title and the bulk of the wealth and land from Burrimummy's father's princely estate. Shaheen, Burrimummy's unmarried sister, with the same shaped face as Burrimummy, the same musical voice, but as dark as me, with a hooked nose and thin lips, lives with Rasheed. They are in divided camps. Their middle sister, Meher, lives in America, and apart from being told she is Mumma's favourite daughter, she is not spoken of.

I can't work out if Burrimummy admires Mumma or hates her.

'My father loved me, you know, and never let me forget Savanur comes from the Persian word Shahnoor, which means "king of light". That's what he named me – Shahnur.'

Burrimummy stops the car in front of a Hindu temple with a sixty-five-

foot statue of Shiva holding a pitchfork and a snake in two of his raised
hands. The two remaining hands are folded in supplication.

'Dekho, look at that obscenity! An entire temple for Sheeva's lingam, his
thingamabob. You know there is an entire path INSIDE the statue's gaaf
filled with marble lingams. They even have one in ice.' She refuses to
pronounce Shiva correctly, deliberately making it sound foreign – 'Sheeva'.

'What's inside, Burrimummy?'

'A HUGE statue of a blue elephant they call god, darling.' She laughs.
'You can't have hundreds of frightening gods like the Hindus, or three
Gods, Father, Son *and* Holy Ghost, like the Christians, even though
Muslims DO acknowledge Jesus as a prophet. STILL, you CAN'T serve two
masters. No matter what happens to us, we NEVER give up our Allah.'

She sings:

> *ONWARD Mohammedan soldiers*
> *MARCHING off to war*
> *With the love of Mohammed*
> *Going on before.*

We drive into the old city, past the markets, dozens of little sari shops and
locksmiths' shops, tailor shops and ice cream parlours. She weaves her car
deftly between peanut vendors, hawkers with carts of thick ropes of woven
jasmine for women's hair, people jumping on and off crammed moving
buses, entire families perched on a cycle, scooters, everyone hooting and
jostling.

As Burrimummy slows down in the traffic, women with dark, skeletal
faces and claw-like hands come to our windows, pointing at their babies'
big bellies, making signs of hunger at their mouths. Burrimummy shoos
them away with a hand that looks like marble against their skin. She stops
the car to point out an imposing, three-domed white marble building with
twin towers on granite pillars and an intricately carved balcony. 'This,
darling, is Jama Masjid, made by the Mughals. It was designed,' she says, 'by
a famous architect in Hyderabad as the seat of Mughal, Turk and Afghan
power. More than ten thousand men can fit in there for Eid namaaz, you
know. THIS is sacred. That other temple we saw is a profane monstrosity.'

I ponder the difference between the profane and sacred in a foggy,
childlike way. Sometimes they feel like the same thing to me. Or parts of
the same thing.

Burrimummy turns into a shady avenue of sprawling old homes with
circular driveways, with large rose bushes shedding petals in gardens
shaded by trees – guavas, sapodilla, jamun, tamarind, mangoes. Branches
of overripe fruit dangle over cracked and peeling walls which have a look
of stricken majesty on the edge of collapse. Rain-damp earth mingles with
rancid, sweetened decay.

Mumma lives with Burrimummy's youngest brother, Wahid, in Davis Road with his American-Jewish wife, Aunt Adrian. Wahid, whom Mumma loves best, whom Burrimummy adores, has gambled everything away on the stock market, and keeps threatening to move to America, to his wife's family in California.

'You know, when he returned from England after getting his degree, Wahid kept a European woman in the garage for months. He once took her for a ride on his motorcycle and didn't notice she had fallen off. She was unharmed, but that was the end of that.'

At a traffic light, we see a man urinating near a tree. Burrimummy says casually, 'Bloody Indians. So uncivilised. The British should never have left.' She laughs, as if to herself, 'My brothers Wahid and Rasheed once urinated into the open mouth of my ayah.'

I swallow, thinking of the urine. People like that lived carelessly, did what they wanted, uncaring of others.

With its faded olive window frames and wood roses on the latticed garage, Mumma's house on Davis Road looks the oldest of them all. Its driveway is covered with weedy foliage.

As we drive into the wasteland of dead trees, fallen leaves and wilting rose bushes, Burrimummy says, 'After Puppa died, your great-grandmother bought this house and ran it with the privy purse until the ruddy Indian Government took that too. Look at the state of the garden! Wahid should care for Mumma's house instead of throwing money at the stock market.'

We are met by a chorus of yapping dogs racing down the front steps, followed by Adrian – an untanned, white, freckled woman in a short blue mini dress, showing solid thighs in a manner Burrimummy calls vulgar. With wiry red hair that looks alive, Adrian is as big-boned and square-jawed as Burrimummy, but her blue, deeply-set eyes are kind, and she seems perpetually distracted as if that's the only way she can deal with the chaos around her. She is hollering at the dogs, 'Abdul, Kismet, Bismillah! Stop! Stop! Sit! Sit!'

'Salaam Alaikum, Adrian.' Burrimummy greets Adrian with an injured smile, looking pointedly at her thighs as we get out of the car. Aunt Adrian doesn't notice and kisses Burrimummy's cheeks and says hello to Angel and me with a little wink of her eyes.

'Walaikum salaam, Burri Bibi,' Adrian responds, in an accent we associate with Anglo-Indians. I don't understand anything she says. Burrimummy is holding Angel's hand. I am squirming around Burrimummy's sari, scared of the dogs. Mummy has passed her fear on to me. When we come across dogs, Mummy digs her nails into my arm, always remembering the Alsatians who bit her, how her grandfather had them put down, the sixteen injections in her stomach and afterwards, how her uncles would make her say salaam to the dogs as their price to keep them away from her.

An emaciated Tamil ayah has been sweeping up leaves and rotten fruit under the laden Jamun tree. As we arrive, she puts down her broom and picks up a bucket, throwing water on the concrete around the entrance, some of which lands on Burrimummy's sari in round patches.

'Oh, GOD, can't you see I'm walking up the stairs?' This is followed by obscenities. The woman cowers, her sari pulled over her face.

My granduncle Wahid walks towards us, holding a glass of whisky in his left hand, raising his right hand in greeting while balancing a lit cigarette in his mouth from the corner of which he says salaam to Burrimummy, followed by a hug. 'Have you found a husband yet, Aapma?' Burrimummy scrunches up her eyes and frowns, but I can tell she likes whatever her younger brother says. He has the face of Marlon Brando mixed with the Bollywood star Dharmendra, except he is more handsome, heftier, taller, with a booming voice.

He gulps the whisky, flicks his cigarette on the steps, picks up Angel and says, 'Hello, Burrimummy's Angel.' All ribbons and bright eyes, Angel beams at our granduncle.

He sings, 'Well, hello, Poppet. You're looking swell, Poppet.'

We follow him into the drawing-room, dark with heavy furniture and a multitude of Mumma's knickknacks. There are photographs of Puppa attending his majesty's levee in London in 1925, in white, wearing a turban and full regalia; Mumma in school uniform looking like an English girl – Minden Hurst Girls' School, Eastbourne; Mummy, a baby in Savanur House with her English nurse; Sir Afsar with Burrimummy; Sir Afsar in uniform at the coronation of the new King-Emperor – Edward 7th, leading the Golconda regiment.

The ashtrays are overflowing, soiled nappies are scattered. Maimanath, a toddler, rolls about on the sofa with some puppies, chattering nonstop, her eyes as green as her mother's. The baby, a boy, is in the crib, fast asleep.

There are dogs everywhere, wandering in and out, leaping on the furniture, sitting at granduncle Wahid's feet, playing with the children. Brown springs sprout from a sofa covered in dog hair, its cushions ripped by one of these canines. Wahid picks up two. 'Look at these beauties. Dachshunds. I got them last week. Cost me plenty.'

Burrimummy sounds annoyed but takes one from Wahid. 'Really, Wahid, this is awfully unhygienic. I don't care if you've paid a packet for them; they shouldn't be in the house.' An old Alsatian sleeps on the dark grand piano, elegantly curved, pedals poking out like paws beneath a velvet dress. 'A Blüthner,' says Burrimummy, closing her eyes, running her fingers over the keys, her hands spread out. 'Out of tune.'

The chaos is dizzying. I feel as if I'm looking on from a merry-go-round. Adrian appears and disappears from the room like a ghostly figure.

'How's your big round arse, Aapoo?' Wahid grabs Burrimummy's bottom, so Angel and I giggle into a cushion. Burrimummy scolds Wahid in an indulgent, flirtatious voice. 'Really, Wahid, what a thing to do to your sister.' Wahid turns away from Burrimummy and shouts for Adrian. 'Where's the bloody soda water?'

'I'll go say hello to Mother first,' Burrimummy tells Wahid, as he downs another whisky, neat, in one shot, his voluptuous lips moistening, his eyes troubled and teasing by turns. I imagine the stocks he's lost as a collection of brilliant, dazzling little bricks made of gold and jewels.

We follow Burrimummy into Mumma's room. It smells of urine, dogs, rotting flowers and Dettol. I edge closer to Burrimummy, breathing in her sandalwood scent to ward off the other smells. Mumma is there – a toothless woman in a red dressing gown that has fallen open to reveal mounds of white doughy flesh. She is half-lying, half-sitting – propped up in bed by many pillows – gulping sweet red sherbet with barley, eating a slice of cake, arguing with herself. 'Why shouldn't I have cake? It sends up my sugar. Never mind – it's a small luxury. I'll be dead before long.'

Mumma lies across from a life-sized painting of her as a young girl in full riding gear on a white horse, her hair flaring like a pre-Raphaelite. She looks imperious and beautiful, unrelated to the woman on the bed.

Burrimummy bends over Mumma, her right hand raised to her forehead in a salute.

'*Asalaam Alaikum*, Mumma.'

'Hello, Burri Bibi,' Mumma says, looking unimpressed.

Burrimummy stands rooted to her place, helpless in a way I've never seen before.

'Why did you come, Bibi?'

'I came because I wanted to see you, Mumma.'

Burrimummy bows her head like a contrite child.

'Like hell, you did.'

Burrimummy takes hold of Angel – pink-cheeked, hair tied in silk ribbons, dressed in frills – and nudges her forward.

'Look. I've brought Angel.'

'Nur's child? I love Nur.'

Burrimummy's face twists into something, envy.

Angel sucks her thumb while Burrimummy grips her shoulder. I look on, glad for once to be invisible.

Mumma's gummy mouth shifts with a crooked smile.

'Angel, is it? I know Angel. It's my name, after all, that you've given my great-granddaughter. She's sweet. A little too sweet. She looks too pampered to me. Does she ride, swim, play tennis? Well, she should, you know. Doesn't she have any manners?'

Burrimummy places her hand on Angel's head, bending down to

whisper, 'Say Salaam Walaikum, with your right palm to your face, Baby.'
Angel obeys and Burrimummy follows this with a quick defensive salvo.
'Mumma, you need a new dressing gown. That gaudy red is ghastly.'

'Never mind, Shahnur, I like it. It will be dark in the grave.' Mumma
closes her eyes.

The moods between the women shift so fast that it is hard to know which
grownup to bat for.

Mumma opens one eye. 'Whose boy is that?'

I hop around nervously, self-conscious of my short hair, inflicted by
Mummy. I am wearing a peculiar dress with puffed sleeves made from
leftover material from one of Mummy's petticoats.

'She's Poppet, Nur's older daughter.'

'I like her,' she says, ignoring Angel, who is as pale as herself.

My heart soars.

'Why does your grandmother call your sister Angel and Sadrunissa? I am
Angel. My mother was Sadrunissa. Doesn't your sister have her own
name?'

She does, but it's Hindu. It's Ishani. I dare not say it aloud.

Mumma beckons me to the bed with her swollen, diabetic hand.

'Come.' She sings with a cracked, heavy voice: 'Hello, Poppet! It's so
nice to have you back where you belong.'

She thinks I belong. Her smile is genuine and gives me the courage to
advance. 'Poppet, boy, you're dark, but I bet you're wild. Aren't you,
darling? It's in your eyes. What do you like to do? Do you ride? Do you play
tennis?'

'I'm not good at tennis, Mumma. I prefer stories.'

'Oh,' she says, 'well, I can tell you stories.' She sounds as if she is weeping
with all her quivering flesh. 'I never thought I would end up here, you
know, dependent on my children. I imagined dying in a roomful of pearls,
married to the Nizam of Hyderabad, the richest man in the world, nowhere
like this wretched Bangalore. He saw me riding in the public gardens and
wanted to marry me but my grandfather, Sir Afsar, made me marry your
grandfather, the Nawab of a very minor state, with not even a *one*-gun
salute. I wanted to study medicine, Poppet darling. But as soon as I was
sixteen, Sir Afsar brought me back from England to marry a man I'd never
met.'

Burrimummy interrupts her mother, 'Puppa's dead and gone now. He
adored you.'

Mumma ignores Burrimummy.

'Darling Poppet, you look like a peculiar boy. I have nothing to give you.
All my stocks and shares have disappeared, and I've no money to pay my
medical bills. I don't know what happened to the money. Your grandmother won't help. She was a difficult child, you know. Very selfish. She

was good-looking, I suppose and played the piano well, Sir Afsar's favourite great-grandchild because she was fat and pink. He called her Rosy, can you believe it? When she left her marriage, she returned to Savanur and tried to act like the Begum of Savanur state, lord it over me. She wanted her own apartments, a blank cheque book. My husband spoiled her, gave her what she wanted, called her Begum Pasha, a queen among emperors. Imagine that… no wonder she always thought too much of herself. I had to bring her down a peg or two. That's why I would rather die a pauper – give everything away than give it to her.'

'Stop it, Mother. It's simply wrong to demean me like that, especially in front of a child.'

Mumma ignores Burrimummy and asks me to pass her silver paan holder.

Mumma continues, 'I had a bloody awful mother, you know. Do you want to hear about her? Sir Afsar forced her and me – both of us – to marry against our will.'

Burrimummy has the same sadness in her eyes as when she plays the piano. She turns around and leaves the room, Angel racing after her. I stay with Mumma.

Mumma catches me looking at a photo of my great-great-grandmother, a young, waif-like woman dressed like an Englishwoman in a delicate lace gown.

She picks it up. 'My mother Sadrunissa, at the Delhi Durbar in 1902. She looks like a wilting flower, but she used to buy slave children whose parents went from house to house during the great drought and famine in India before the war. She had their heads shaved and, as the girls grew, their breasts bound. She made them work all over Mumtaz mansion. Woken by cries, I saw her whipping one of them one night. I always thought it was the peacocks in the gardens, but it was her beating one of them over something or another. She beat me too, for wetting my bed. She couldn't love me, you know. Even when she was dying, she went on and on about how my father Mumtaz broke his promise and never divorced his first wife.'

'Adrian,' she shouts for her daughter-in-law. 'Adrian!'

Mumma is done with me.

The ayah who had been throwing water in the veranda earlier comes rushing in. She has the ubiquitous look of India's destitute millions: dark, bony-faced, broad-nosed, nose-ringed, emaciated.

'Yes, Maa, you called, Maa?'

'Can you tell Adrian Memsahib I want chicken sandwiches? I'm tired of Indian food.'

Mumma spits orange tobacco out, but it misses her silver *paan-daan* and lands on the floor.

Burrimummy walks into the bedroom alongside her dark replica, her sister Shaheen, who lives with the Nawab of Savanur, their elder brother.

'Mumma, darling, I'm here.' Her voice sounds like Burrimummy's but higher, petulant, expressing a lifetime of disappointment. Puppa rejected suitor after suitor for her because they were Hindu or not Sunni Muslims.

'Darling Shaheen, you're here.'

Shaheen kisses Mumma then turns to her sister, 'Salaam, Burrimummy. I see you've brought your granddaughters.'

Burrimummy does not respond.

'Why did you really come?' Shaheen asks Burrimummy, 'And have you appropriated both of Nur's girls now? They should be with their parents. I'm sorry to say, Shahnur, but you really can be like shit wrapped in silver.'

'You should talk, Shaheen; you never married.'

Mumma says, 'Why *did* you come?'

'I came to say goodbye. I'm going to the West Indies with Nur, Ved and the children.'

Mumma says, 'Oh God! Why can't you leave Nur alone and stop interfering?'

I switch off from these conversations, thinking about the tiger skin in the drawing-room, the one Mumma shot in Gwalior. I quietly leave the bedroom to look closely at the tiger's face again. Its uneven teeth are reflected in the gilded mirrors of various lengths on the walls. Voices in Mumma's bedroom rise and fall like piano notes. I catch my reflections in the mirrors, reflected into infinity. I pretend I am a magician, spinning myself in this grand room, dizzy, my spinning merging into the black and gold of the tiger skin, the crystal chandelier splintering with each swirl. I hear footsteps and rush to hide, but a large hand clasps my shoulder. Orange tobacco lands on my cheeks. 'What is Nur's little black girl doing dancing in the drawing-room like a Hindu monkey?'

It is Shaheen. I am terrified, knowing this is not the time to cry. She hauls me from the drawing-room out to the veranda. Another scream ensues, this time from Burrimummy, who is running in, betel-nut juice spewing from her mouth.

'This is the limit. Poppet is a small CHILD. YOU are the blackie, Shaheen. YOU are.'

On the way home, Burrimummy talks to herself.

'Mumma is a self-indulgent woman, darling, terribly unhappy in Savanur, you know. Puppa built a castle for her, but she said it was a castle in a village. She'd never have been married to the Nizam, but just part of his huge harem. I'm fed up with Shaheen saying she got a proposal from Zulfikar Ali Bhutto, which Puppa turned down. Bhutto got over it easily. After that, Shaheen never married. Rasheed is a saint putting up with her.'

We haven't had a chance to kiss Mumma goodbye. I never see Mumma, Wahid or his children again.

*

I wake to my own screaming – a night-fright, an advancing invisible menace I can't see or describe. I'm comforted to smell cigarette smoke, fragrant tobacco and grab Burrimummy's dressing gown.

She puts her arms around me. I touch her face. She squeezes my shoulder like it's a piece of dough and I am loved again.

SIX

St Lucia, 2016

The seatbelt sign is off, and I look down on the ocean, reaching for a copy of *White Egrets*. Angel said she was reading it when I called her after I booked my ticket to St Lucia. Reaching her is always my first impulse, and I don't know if it's to share or compete or both. Our love, Angel's and mine, feels like a tattered accordion, unbearably close at times, stretched wide at others, with the rare pure high note, more often negotiating discordant semiquavers. As much as we want to break free from one another, we are interchangeable and intertwined; to hurt the other is to harm ourselves. After not seeing or speaking for months, we meet in doctors' offices to accompany Mummy and Daddy to their appointments and find we are reading the same books. They live their lives as they always have, impervious to our concerns, with rounds of bridge, dinner parties among the ex-pat Indian community and Indian High Commission events

'Puppa…' – I sometimes addressed her the way Burrimummy did – 'imagine, Derek Walcott wants me to visit.'

Pause. 'Will you go?'

She says it as if it's a moral issue.

'Of course.'

Another pause.

'I took Mummy to the doctor today. Her sugar is high, but I sorted her medication out for the next three months. It's been an exhausting day.'

'Well, I sorted out her facial and nails last week, so at least she wasn't unkempt.'

Silence. Angel always defeated me with hers.

'I'll call you when I get back.'

'Okay. I'll look after Mummy and Daddy. Don't worry.'

She had won this one. After Burrimummy, Angel had felt a need to belong and tried extremely hard to be the good daughter. I tried, too, but spoke out a little too much to have an edge in that competition. We had both returned to Trinidad from England – where we had both planned to settle after our degrees – when Winky fell ill with a rare disease, and we had to support him and Mummy and Daddy through that terrible time. We were both married within a year of coming home: she to the Englishman she'd met at university and me to a Trinidadian man.

The seatbelt light comes on, and the island's pitons rise like castles circled by the ocean in swathes of blue and green. The plane shudders, drops, floats and drops again, and I brace for the landing.

My eyes find Derek first, in the wheelchair, dressed for the beach in shorts and a T-shirt. Sigrid is standing next to him, waving frantically at me, and as I go towards them, I see her yellow hair darkened by sweat, her face, pink and luminous in the afternoon heat. She's dressed in comfortable trousers and a bright cotton blouse.

Sigrid comes forward, and encouraged by her smiling light-blue eyes, I move tentatively towards Derek, bend down, and shake his large hand, surprisingly sturdy, covered in dark liver spots. His eyes, narrowed as if to escape the sun, seem to take in everything at once, yet the air around him is dense, an invisible force-field barring entry, his expression aloof. I hesitate, uncertain if he meant me to come here.

He smiles suddenly – the smile of the man he once was, the stud with the golden skin. He could be a Mexican farmer with that face. As I return his smile, his turns lopsided, self-conscious. I look away as Sigrid and the driver manoeuvre him into the car.

Their driver steps forward and takes my bag. 'Thank you, Malcolm,' she says, and I follow suit, as if parroting Mummy.

Settled in the front seat, he puffs himself up and throws his chest out as if he has nothing to do with his body in the wheelchair, his taciturnity there to override any shred of pity for his immobility. I wonder if the service of care he is forced to accept from Sigrid is a drain on them both.

From the back seat, the rear-view mirror shows his profile, closed eyes as if in some conversation with himself. Abruptly, he cranes his neck towards the sea with an alertness that reminds me of Burrimummy.

'You okay? Good flight?'

'Yes, thank you, Derek.'

The humidity hits me, the sea air whipping through the open car windows – so different from the dry Trinidad heat. My eyes cloud up.

I spend the rest of the dizzying mountainous drive to his house in a semi-hallucinatory state, cooling air on my face, eyes blinking at the dazzling heaps of canary-yellow bananas, crates along the road covered in bright-blue canvas, thick green vegetation, the ocean's wide broad bands of cerulean and jade fading into the powdery hot morning sky. A great black hawk cuts close to my window, startling me. Sigrid, in the back seat with me, asks the driver to stop by a Minimart – on a narrow street where boys play cricket with a makeshift bat. 'Our guests make their own breakfasts,' she explains. I take the hint, open the car door and get out.

Derek must stay put, but I imagine him walking out, striding ahead of me, taking charge. As Sigrid reaches out to the front seat to put a protective hand on his arm, I get out of the car.

The grocery shop is dark inside, the atmosphere thick with the smells of camphor balls, incense and earth from the yams. Papayas, green figs, bananas and bags of shrunken grapes are suspended on strings. I race around, not wanting to keep them waiting. They stock the usual fare of pickled plums and salted prunes, peanuts and tamarind balls, white bread, salted fish, cheese and eggs.

I grab eggs, bananas, milk and bread, pay quickly and head back to the car.

We scrunch up a long driveway leading to a house that stands blinding white on the flattest part of the land sloping down to a wide lawn, bordered by flowers, heliconia, tiger lilies, shaded by fruit trees – mango, zaboca, orange, lime. The swimming pool on the lower layer of the land appears to merge with the bleached light of the bay. The ocean crashes at the cliffs below.

Snug in the corner of a bright leafy garden, a grasshopper green hammock sways between two trees. A path and steps lead to a small cottage. Perfect for Little Red Riding Hood.

We approach the main house by the side gate and enter through the kitchen, straight to the study, the heart of the home. The light filters through French windows and cream curtains onto white sofas and weathered books, giving the room the luminosity of a theatre. There are thousands of books, yellowed by sunlight and sea breeze. Another partially open door shows glimpses of a more formal dining room with antique furniture and yet more French windows. This house was designed to make the most of the St Lucian light. Sigrid disappears into the kitchen. I can hear her discussing something that needs fixing and the fish required for lunch with Malcolm, the driver.

The walls are hung with watercolours, mostly seascapes in teal and sapphire, rimmed by caked earth and pewter rocks. Some are peopled, with a fisherman or a solitary beach walker. I wonder which paintings are his, which his father's.

I examine a heavily annotated, old Faber & Faber edition of T.S. Eliot's *Four Quartets* from his bookshelves, as if his books are a doorway to his mind.

This space is a shrine of his life – the formative books: Chaucer, Shakespeare, Maugham, Pound, Eliot. His own work, several editions of *Omeros*, plays and poetry collections take centre space on the shelves.

Derek approaches me in his wheelchair, looking at the worn Dickens in my hand.

'My father's. He died before I knew him. Young. Just thirty.'

'He wrote?'

'Not exactly, although there were some jocular poems and prose. My father painted watercolours, composed poetry, left me some good records, – I felt I needed to continue the work, you know.'

So even Nobel Laureates write for approbation from parents, alive or dead. Naipaul did the same for his journalist father with writing ambitions, even briefly writing for the *Trinidad Guardian*. His father never achieved the success his talent deserved. How much of Naipaul's writing was the loving act of a child wanting to complete his father's truncated ambition – the son finishing off his father's business?

I think of Burrimummy – born in 1915, a full fifteen years older than Derek – who was stopped from going to Vienna to take up her music scholarship, how her Anglo-Indian piano teacher said Burrimummy was gifted with acute musical timing and photographic memory. But in the 1930s, a woman leaving India to live and study in Europe was unthinkable. As I've recorded, she was married off to a widower almost twice her age – a beautiful philanderer who broke her heart, and from whom she never recovered. In the end, she lost both – the music and the man. I was here to salvage something for her and maybe myself.

He is saying, 'My mother influenced me, always reciting Shakespeare, lending me money to publish my first collection of poems when I was just eighteen.'

His mother, then a young, widowed teacher, a seamstress and actress, had seemingly denied him nothing and for a woman carrying the entire household to invest that much in her young son's poetry was remarkable. With no obstacles, he finished the incomplete work of the dead. He did what he wanted and had probably never felt a duty to look after anyone. His first and last duty was to his art. I thought this resentfully as he spoke. I had spent my life playing by the rules of wife, mother and part breadwinner. When was I to learn to wrestle for myself such expansive time?

When he turns his attention on me, I feel the same way as I did around Burrimummy: awed and terrified, but transfixed, as if no price were too high to win her love. I lived for those small moments with Burrimummy.

'Sigrid, Sigrid,' Walcott yells with increasing urgency.

Malcolm rushes in with her, his eyes scanning Derek, alert to his needs.

'I need to go to the bathroom.'

'Let's go, dear. Or do you want Malcolm to take you?' she replies cheerfully.

Derek glares at her as if it is all her fault as she wheels him to his bedroom. She doesn't stop smiling. 'It's okay, Malcolm,' she says. 'See you on Monday.'

Malcolm hesitates, gives me a suspicious look and leaves the room.

I return to his bookshelves, pick out Hemingway's *The Old Man and the Sea,* and inspect Walcott's sprawling handwritten annotations.

'He's resting. Would you like a cup of tea, dear?' Sigrid's voice sounds faintly tired. It feels familiar as when, after a bust-up, my husband some-times turned to me and asked casually if I wanted a cup of tea.

Back in the kitchen, she talks as she works, washing vegetables, putting things away, checking her iPad while I sip tea.

'The vegetables are all local and Derek loves fish which I get from the village. We like everything fresh. I give the housekeeper a day off on Saturdays.' She tells me she runs the house, pays the bills, rotates the staff, sorts out the meals, pays the drivers, sorts out plumbing, deals with agents, and is in the midst of organising his annual birthday cruise a few weeks away, which will include five Nobel Laureates.

They've been together since 1986. She was an uptown New York girl – an art curator. They met at an exhibition at the Carnegie Library in Pittsburgh. 'You know what got me? He was more knowledgeable about art than I was.' She is the daughter of Latvian immigrants, she says. Her father was a psychiatrist, her mother a nurse. Curative, caring professions, both dead.

'I have come to love this island more than any place on earth. It is home now. So no, I don't miss New York at all. Derek is a workaholic, and I'm here to enable the art.'

I sense Sigrid as an alter ego to Derek – subsuming her own fine intellect with ordinary tasks and wonder if she makes herself smaller for him. I feel terrible that I have this view of her and decide she is where she wants to be, does what she wants.

Malcolm leaves, shutting the door quietly. I sense how vulnerable these two are here – an infirm older man and his foreign wife in their expensive home, alone at night.

There is a shout from the bedroom.

'Sigrid!'

She disappears. I will not look at the wheelchair, I decide. I will look at Derek's books until he is ready to see me. I'm still looking at his books when she wheels him onto the veranda. 'Why don't you come out here and talk to Derek?' she says and leaves.

My legs go wobbly from a sudden pang of hunger and feeling that I don't deserve to be here, worrying that I must perform and will come up short. I sit down in a well-used, cushioned rattan chair opposite him, glad for the table between us, piled with his books. I'd left Trinidad when it was dawn, and the morning was already ripening.

My eyes sting at the glare, the rippled surface of the shell-shaped pool, shimmering in the breeze, and beyond it the distant curve of the bay on the other side of the island. A low white picket fence closes off the veranda to the garden where the green hammock is eerily still, as if defying the wind.

Sigrid returns. 'Let's get you settled,' she says to me. 'Come this way.'

All this beauty, and I suspect he hasn't been able to walk on the grass for a long time.

Derek looks out at the pool.

'Let me show you to your room, dear,' Sigrid repeats and leads me across the garden along a path shaded by a giant dark-green tree, its roots running along the path. I admire women like Sigrid, their tireless service to art, but I wonder why they don't bother creating their own legacies. Maybe this is hers. I chide myself for speculating on her life, given I know so little about her, and can't shake off the feeling that I am a chore managed with polite grace.

'I brought the rest of the manuscript with me,' I say. 'Just in case he didn't receive the one I posted.'

I am dissembling, not entirely understanding why. I know he received it. He told me he had when I called to give him my flight details.

'He's been reading it, dear.'

The 'cottage' is like a bedsit, a single room with a kitchenette, with a stove, sink and miniature counter, and ahead, the en suite bedroom.

'This is where you will be staying. There's water in the fridge. Freshen up, make yourself breakfast.'

As she turns to leave, she points to a table and chair on the veranda, with the view of the water, the pool, the cleft on the lawn, leading to the cliffs, the sea. 'This is where our writers write.' When she leaves, I shut the door and can't tell if it's the waves or thunder.

I unpack my groceries: bread, eggs, bananas and milk, fill a pan with water, put in an egg, turn the stove on, return to the bed and lie down on the faded patterned bedspread in the poets' cottage, waiting for an egg to boil. I know Arthur Miller was Derek's friend and visited him here. Like a tabloid journalist, I speculate whether Marilyn Monroe herself lay here once with Arthur Miller. There are always reports of his buddies Seamus Heaney and Joseph Brodsky on his birthday cruises. Where do I find the gall to sleep in the same bed as those great dead and living poets?

The sound of shattering.

Gunshots? No, this is St Lucia. Not Trinidad.

There's glass on the bed and on the floor. I remove a shard from my slippers, put them on and walk to the stove covered in shattered glass gingerly dipping a finger in the pan on the stove.

Mystifyingly, the boiled egg is cool. The glass covering of the stove has exploded – I forgot to lift it off before putting the pan with the egg on the burner. The cover must have prevented the heat from touching the pan. It has blown up.

I take a few steps to the front door and inch it open, peeping out like a criminal. It's quiet. Eleven o'clock. Two hours till lunch. The ocean beyond the swimming pool is a brilliant ice blue. The door to the great white house is shut. After closing my door, I head back to the bed, pick my way around the shards of glass, and lie down. Don't overreact. Remember, you've been diagnosed with things that make you jumpy. A touch can feel like a blow.

I raise and dismiss solutions.

Should I call my husband, Sadiq, in Trinidad, to look up electric goods places in St Lucia? But there is the problem of the delivery of the stove.

I could sweep the glass and pretend it hasn't happened. No, God, what am I thinking?

I could slip out and leave for the airport and get a flight home, leaving them all the cash I have, but I don't have enough to pay for the stove.

I could walk over at teatime and confess, offering to order another stove online, but that will take days.

I do nothing.

My face burns with shame. I bet none of the other writers and poets who stayed here did anything this undignified, nor would they worry if they did. I'm granted one weekend to spend with a Nobel Laureate, and I fuck up the stove and fuck myself up even more for doing so.

He is reading the MS I gave him, and here I am, an unworthy visitor to this cottage, vandalising the stove of two old people who have no help on the weekend.

He didn't invite me here for my poetry as I've written none. I'm a journalist – his daughter's friend. He asked to see my manuscript, but something within himself, his own vulnerability at the end of his life, may have intuited my need for approbation, the kind he and Naipaul sought long after their fathers were dead, something unresolved that moved us towards one another as if recognising there is comfort in knowing we aren't alone?

Did he, too, have unexamined, troubling memories – like the dregs of rose water in which my sister was submerged, and the python shot in the head in my father's dressing room, a sight that directed my adolescent dreams towards deathly desires? Did his dead mother and father appear to him as if a mirage?

Peering out of the window of the cottage at the sunlit garden, at the deep swaying, patterned shades of the weighty tamberin tree, the sturdy frog-green hammock with its own life, I also wonder uneasily whether Derek asked me here to remind himself of the power he once had over women, or if he really saw me struggling to belong somewhere.

Something about this garden, the phosphorene green of filtered sunlight through leaves, the purple shadows of mango trees, fetid rotten half-eaten fruit submerged with dead leaves on the earth, reminds me of Cubbon Park, of Rest House Road. I want to go out but am frozen, afraid of being found out.

PART TWO

Tobago

'Break a vase, and the love that reassembles the fragments is stronger than that love which took its symmetry for granted when it was whole.'
                                                                    — Derek Walcott

SEVEN

Bangalore, Tobago 1976

17 Rest House Road is slowly being emptied. Burrimummy is sitting in her dressing gown, supervising the packing, meticulously recording everything she is leaving behind in a little book.

She has had nine massive black trunks cleaned and lined with newspaper. They have been filling up with household things – silver, saris, crockery – sorted and then locked and stored in her guest room. She empties her glass-fronted cupboards of miniature teapots with matching cups; teapots shaped like peacocks' houses; blue and white soup bowls with dragon shapes. She carefully wraps each one with newspaper and puts them in a trunk marked CHINA.

'Sir Afsar wanted me to have these from when he fought in China in 1900. The others got most of it – I got the dregs. He was on the staff of Count Von Waldersee during the Boxer Rebellion in 1901. The British looted the Emperor's palace.'

She supervises the removal of photographs from walls, wraps them and places them in a trunk marked PHOTOGRAPHS.

'Look at this, my two eyes.'

It's a framed card. Mumma. She's leaning on a garden urn, swathed in pearls, a diamond in her hair. The card says, in italics, 'To wish you not great grandeur, nor store of worldly wealth, only a mind contented, peace, happiness and health. The Palace. Savanur. 1915.'

'The grand Begum of Savanur, Khaleequnissa, sulking as usual.'

Burrimummy uses her mother's title with irony. This is Mumma, whose flesh spreads like melting lard, who gives us terrible toothless smiles in Davies Road, whose bills nobody can pay. With no concept of time, I understand how that happened to her.

'Does Mumma love you, Burrimummy?' I ask.

'No, darling. She does not. She thinks my father ruined me. I had a younger brother, Maqbool, whom she loved more. One summer, when Mumma and Puppa were in England, Maqbool died of diphtheria. On her return, I heard Mumma telling Puppa she wished I'd died instead. She said I was shit wrapped in silver.'

I look closely at the photo of Mumma's profile, the smug smile, pearls down to her knees, diamonds in her hair. What a terrible inheritance: all these unhappy women passing along sadness with their jewellery. Love can be shit wrapped in silver, but who's to say some of the shine doesn't rub off on the shit and make us yearn for more?

With Khaja's help, Burrimummy empties the contents of a trunk on the floor by the windows of her drawing room. It's a heap of alive, bright mauve, dust rising where the threads have come apart. 'Mountbatten pink-and-gold brocade curtains from Majid Castle', she announces as if we were at the auctioneers as she stands amidst furniture piled high, gilded chairs leaning on huge dressers, faded Persian carpets rolled up.

Burrimummy caresses a photo of her Puppa, dressed in his achkan and sword, on his way to his Majesty's levee in London.

'I need to replace this frame,' she says, 'but it can wait till we return. When that man in the dhoti, Gandhi, began agitating for self-rule, his great friend Dickie Mountbatten reassured Puppa that he and all the princes of India would keep their autonomy, a privy purse, and titles.'

Burrimummy picks up another photograph of an older man in a garden in a knitted vest, smoking a cigarette.

'You know you can die of a broken heart, darlings. This is Puppa after 1947. The worst betrayal came from Dickie. He said he would expel any dissenting princely state from the Commonwealth. Puppa's hair went white overnight.'

Light is pouring in; without curtains, this is the brightest Rest House Road has been, turning dust into diamonds. The servants are quiet. They are looking at Burrimummy differently. Khaja's eyes are full of tears; Ansia is staring at her as if to memorise her. How she speaks to them and what they hear are two separate things. They love her. Burrimummy's rage is part of what they must accept to survive. Love and violence are one. They nod as she speaks as if she is a preacher at a pulpit.

'Puppa knew it was over when Nehru said he would not accept the divine right of kings. Of course, by then, Nehru was sleeping with Dickie's garish wife, Lady Edwina. She reminded me of a hyena, that woman. I saw her at a party in Vienna at the British Embassy when I was with that damned Saied.'

'Why didn't Nehru sleep in his own bed?' Angel asks.

Burrimummy says, 'Dickie often said himself that although they were a couple, they spent more time in bed with others.'

Angel looks puzzled. I think of monkeys.

'Those bloody shits Gandhi, Nehru, Vallabhbhai Patel, Jinnah, Mountbatten, slashed India into bits. They were responsible for a million Hindus and Muslims butchering one another on trains on 15th August 1947. Puppa swore in '47 that he would never return to Savanur alive. He got the packers in to Majid Castle and was off to Bangalore even before the paintings had been taken off the walls, leaving Mumma to supervise everything. It was the one time she stayed there longer than he did. She was terrified people would steal things. That's when I took the curtains and brought them to Bangalore.'

The ragged heap of blush-gold material on the floor seems to be alive, emanating bright dust.

Angel puts her arms around Burrimummy. 'Did he die?'

'Yes, darling. He had been in bed for a year, suffering from a heart condition. His pulse was shallow. It kept dropping until he was bedridden. Puppa, once so active, became sedentary, quiet, smoking cigarette after cigarette and writing letters. One afternoon, Mumma smelt burning in his study and found Puppa on the floor, his cigarette on the carpet. He had a heart attack.'

I remember Daddy's heart attack and ache for him, and wonder who broke Daddy's heart.

'For two weeks before Puppa died, he said he saw his mother's face all over the house, looking at him. He cried out, "My mother is here; my mother is there." His mother and father had been murdered when he was two by an uncle who wanted to be the Nawab.

'That same night, they carried him in a lorry to Khadarbag in Savanur, where generations of Nawabs of Savanur were buried. Only men were allowed at the funeral. Rashid and Wahid kept him company in the car. Miles of streets were lined with his subjects waiting to receive his body; every able-bodied Muslim man in Savanur was there.

'The women went to Savanur to visit his grave a few days later. Majid Castle was locked up; there were no guards; the garden was overgrown and the roses were dead. It was desolate. Some old servants came and cried at Mumma's feet and she couldn't bear to see it, so when an official offered to open up the place for her, she refused, and we took the next train back to Bangalore.'

Angel and I start crying as the piano is taken away by four men, leaving only the piano stool with all the sheet music inside it. Khaja hugs Angel, tears falling into Angel's dark hair, her frail hands around Angel's waist.

'Don't cry, girls – Poppet, Angel, don't cry. Only two days; then we fly.'

'Only two days; then we fly,' says Angel, in Burrimummy's voice, breaking free from Khaja. She starts running, her chubby fingers making piano-playing movements in the air as she wades into the old brocade curtains from Majid Castle that have been locked in a trunk since 1947.

I am surprised to see the tears in Burrimummy's eyes when the ayahs line up to say goodbye to us. She hands them little envelopes with money. 'Don't worry. You can stay here. You'll get a monthly salary. Just don't give it to your damn men.'

Angel is shouting, 'Fairy dust, fairy dust!' She is spinning in circles in the curtains, watching with shrieking delight the brocade disintegrate into bejewelled smoke as it spreads into the room and floats out of the windows.

'Oh God, Mumma's curtains, falling apart, in bits, the last of Majid Castle. Mumma, Puppa, all gone, gone.' Our laughter smothers her wail as she draws our faces close to hers. I can't tell if Burrimummy is laughing or crying, blinded by the swirling, ascending dust.

Briefly, 17 Rest House Road is a goblet of electric blue light.

We are leaving Rest House Road for the airport, our suitcases strapped on the top of the taxi. We stare through the back window until the house is out of sight. Burrimummy looks straight ahead, wearing oversized sunglasses. She puts Angel on her lap and says, 'Don't be sad, darling, everything will be the same when we return. We are going on an adventure on an island. We will go to the seaside. Would you like that, my darlings?'

Angel puts her thumb in her mouth. We would go anywhere with Burrimummy. If she can leave Rest House Road behind, so can we. Maybe, finally, we could be a proper family with all of us together.

Burrimummy sings.

> *'Just Poppet and me*
> *And Angel makes three*
> *Together we'll be*
> *In our sweet heaven.'*

In Bombay, we stay at the Taj, where the managers seem to know Burrimummy well. Angel and I are open-mouthed at this, at Burrimummy in imposing black silk and pearls, with her usual crimson lipstick, paan exchanged for cigarettes with a long holder, commanding even here amidst the gleaming marble floors, high ceilings and unending stairwells.

She smokes, crossing and uncrossing her legs, telling hovering, liveried bearers to heat her milk, take this away, bring that, crumpling fine linen as casually as if she did this every day. One evening, she tells the pianist she'd like to play and, as if there was no one there – no tourists, no strangers – in that plush Victorian tea room, with the view of India Gate and the ocean, she plays some Bach, always that Brandenburg Concerto, and closes with Dr Zhivago, her eyes closed.

In India, we'd heard that London was always damp with a cold that got into your bones. I wanted to know how that felt, but we landed in London to stifling heat – nothing like Bangalore, cool all year round. The streets looked ordered and bare, the city as magical as a storybook: Harrods, Big Ben, the Houses of Parliament, the Thames, Buckingham Palace, Hyde Park, the Victoria and Albert Museum. Burrimummy points them out from the taxi, in the day and at night when she takes us around the city.

We stay at the Dorchester for two nights. Again, Burrimummy behaves as if she is a permanent resident of the hotel. It is strange not having the ayahs to help us all to dress. As she looks out onto Park Lane from our hotel window, she tells us, 'You know, girls, I once had a flat here in Knightsbridge. I really wish I hadn't sold it. Everything worth having is finished.'

We take a taxi to Golders Green, where she meets a relative from Hyderabad, another great-grandchild of Sir Afsars – there are plenty of them. I am starving. The lady offers us sandwiches. Remembering my manners, I refuse, expecting her to press them upon me, but she accepts my 'No thank you' and moves away with the tray. The same thing happens to Angel and Burrimummy. Afterwards, eating at the hotel, Burrimummy says, 'They lose all their grace when they come to the West. They've forgotten all their courtly manners.'

On the tube back, I am struck at the sight of a couple kissing passionately, wondering if love can be this open. I know it as a dark secret thing. I stand, staring at them until Burrimummy pulls me away roughly.

The passengers on the plane from London to Port of Spain look to me like South Indians but darker. I am confused, questioning. South Indian women have long plaits coiled with oil and jasmine. They wear bright silk saris. But these women have short hair and wear dresses. 'It's because they are African, darling,' Burrimummy pronounces. 'See, their hair is so thick and curly.'

'Like mine?' asks Angel.

'No. Theirs is thicker'.

Angel sets up her face as if she wants to cry but sees Burrimummy is too distracted to comfort her, so puts her thumb in her mouth instead.

At Piarco airport, we walk out of the aircraft into heat so powerful we are pushed backwards, then the blast from the aircraft engines throws us forward into a furnace.

In the carousel area, Burrimummy beckons to a dark, thin young man of Indian descent to pick up our bags and carry them through. She says, 'Coolie! Take these bags. I've got no money to give you, but my son-in-law is outside. He will pay you.'

'Nah,' he says, 'I'm not an attendant. I'm a medical student. We don't use that word here, madam.'

Burrimummy looks confused. He helps us anyway.

We enter a chaotic customs hall with a long, raggedy queue. Burrimummy goes straight up to the top of the queue, but the customs officer points for her to go back.

'My granddaughters are very tired.'

'Everybody tired. You cyar break de line. Go back.' People throw us curious looks, but Burrimummy doesn't notice.

'What did you say? I don't understand you.'

'Look, lady, just go back.' The officer points to the long line, but she waits beside him, sighing until some kind people let us go to the front of the line. The customs officer eyes her doubtfully. 'You come for a holiday?'

'Absolutely not. I'm here to meet Colonel Ved Nath. His daughters are my wards.'

'Well, call it what you want, you know you can't stay for more than three months, right?'

'Don't be impertinent, young man. I'm a guest in your country.'

He shrugs and lets us through.

On our way out, she pushes past the crowds impatiently. 'Let me through. The children are tired. Let me through. Please.'

I'm relieved to see Daddy's deeply tanned, handsome face in the crowd, coming towards us, his white teeth glinting. He gets us through formalities and takes us onto the Tarmac, where we climb into a small helicopter – a perk we take for granted, the hot wind throwing grit in our eyes. I am exhilarated as we fly jumpily through faint wisps of candyfloss clouds. The sea is a slate-grey slab of thrilling, dangerous choppy water.

In Tobago, we are back out on the Tarmac, walking towards a waiting car. Angel and I hold hands tightly in the back seat as Daddy drives along the seafront in the grainy evening light, the palm trees bending in the salty breeze as we pass vast tracts of land and tiny homes on stilts in the hills. Soon we are climbing up past a rectangular hospital, up towards a fort lit by a single neon light, then onto a plateau at the top of a hill where we stop at a small house with bare, lit rooms.

Mummy greets us at the door. I expect her to be more excited. 'You're here! Hello, My The, Poppet Dait-ny, Angel child.' She kisses us, but I can tell she's distracted. There is no ayah to greet us with offers of refreshments.

Winky rushes at us. 'Burrimummy, Poppet, Angel, come and see the fort.'

We have cheese sandwiches in a room with one small table and a single ceiling bulb. Winky is shoving bread into his mouth, saying, 'Poppet, Angel, want to go on the go-cart? Down the hill?' Angel hides behind Burrimummy. Winky slams out of the house, joining other boys' voices, yelping. Mummy makes instant coffee for Burrimummy while Daddy heaves our suitcases into a small room with a double bed.

Angel and I fall asleep on either side of Burrimummy. During the night, we kick off the cotton covers, sweltering in the unaccustomed humidity.

We wake to Daddy's voice, a slamming door, the car starting. He's driven off, taking Winky to school. Angel and I follow Burrimummy outside, squinting at the glare of the already hot day, at the curve of the bay. We taste briny air and look around. The back of our house faces the edge of a plateau that slopes into a guava orchard; the front looks over a valley. To our left, on a vast expanse of lawn, dotted with hibiscus and bougainvillaea, there are four cannons, their muzzles neatly slotted into the wall, pointing at the ocean.

Burrimummy sounds like a general exploring territory.

'Look, we are on a fort! Come on, let's go look at the cannons.' She leads us off.

I stroke the smooth black cannon and look out at the dazzling ocean. I've never seen anything this bright – the sky, the sea, the air.

Burrimummy reads the plaque. 'This fort was built by Sir Thomas Hislop and named after King George III, in 1804 to secure the colonial territory from foreign invasions and prevent internal revolts from the slaves.'

A heavy woman approaches slowly, her floral dress whipping around her legs. As she reaches the door, Mummy says, 'Oh look, it's Beulah. Thank God you're here.'

Beulah breathes heavily by the front door where we are now congregated. She looks Burrimummy up and down, then brushes past her with a 'Mornin'.'

Enraged, Burrimummy opens her mouth to chastise her. Mummy whispers urgently in Urdu, 'Don't say anything, Mother. She won't like it.'

We look on aghast as Beulah sits at the table and serves herself breakfast. Burrimummy says in Urdu to Mummy, 'This is unheard of for a servant in India.'

Mummy says dryly, 'This is not India My-The.'

Beulah, unaffected by our staring, calmly sets about consuming half a loaf of white bread and butter, washing it down with a fizzy orange soft drink mixed with condensed milk.

Mummy approaches her tentatively, sweat on her upper lip. 'Do what you can; cook something and maybe dust – after you've eaten...' vaguely gesturing towards the kitchen and the bedrooms.

Angel and I remain at the door, staring until Beulah finally rises from the table and begins the housework at a stately pace.

We have sandwiches for dinner. Mummy collapses on the stairs with the effort of folding her own saris.

Burrimummy adjusts to the heat by wearing her thinnest saris, clipping a bedcover onto the curtains to block out the light, and drinking gallons of iced water – muttering about the lack of servants.

'Beulah is no servant,' she says sharply. For hours after Beulah has gone, I wonder how I should address her, as I am as scared of her as I am of Burrimummy.

Something builds up in Burrimummy, and the Beulah wars begin.

Burrimummy turns supervisor. 'You haven't tucked in the lower sheet.'

Beulah sucks her teeth, ignoring her.

Burrimummy thunders at Angel, Mummy and me the following day, as if Beulah is not in the room. 'You know she sweeps around the furniture instead of moving it. You can't take shortcuts, you know.'

This has no effect on Beulah, who sits down for a cup of tea and leaves the dirty dishes in the sink. Burrimummy starts washing them with exaggerated slowness. Instead of being shamed, Beulah allows Burrimummy to continue working.

Burrimummy's voice turns increasingly polite and supercilious. 'Would you mind, awfully, if you please, sweeping beneath the bed? If you have time between your other important work, of course.'

Beulah responds coolly, 'I go see. Eef I have de time.'

Come washing day, Beulah ruins several of Burrimummy's cotton saris by immersing them in bleach. My grandmother shoves them under Beulah's face.

'THANK you so much for putting these spots on my saris.'

'You want me put spots on all?' Beulah responds.

Beulah irons only once a week. Mummy accepts this rule. One stormy day we return from school to a crisis. Burrimummy has no more pressed saris to wear. She asks Beulah to iron one for her.

Beulah refuses. 'I don't iron when it rains, or when I wash, or when I get dew on me.'

Burrimummy says, 'So when DO you iron?'

Beulah says patiently with due dignity, as if Burrimummy is a halfwit, 'I cyan iron after I put my han' in water. The hotness of the iron after the coldness of the water does make me sick.'

'What rubbish.'

'I ent doin' it.'

'You HAVE to.'

Mummy comes across them facing one another like warriors and says in Urdu, 'Mother, please don't say anything. If you talk to Beulah like that, she'll leave, and then we'll have no one to do anything. I'll be left with EVERYTHING, and I can't cope.'

Beulah looks Burrimummy up and down, moving her mouth as if chewing air and says, 'Watch me go. And call me when you learn some manners, okay?'

Mummy begs Beulah, 'Please, stay.'

'Okay, but I NOT ironin' today. And if that woman talks to me disrespectfully, I will box her.'

Beulah leaves early with a swagger and is absent for a week, after which she makes a smug return. Burrimummy's battles with her intensify. We stand, as always, a hushed and enthralled audience. Winky doesn't care. 'What's there to hog yaar?' he says in Indian English.

One evening, as she watches Beulah cooking, Burrimummy says, 'Must you put sugar in everything – the chicken, the beans even?'

Beulah stops and holds the ladle midair and throws it in the sink.

'I not cooking again.'

For weeks, the house is on tenterhooks. We eat more and more sandwiches. Burrimummy is forever lurking in the bedroom doorways watching Beulah in silent fury.

The end comes over a raw chicken which Beulah is cleaning.

Burrimummy grabs it from her at the sink and says, 'She shouldn't touch it with bleach on her hands.' The two women wrestle over the pink carcass until Beulah finally drops it disgustedly in the sink.

'Clean it up!' Burrimummy is at her most imperious.

Beulah picks up the chicken slowly and drops it on the floor.

'What are you doing, you blackie?'

Beulah fixes Burrimummy with a hard stare, straight up to her face. 'Who the hell you talking to like that, eh ole lady? Who de arse you think you are? De Queen of Sheba? I black? I black and proud. You ever hear what our beloved prime minister, the great Dr Williams, say? "Massa day done." Go back to India or wherever the hell you from.' She gathers her things with a parting shot: 'Blasted coolie.'

Shocked and sweating, eyes fixed on the chicken splayed on the bleached floor, Burrimummy turns in confusion and heads for her room to pray. In Beulah's absence, the small house on the fort in Tobago grows increasingly filthy, the floors sticky. The dishes are dirty, and beds unmade for days. The garbage piles up. I don't think anyone knows what to do with it. I throw it over into the chicken farmer's yard next door. The grass is high there so no one will notice. Winky is freer than ever, go-carting down the hill, returning from a beach outing with sand in his hair, and spreading it across the floors for Angel and I to mop. No one asks him to do anything.

Mummy is disengaged, even contemptuous of Burrimummy's need for order. She emerges from a messy bedroom looking like she's ready for a Vogue photoshoot. She has cups of tea, bits of toast and jam, lives comfortably with chaos, as if order would require her to do the accounts and reveal her losses; she couldn't risk that.

Burrimummy cooks for a few days, but then announces she will no longer cook as Mummy has accused her of finishing off the butter.

'I'm not a thief. I won't be spoken to like that by my own daughter.' Burrimummy shouts within earshot of Mummy, but not quite at her, which is a change.

They fight continuously, uttering the same accusations.

'I sold my piano, impoverished myself to come here, and you make me live like this? This is the thanks I get. This dry chapati and cauliflower – my servants in Bangalore ate more nourishing food. I'm starving here. If I carry on like this, I'll be dead.'

Mummy responds in an injured, theatrical tone as if she were in a Bollywood melodrama. 'Ved can't afford to buy meat every day, Mother. ONE man is supporting FIVE people on a small salary. He's just an engineer building a highway, not a Nawab. We do what we can. Today I COOKED so much my back is breaking.'

She speaks like she had been sentenced to working in a chain gang. 'Two vegetables, fried fish, a nourishing salad and rice for our lunch. That's plenty for our small needs. I can't give you lamb, chicken, minced meat and pudding for every meal.' She's outdoing every Bollywood actress I have ever seen.

Now that Mummy has power over Burrimummy, she uses it mercilessly. Mummy's look of wide-eyed, childlike vulnerability, her absent air, and full lips give her the appearance of malleability. It comes as a considerable shock to Burrimummy to finally realise that Mummy is totally uncaring of her disapproval of her domestic shortcomings. The antagonism between them is a heart-hammering, living thing.

'No servants. There is no one even to scrub my back. Not one comfort. Not only that, but I must also carry HEAVY buckets of hot water up these stairs to the bathroom by myself. I'm not a young woman, you know. One day I will just drop down and die. But you don't give a damn, do you?'

Mummy doesn't; she has other things on her mind.

In her floaty chiffons and parasols, she effortlessly gets people to admire and look after her. A kindly woman whose son would one day be prime minister, takes us in and offers us water in a parlour, with a piano, that looks like 17 Rest House Road. She tells us her son is a lawyer and politician called A.N.R. Robinson; she becomes a second 'granny' to us and Mummy Robinson to Mummy.

Just as Mummy's beauty has caused a minor sensation in Tobago, Daddy charms women and wins the respect of the men with his stories of the trenches and his engineering knowledge. They are catapulted into the cream of society, sought-after and fêted as an ultra-glamorous addition to the circle of former plantation owners, descendants of European colonisers with their cocoa and coffee estates, Indian businessmen and high-ranking African civil servants. My parents don't see race, just charm, which they ooze, and to which they gravitate.

Soon they are as busy as they were in India. Their social diary is full: golf, moonlight picnics on the beach, dances and cocktails, dinners and garden parties. This time, instead of his colleagues belonging to different states of India, they belong to other continents.

Another maid arrives. She is Patsy, dark-skinned, slim, a tall student with spectacles and ambition. Winky is star-struck and follows her around.

She is studying part-time for her accounting exams and does just enough to keep the house from apocalyptic chaos. Warned by Mummy not to interfere with Patsy, Burrimummy retreats.

Daddy buys groceries when he remembers, but there is no one reliable to cook, clean, wash and iron clothes – not Mummy, not Burrimummy, not even Patsy. We might eat dal for a week, bread and jam or cheese for supper. Sometimes, someone boils some rice.

It becomes a habit with Patsy – on the rare days she does come in – to take one look at the kitchen and say, 'Oh God, I have so much studies to do,' swiftly followed by complaints of dizziness before making an early exit.

On a school afternoon, Angel and I come home to find Mummy is in bed with a migraine. Angel goes to Burrimummy's bedroom and I to Mummy's. Winky is, as usual, on a beach somewhere, meandering home, taking his own sweet time. Burrimummy is quieter, angrier. She spends a lot of time on her prayer mat. She mutters and paces, holds Angel close to her. The two are locked up in the bedroom for hours. I don't mind as much as I did before. She's losing her power.

'What's the matter, Mummy?'

'I've had such a shock. Baig is dead.'

'Burrimummy is dead? She's dead? But she's in her room, isn't she?' I'm shouting, and Mummy restrains me from running to Burrimummy's room, waving about a blue air-letter with an Indian stamp.

'No, not HER. Her husband, my stepfather. He's dead. When I got the letter, I wasn't at all sorry. I hope Baig burns in hell. My stepfather and I loathed one another. She would still have been married to him if he weren't dead. Please press my head, Poppet. Take a hammer and hit me with it.'

I lie down next to her and remember what Mummy told me about her stepfather over the years.

★

Still in her twenties estranged from her parents, between homes, living at the Taj, Burrimummy met her second husband, Col. Sikandar Ali Baig at the Bombay races. On the day of the proposal, she was in an unusually risqué sari, artfully simple, taupe, but transparent so her petticoat showed, with a narrow gold border, shades and Puppa's pearls. Her hair was short and crimped, lips stained. A rider fell off his horse, landed at her feet, looked up, saw her, and asked her to marry him. He was a handsome, well-built polo player, a cousin of hers, a great-grandson of Sir Afsar's and a colonel in the Pakistani army. The trouble was he was already married, but that didn't stop him. He began visiting Burrimummy at the Taj hotel daily.

Mummy told me she'd thought nothing of it because Baig had also brought his wife, a pretty, kind woman called Zainab, and their two children, just five and six years old. The children treated the Taj like a large playground, racing between its marble pillars, corridors and around the pool as Zainab, Baig and Burrimummy chatted.

Eventually, Burrimummy left the Taj and took Mummy, then a child of ten, to see her great-grandmother in Hyderabad. Sadrunissa was all grace in Mumtaz Mahal, a haveli, built in the sprawling Mughal style, with a courtyard connecting apartments, trees, rose garden and durbar hall. Sadrunissa, Sir Afsar's eldest daughter, wore white saris, her hair suffused with sandalwood, skin rosy and wafery as the petals in her garden, and always had two baby cheetahs by her side. She still lived in the women's quarters, the zenana, where dozens of women had lived for years. Sadrunissa told Mummy stories of the days when Hyderabad was a princely state, when the Nizam of Hyderabad tried to abduct Angel, Burrimummy's mother, and how, for Angel's wedding, invitations were sent out in Persian verse. It was a time when slaves could be bought cheaply, and women dressed in velvet pants rimmed in silver. Mummy said she had never been happier. Then Baig arrived.

Burrimummy went riding with Baig every day, all around the Golconda Fort and the old city, and the two returned flushed and famished every evening. One day Mummy heard shouting. Sadrunissa was saying to Burrimummy, 'It's entirely wrong. I WON'T have you ruining Baig's marriage. He's a MARRIED man.'

Burrimummy retorted, 'YOU married a man with two grown children, so why do you think it wrong?' Mummy never saw her great grandmother Sadrunissa again.

Burrimummy packed up and followed Baig to Pakistan. She put Mummy in Queen Mary College, a boarding school in Lahore, established in the time of the British for aristocratic children. Mummy was terribly lonely. On one of Burrimummy's visits, she casually said, 'Oh, Nur, I've married Sikandar, you know, my cousin Colonel Baig.'

At sixteen, Mummy hated the idea of this man becoming her stepfather and of her mother being a second wife. She asked what had happened to Baig's wife. 'He's sent Zainab packing to Lucknow,' Burrimummy said.

*

When Mummy goes to the bathroom I race down to the kitchen and get her some water and biscuits.

Back in bed, she pulls at my ribbon and says, 'I was a schoolgirl, a year older than you when your grandmother came with a military chauffeur to pick me up. She was waiting for me in the visitors' drawing room, holding a long cigarette in her hand; she blew smoke rings around her painted mouth, like an actress.

'I was ashamed. The girls gawked at her velvet kitten-heels, her beaded handbag, her silver cigarette holder. She carried on smoking calmly while talking to the teachers and other parents, and later, even in the car.'

'Why do you hate him so much, Mummy? You never told me.'

'She took me back to Baig's house. It was beautiful, sprawling, with a wraparound balcony and a lovely garden in an exclusive area for top Pakistani officials, where the British once lived.

'When we got to the house, she said she was sorry, but he didn't want to see my face. He was in the Pakistani army and didn't want people to know he had a stepdaughter. I wasn't allowed anywhere in the house, not even the dining room. She would hide me, and I was to be a good girl, stay quiet, and read the books she'd bought me.

'She had the chauffeur take me around the back entrance. We crept to a bedroom which she'd arranged nicely with flowers, Emerson's essays, and my favourite Jane Austen, *Emma*. She had a hot meal sent up for me, spent some time with me, then locked me in the room.

'For four days, a servant brought my meals. She would visit me when he was out of the house, covering me with kisses, feeding me leftover sweets from parties, saying a prayer over me. I could hear her playing the piano and laughter; I heard her singing when they had guests. She composed all the war songs you hear Pakistani soldiers singing today.'

I keep pressing Mummy's head.

'Press here, no here, harder. Yes, like that,' she carries on between moaning.

'I was packing to go back to school when Baig found me. He followed the servant who was bringing juice for me. Mother wasn't there. He shook me and called me "a black bitch" and said he never wanted to see me again. When Mother heard the commotion, she came running up the stairs. Baig slapped her hard across her face, and your Burrimummy looked terribly sad, and we both cried when she left me in school. She said I was her beautiful Nur, her moonchild. She said, "Just you wait, I'll talk to him. He'll see how beloved you are, how beautiful."'

I am crying now, silently, thinking of Burrimummy at the piano, how she defended me when Aunt Shaheen called me black.

'She didn't visit me for months; Baig didn't allow her to see me. You would have thought she would have left Baig after he started hitting her. She took me out of boarding school, sent me back to Bangalore to my grandparents and followed him to London where she bought a flat in Knightsbridge with her father's money.

'My beloved Puppa died when I was sixteen. I was destroyed for months and months. Your Burrimummy stored all the things Puppa had given her from Majid Castle in one room. I saw them disappear bit by bit: silver teapots, Persian carpets, tapestries, jade clocks and dozens of gold plates. She often went to Pakistan, taking more things out of her locker. Silver and carpets, furniture, jewels.

'Baig wanted more, so she came back and forth to India to get her valuables. On her final trip, she discovered that, in her absence, Baig had married another rich woman with land and property. Your grandmother went back to him, willing to be his second wife. A month later, she wrote to my uncle saying she had been severely beaten and was locked in her room. My darling uncle Rasheed, the late Nawab of Savanur, with whom she fought so often before he died, helped her to escape somehow.'

I feel faint as if the Burrimummy in me was falling.

'The thing was, he kept all her jewels: Sir Afsar's diamonds; Sadrunissa's blocks of gold; Mumma's emeralds. There was nothing left for me,' she says. 'That's when she bought Rest House Road. All her property and fixed deposits were in both our names. Now she's destroyed everything, so I won't get anything. She left whatever she didn't give to Baig in a safe in Pakistan and sold the Knightsbridge flat. The government has confiscated it. But you can't have everything, you know. Life is a package. And look, Baig is dead.'

As Mummy's voice fades, I hear a gasp, see Burrimummy's sari, and smell her sandalwood. She'd been listening at the door. Mummy doesn't notice.

Mummy looks happy. Her headache has vanished. I follow her to the kitchen, where she cuts a slice of the cake given to us by our neighbour, Mrs Waterman. As she wipes away the crumbs from her mouth, I see she is celebrating the end of something awful. But Burrimummy gets grimmer and sadder.

We all fall into the crevices created by one another's neglect, and Burrimummy falls the hardest.

EIGHT

The Beulah wars over; the religious wars begin. Daddy doesn't allow Burrimummy to teach us the Quran or Arabic in the house, so she does it stealthily, teaching Angel at night while sweating in drenching humidity, with a fan blowing over the bed and muffling her words.

There is a Gita in Daddy's room, with a framed photo of Lord Shiva, with a garlanded serpent around his neck and four hands raised in benediction, that Daddy tells us to face when he makes us sit down to meditate for five minutes every day. I see again that not everything is in Burrimummy's power. Late at night, she seethes, telling us of Allah's terrible retribution towards kafirs.

In the afternoons, in her expansive moments, Mummy adds to our religious classes, telling us about another kind of Islam, another Jihad, a war, she says, looking at Burrimummy, that is not against other people, but against oneself, against one's own rebellious nature.

I am torn at the sight of Burrimummy's distressed face each time she glimpses the image of Lord Shiva in our parents' room. I know this image means a lot to Daddy. She shudders as she passes their room and invokes Allah's judgement and mercy. Again, the only protest available to Burrimummy is to stop helping. It doesn't work because Mummy never notices anything and has the power to decide everything.

It is Burrimummy's first Ramadan in Tobago. I wake early and go downstairs to a kitchen table full of rancid cheese toast and dirty dishes from the night before. A cockroach darts from the sink to the fridge. It has been another fractious day of quarrels between the grownups.

Burrimummy must have woken at three in the morning to pray and eat, but no lace-covered table filled with food awaited to nourish her before the long day of fasting. It would be the same at sunset. Ramadan here is so different from Ramadan in Rest House Road, with the Hyderabadi dishes emerging from the kitchen at dusk, being laid out in the proper dining room: lamb cooked slowly; desserts, cakes and pastries stuffed with crushed coconut, fresh cream, pistachios, rose water; the evening prayer; Burrimummy fragrant with oudh and afterwards the recitation of the Quran in her musical voice.

That Friday assembly at school, during the silent prayer, I resolve to recreate 17 Rest House Road, to learn to cook and clean. At the weekend,

I cross a courtyard to our neighbours and our first school friends. The boy, David, is in Winky's class, Suzie in mine, Debby in Angel's. Sharon is the baby who Mummy pets up and calls 'Mouse'. Their mother, Mrs Waterman, is a prominent civil servant and a strict single parent. The Watermans have clean, ironed clothes and schedules. They go to church and have baths and bedtimes. Instead of playing, that weekend I ask Mrs Waterman if I could keep her company in the kitchen. I watch as she stews plums, burns sugar for a stewed chicken, bakes macaroni pie, simmers crab and callaloo. I learn to feed the crabs with hot pepper as they crawl around in a bucket and watch as Mrs Waterman cleans them before dropping them in the boiling callaloo pot with the coconut milk.

On Monday, after school, I buy little treats – sugary breakfast buns and rock-hard coconut drops from our school bakery. I ask Daddy to stop off in the market for vegetables, chicken, flour, callaloo, crabs, rice. Burri-mummy has been too weak from her fast, waking daily at three and not eating all day.

I make it a game with Angel; tell her we are like the secret shoemakers in children's stories. We will creep out of bed at midnight – to clean the kitchen and bake a cake, wash the clothes and lay the table. After Burri-mummy is asleep, we wait till midnight, nudging one another to stay awake. In the kitchen, I stack the dirty dishes in one of the sinks and wash them. I tell Angel to dry and wipe the oil and turmeric from surfaces. I learnt how to boil the steel pots with their burnt remnants of turmeric, saffron, cayenne, garlic and onions until the debris is loosened, and then scrub them furiously.

Sounding like Burrimummy, I say, 'Wipe under the toaster – and don't forget the corners of the stove.' I go down on my knees and mop the floor with a rag like I had seen Ansia do. I give Angel a dishcloth. We clean separate sections of the room, scrub the bathroom floors and tidy the drawing room.

I make Mrs Waterman's stewed chicken, macaroni pie and fried rice. Angel surprises me with her neat ingenuity, producing mountains of chapatis cutting out perfect round edges with a steel bowl. We cover the decorated coconut treats and the still un-iced cake in cheesecloths for Burrimummy's morning *Suhoor* and evening *Iftar*. Not knowing what to do with the garbage, I empty it again into the chicken farmer's yard next door. The grownups never notice. We hear the cocks crowing and have just enough time to fall into bed when we hear Burrimummy wake to prepare for her fast and wake bleary to Daddy shouting for us to get in the car for school.

On Tuesday after school, I discover Winky has polished off most of the cake I planned to ice. 'Stop me if you can,' he says, stuffing it down his face. 'You selfish boy, you do nothing, and now you've gone and eaten Burri-mummy's cake. I hate you.' He lunges at me, and I pull his hair. Burrimummy separates us, saying, 'It's only a bit of cake. For God's sake, leave Zafar alone.' Zafar is her Muslim name for him, after our grandfather, the only man she loved. Angel sees none of this as she's quietly finishing the homework Burrimummy has been supervising.

Before bedtime, we clean her room, change her sheets and pillowcases. We fold her saris, each holding an end, walking towards one another to fold them, fix her mosquito net and spray the room with Mummy's Chanel perfume to surprise her.

Finally, we gain our reward when she lavishes us with praise reminiscent of 17 Rest House Road days. 'You have hearts of gold, my two eyes, brought to me by angels in chariots.' But the warmth barely lasts an hour. Burrimummy looks out of the window and says, 'The roses, gone. I tried to plant them under that mango tree, but this sun and the rain here are too strong. Oh, God.' Nothing can stop the avalanche of disappointment pouring out of her. Our faces crumple with sadness as we separate from her each morning.

The sharpness of her distress is ever-present. There are muffled ends of complaints about meat, servants, the heat; regret about leaving Rest House Road, her piano; the ruin that comes from marrying out of Islam; the loss of the love of Nur, of her mother. It never goes away.

Things change when I bring home a friend who tells Burrimummy there are Muslims here, that her father has built a mosque. A visit is arranged, although Angel, Mummy and I are not allowed to go. Burrimummy returns with shining eyes, holding two large avocados and a bag of fruit.

'Darling, what a time I'm having! Women are allowed into the mosque here, Subhan Allah! I wept when I prayed there in the women's section. A lady doctor, the wife of the imam, took me home. It was enormous, with marble floors and a garden. She showed me her mango, guava and lime trees, terrific flowers – anthuriums, orchids, tiger lilies. Here, Poppet, guavas; Angel, look! Limes, green mangoes for pickles. They have no one here, you know, who speaks or reads Urdu. They've asked me to start a small school for children; imagine teaching the Quran, Arabic, in the month of Ramadan.'

I have never seen her this happy. She's starching her own saris now, wearing them with pearls, applying her precious oudh behind her ears.

Each evening she returns from the mosque smiling, carrying food – huge rolled West Indian rotis filled with dal; curried lamb; gulab jamun; mango pickle. While she is preparing to break her fast, Daddy is preparing to meditate, and Angel, Winky and I join him at the brief meditation in front of Shiva, followed by Daddy reading a verse of *The Gita*, our only religious instruction.

Afterwards, while Daddy and Mummy prepare to go out, Burrimummy,

Winky, Angel and I fall upon the food after dusk when she breaks her fast.

Burrimummy whispers loudly, as if telling us a secret, 'You know, darling, such shocking things and a miracle. These people with huge cars who took me to the mosque were like Khaja once. Completely illiterate. Worse. Many came from Bihar, that impoverished state crammed with horribly oppressed people. They came with nothing, just bundles on their backs. That Hindu caste system is terrible, you know. The worst of the lot, the untouchables, aren't allowed to do anything but clean toilets and weren't even allowed to drink water from the wells owned by Brahmins. They told me that's why so many of them converted to Islam. Isn't that a wonder of Islam? Someone like Khaja's daughter could come here with grandparents who worked in the fields and become a lawyer or a doctor.' Her eyes are glowing. 'They are so free here, darling. Look at all these lady doctors, free to complete their studies, to do what I couldn't. It's all Allah's will.'

I hear in school from a Muslim girl that nobody has met anyone like Burrimummy.

'A real Indian princess. My father says the men are secretly in love with her.' I'm shocked that men still look at her like that.

One searing Sunday that month, hungry from fasting, she piles in the car with Angel on her lap on our family trip to the beach at Pigeon Point. We hop at the heat of the melting pitch beneath our bare feet in the car park and grind them into the soft warm sand, avoid walking under the coconut trees, and rub our cheeks against smooth sea shells and stones. With the wide ocean before us, Angel and I hang back. We are afraid, and don't own swimsuits. Burrimummy holds our hands and says, 'Come.' We walk towards the breaking waves gingerly, squealing at the water on us. She takes us further and further out. We follow her, the water now up to our knees, then our waists, until we are almost submerged. Our dresses rise. Burrimummy's white sari blooms high, and she leans back in the water. Her hair is wet, her cheeks pink, her eyes closed. We yelp, the three of us, amidst the sting of salty sprays, and slowly walk out of the sea. Angel says people are staring at us, but I'm short-sighted and only see a blur of green and khaki. Burrimummy's elation becomes ours, and we sit stunned on sodden towels for the drive home as if we've been submerged in magic. 'I once went swimming in the ocean in Bombay', she says, and closes her eyes. There are things we will never know about her but we will be made to mourn their loss.

On the day before Eid, a teenager to whom Burrimummy is teaching Arabic drops off food. He tells Mummy, 'Don't thank me, aunty. We must be charitable during Ramadan. It's sad Burrimummy doesn't have enough to eat.'

Mummy says to Burrimummy, 'You're eating our *salt* and betraying us like this? You haven't lost weight. You are humiliating us.'

Burrimummy's lips go back to being so pursed it's as if she's swallowed them entirely, her silence heavy with unuttered abuse.

Later that night, Daddy comes to the bedroom we share with Burrimummy. Mummy is following him. Staring at Burrimummy on her prayer mat, Daddy says, 'I found the photo of Lord Shiva turned upside down in my prayer area. This is a Hindu house. Do I tell people here not to go to the mosque? Who desecrated this?'

Mummy says darkly, 'We should respect people's religion, especially if we live in their house and eat their food. I'm a Muslim and I would never disrespect anyone else's faith.'

He orders us to leave the room. We stay close, listening to the weeping and shouting behind closed doors. Burrimummy invokes Allah and says she would never do that to Nath Saab, but we all know it was her.

'I may have allowed you to brainwash Angel for years. I can do nothing about the way you've treated Nur. But this is not Rest House Road. It's my house, and you're no longer welcome here.'

We understand then that Daddy is kicking her out.

Angel and I follow her to her room, crying. 'Burri, don't go, don't go, Daddy didn't mean it,' while she packs up her two suitcases.

Early in the morning, a taxi arrives for her. We watch as she hauls herself, holding her big black handbag, into the taxi and eases herself onto the cracked seats in the back, her shades on, her mouth a slash of red on her face. The radio blares a reggae song: *'Hey fatty bum bum, sweet sugar dumpling.'* Daddy and Mummy continue to drink their tea and watch with interest and without alarm – which they would do even if the world was falling apart. Angel runs after the taxi, its bumper open with Burrimummy's suitcases. She stands in the middle of the road, until the taxi turns the corner and I bring her in. For days, weeks and months, Angel alternates between weeping when everyone is asleep, and silence. We are forbidden from having any contact with Burrimummy, but Angel and Burrimummy are like dying plants that need the oxygen and water of each other to survive.

NINE

The sea fills the void that was order: Bangalore, Burrimummy, Simla, the perpetual snow on the mountains, our mannered army lives. We recover slowly from these absences, drawn by the thick salty humidity, the whipping breezes on the fort, the everyday view of the changing ocean, the long Sundays on the beach.

A year has passed since Burrimummy's departure. Daddy forbids us to write to her, but Angel, Winky and I write anyway, begging her to reply. No letter arrives from 17 Rest House Road.

More people claim Mummy and Daddy. French Creole landowners respect Daddy even though he preserved villages and cut into their land to construct the highway. As if faced with equals, they are eager to show my parents civility with walks on their cocoa estates, drinks by palm and bougainvillaea shaded swimming pools, dinner in colonial homes built with white coral from Barbados, intricately carved balusters, the dull gold of their chandeliers mingling with the tropical light. Dinner and golf course invitations arrive from African professionals, immigrant Arabs and Filipino and Indian ex-pats here on government contracts.

Every afternoon, around six, Mummy and Daddy are changing in their bedroom as if they'd never left India. Mummy's room looks like a ransacked sari shop, but she emerges looking like a movie star, her hair silky, tucked behind her ears, lips a deep mulberry, in her understated chiffon saris and pearls. They only stay in when Mummy has a migraine. Then, she is locked up in a darkened room for days, vomiting, unkempt, unbathed, groaning, weeping and asking for someone to break her head open with a hammer.

With even less supervision, Winky, Angel and I dive into life in Tobago. On Sundays, we swim in the ocean while the grownups sit on sheets in the shade, amidst picnic baskets, under the scant shade of coconut trees silvery with the morning sun. Once a month, we head to the ocean to picnic under the full moon at night, diving and delighting in the occasional psychedelic luminescence of the sea. Turned island-children, without ayah or umbrella, tanned and lean exuberance is ours. Exploring the guava patch opposite our school, we shake trees for fruit, examine for worms and eat and stuff in our pockets. We walk along the beach, picking up pink and green almond fruit on the sand. After rushing through homework, we climb mango and cherry trees on the fort, looking out high from their branches at the blue ocean disappearing into the horizon and Winky go-carting down the hill with the boys.

We miss Burrimummy's cooking. Mummy waits till the last possible hour, till Daddy is due to come home, and cooks, resentfully, distractedly. The results are unexpected and startling. Her chapatis are burnt on the outside and raw inside, in peculiar abstract shapes. The peanut butter pizza is baked to the consistency of concrete and, once, a neglected pressure cooker filled with lentils careens into the ceiling, splashing yellow stains around the kitchen, drilling a hole large enough in the roof to be able to see the moon. Supper is often bread and butter.

Patsy takes time off for her exams, leaving me to tackle the chaos at home. Angel helps me clean the kitchen after school, always a mountain of disorder. Angel and I are now experts and do the laundry on a Saturday, scrubbing stains on shirts on the ribbed boards, drying them on a clothes-line at the back of the house, folding petticoats, uniforms, shirts.

With no Khaja and no Burrimummy, Angel follows me blindly, as if looking for her footing from someone familiar. I shower her, lather her hair, scrub her back, show her how to wash and iron clothes, and scour and polish her white school shoes. She's no longer Burrimummy's Angel. She's our Angel. Mostly mine. Mummy and Daddy often wonder if Burri-mummy has completely brainwashed Angel against them when she doesn't respond to their mercurial demands for hugs and kisses. I defend her like a tigress, in sisterhood.

'You left her. Burrimummy is all she knows and Burrimummy is gone. Don't be so mean. No one knows what she feels about anyone else, but I do.'

I try making us a proper family – as if by laying the table, as I'd seen the housemaid do in a sitcom, I could become the child and Mummy, the mummy. Mummy says, 'Poppet, you're such a comfort to me. You're my little mummy.' That makes me clean harder.

Mummy writes long letters and spends hours praying and reading the Quran, reminding me of Burrimummy. Once, I saw her crying while sitting on her prayer mat in her bedroom. 'Your grandmother took away everybody I loved. I longed to see my father and she never let me see him. She was spoilt and wanted everything at once, ruining her life, ruining mine, running away from Bhopal, the most powerful state in India where women ruled for two hundred years. My father liked women and horses, but she could have disregarded that and kept her respect. She could have had it all. After a terrible fight with my grandparents, I was never allowed to see them. She's denied me my inheritance as a princess of Bhopal, and now she denies me Rest House Road.'

'You have your own money, Mummy,' I say resentfully.

'I'm entitled to it, you know. It can barely pay for a maid.'

I find it hard to pity Mummy, who looks lovely even while resentfully frying an egg. I see myself through her eyes and feel small, insignificant, dark and scrawny. People who look like oil paintings don't have the right to feel any pain.

Mummy passes on the news of Burrimummy she gets from Aunt Shaheen. 'Your grandmother has sold Rest House Road for a song; she was so worried I wanted it. When she saw I wasn't claiming it, she changed her mind and told her buyers it wasn't hers to sell because she had already gifted it to Angel. But it was too late. It's a terrible mess. All to spite me.'

More news. Mumma has died. Wahid and his Jewish wife lost everything on the stock market and have gone off to live in California with their children.

Another letter. Mummy says, holding up the blue aerogramme, her eyes full of tears, 'Mother has cancer and had to have her left breast removed.'

Daddy says it is all a ruse for sympathy, and my alarm subsides. I choose to believe Daddy. Angel is mute, which suits me.

Mummy's migraines intensify. Twice a month, we come home from school to find her lying in bed in her dressing gown, her hair uncombed, getting up to vomit every few minutes.

We hear raised voices in the bedroom. Mummy: 'My mother took everything from me; my inheritance, my daughter, my jewellery. Shaheen writes to say all Bangalore is talking about me. Did I mistreat her? I have nobody. I'm an orphan. Even if I was rude, shouldn't she protect me?'

Daddy says, 'Come on, Nur. She's right, in some ways, you know. You're not the world's best housekeeper, and you weren't right to let Angel go.'

The following Sunday, she disappears for the entire day.

Daddy is about to call the police when an Irish nun rings from the convent.

'She's here. You'd better pick her up.'

It has become a pattern with Mummy. She walks to the convent and returns, her face hot from the walk, sometimes meeting us as we walk home from school. She carries a parasol to shelter from the heat, wearing flimsy shoes fit only for the drawing room. People stop at the sight of her – in cat shades, chiffon wrapped closer by the wind around her slim waist, like a second skin. She stops to rest and stands frozen on the steaming road as if seized by terror, looking out towards the ocean beyond the slope of trees.

I am directed into a small room in the dark interior of the convent where the yellow light that filters through the stained-glass is the only clue to the white heat outside. Sister Mary is with Mummy. She is Irish, her rose-yellow skin set off by her black habit. Her face is wrinkled and chalky as if she has never been young, but her sky-blue eyes are as bright as a child's. Mummy is hugging Sister Mary and sobbing in her arms.

'What's wrong, dear?'

'You know, sister, I feel terribly alone. No father. My mother is like my enemy.'

Sister Mary sits Mummy down opposite her on a small bench. I squeeze in.

Looking at Mummy, lit by an arrow of motes through stained glass, I say, 'She's feeling sorry for herself again.' Mummy looks furious, and Sister Mary pretends she hasn't heard me.

She says gently, taking Mummy's hand across her desk, 'You must remember a time when you felt loved.'

'Oh yes, when I was a girl living with my grandparents in Savanur. I was the only child there, and my grandparents pampered me. Sometimes I'd look down from the balcony as my grandfather held his durbar, and a stream of villagers poured in all day with complaints. I never went to school, but tutors who lived on the compound taught me at home. A tutor from Pakistan taught me Arabic; the English teacher taught me comprehension, literature, math and the piano; a PE teacher taught me swimming and tennis. Mumma sang and read to me and played the piano to me. We slept with our arms wrapped around one another.'

'How lovely, dear.'

Mummy has a wan, childlike smile on her face.

'My grandfather had a dolls' house made for me, a replica of Majid castle, with tennis courts and winding staircases, drawing room and music room, and I could crawl inside. For my birthday, he had twenty-six sets of dolls made for me, a girl and a boy, from different states of India. Every year in the orange orchard, he would marry off my dolls and sixteen poor families, and I was made to give them saris, utensils and a deed for land. He would do the same for my dolls. The Pundit or Maulvi prayed over them, and I would gift them small saris and tea sets.

'I went for walks with my grandfather outside our grounds, and whenever we saw an unfortunate man, a beggar or a leper, he would say, "There go I but for the grace of God." So I'm not ungrateful, you know, just sad.'

'It all sounds lovely, dear.'

'Mother only began hitting me when I was six when we left my grandparents' home.'

The bench feels hard, and I stare hard at the white haze at the entrance of the dark church, wanting to be outside.

Sister Mary holds Mummy's gaze.

'There were hundreds of skirmishes between my mother and grandmother. My grandfather had diabetes and a weak heart, so he would walk away to another part of the house where he couldn't hear her. One night I heard Mother telling my grandfather, "Get rid of Mumma. I'll get you a better wife." I heard Mumma saying, "No, Shahnur, it's time we get rid of you. Your beauty is just a piece of shit wrapped around with silver paper.

You have never understood that heaven lies at your mother's feet and will always be the dust under my feet."

'That night, Mother packed me into a taxi to the train station in Savanur. My mother didn't look back, and the car went on towards the train station to Bangalore.'

'And then?'

'We went to Bombay. I sat in a chair all day in the hotel room at the Taj while Mother rowed on the phone with my grandparents and cursed my father with her friends. She got terribly skinny, her blouses falling off her shoulders, and she paced and smoked and cried in the room, saying she wished she were dead. That's when she began hitting me, blows to my head, slaps on my face. Why did I speak rudely to a waiter? Why did I read a book? "Haramzadi, kambakhath, wretch, just like your father." Seconds later, she would kiss, cuddle and hug me, put my head on her lap and croon that I was her life, her moon, say she was sorry, and die for me. My migraines started, terrible migraines, which felt like a dozen hammers on my head. They lasted for days. Afterwards, she cried and hugged me tightly, saying I was all she had, that never mind we had no home, at least we were together. She asked me what I would do if she died, and I clung harder than ever to her.'

Maybe when Mummy got angry or went somewhere else in her mind, it reminded her of somebody who hurt her badly. Strangely, she could comfort me when I felt a sickness deep down in that space where you feel everything.

Sister Mary says, holding Mummy's hands, 'Child, it was terrible, the way terrible treatment was mixed in with love, so you didn't know the difference, but now you must be happy for the sake of this child.' She looks at me. 'Do you like Tobago, dear?'

I smile weakly, not knowing what to say, and Mummy carries on speaking as if Sister Mary hasn't said anything.

'I'm glad Poppet has stability, school, parents who love her, friends, siblings. I never had it, you know. After Mother left my father and Savanur, we lived in hotels, and I never went to school, nor did I have tutors. At night, I heard her crying for my father, the man she left voluntarily, saying, "Saied, I loved you. I loved you." And then, "I hate you, Saied. I hate you; I wish I didn't love you."'

'Oh, you poor, poor child.'

Sister Mary didn't seem to understand that that was what love was; you couldn't have it if you didn't have the terrible thing – perpetual longing mixed in with hate. Everyone knew that.

'Soon after, she met a man, her own cousin, who dazzled her when he was half addled himself – after falling off a horse – imagine, being that easily impressed – and they bunked off to Karachi where she left me in a boarding school for girls, all from Pakistan's elite families. They all went home to their families for the holidays, and I sat alone in the dormitory, had my meals alone in a vast dining room. Even the sweeper felt sorry for me and brought me pickles, and sometimes just sat with me under a tree. I'll never forget her, a woman called Mohadin-bi whose children, lived with her on the compound. So happy they looked together, and that's when I understood position, wealth and even looks meant nothing when your mother doesn't care for you.'

Mummy must be exaggerating. No one who looks like that, with the stained-glass light falling on her face, like an actress on a billboard, could be sad. I sigh loudly, open the parasol and shut it again. I want to go home

'Are you hungry, dear?' Sister Mary asks.

'No,' I lie. I knew Mummy wouldn't like me taking food from the nuns. 'Mummy gets tired easily,' I offer to Sister Mary. 'She may want to go home now and rest.'

Sister Mary puts a hand out to me as if saying: be patient.

'Was there anyone in your family to comfort you, dear?'

'Not after my grandfather died, and my uncles got married. Then Ved saved me.'

Sister Mary moves her chair closer to Mummy, and she pours glasses of water for us all. She covers Mummy's hand with hers. 'Don't look back, dear. Look outside. You are on a beautiful island with the ocean always in sight, far away from all that. You have your husband, your children.'

Mummy's 'yes' comes out like a sob, and I put my head on her shoulder.

'Your mother must have had her troubles, dear. Anger is always misdirected pain.'

Sister Mary asks, 'Do you mind if I pray for you, dear?'

'That would make me happy, sister. Islam and Christianity are of the same family, but I can't face any images.'

'We will hold hands as we are, dear, not facing the cross.'

Sister Mary, Mummy and I hold hands and bow our heads. Sister Mary prays, asking Jesus to help Mummy, for the Holy Spirit to bless her and me. There are tears on Mummy's face like a fine sheen in that dark church, her lips red and swollen from crying. I want her to stop. She rubs her streaming eyes like a child, and when she stops, taking sharp breaths to recover, Sister Mary says she must go, but we could stay and pray in this house of God. Mummy and I sit quietly for a few minutes, then she takes out the compact from her purse, reapplies her lipstick, and I follow her out into the hot day.

On our walk home, Mummy holds her parasol over her head with one hand and my hand with the other. I can't bear the thought of Mummy being my age, getting blows on her head. I clutch her hand tight, coax her out of sadness by picking a green mango and saying we could have that later with salt. I run and pick a sprig of bougainvillaea and give it to her. She smiles weakly and puts it behind her ear.

They are like Russian dolls. I understand now. Mummy blames Burri-mummy for being unkind. Burrimummy blames Mumma for ill-treating her, and Mumma blames Sadrunissa for thrashing her. They all took out whatever anger they felt over their own lives on their daughters. No one is responsible. It goes back and back. Elided are the wrongs of patriarchs, husbands, and fathers' treatment of their daughters. I quietly take some of Mummy's lipsticks and go to my room, staring at myself in the mirror, wondering why I was so dark. I put on and rub off the lipstick that looked so beautiful on Mummy's lips; I rub some on my cheeks.

When Daddy comes home, I think he looks like Omar Sharif; his face is a handsome brown, his teeth whiter in contrast to his sunburnt face and alert brown eyes. Even in mufti, plain white shirt and khaki pants, he looks like a dashing army officer home after a game of bridge. He puts his briefcase down, looks at me, and says, 'Poppet Polly Pudding and Pie.' As I run to him, he dashes away to the ringing phone. He pulls out a map where he has drawn a highway across cocoa and coffee estates. He accepts an invitation with a broad smile and says, 'I'll agree to have a scotch with you, but not to changing my plan.' He laughs so charmingly that I can imagine how the person on the other end melts. When he hangs up and looks at me, I can tell it's not his Poppet Polly he sees but another creature.

'Is that lipstick you have on?' he says. 'Red on your cheeks?' My face burns. 'What are you? A whore? Trying to attract men? Don't you know all men are bastards? They will let you down. If you fail all your exams, you'll be a nobody. Go and study.' I feel a churning in my stomach. I will never look like Mummy, and Daddy will never love me.

Later that afternoon, Daddy says to Mummy, 'Nur, please be on time for cocktails at the golf club. This evening is for the Knots' birthday party.'

Poor Mummy; she can't get out of bed and leave the house. I hear her say, 'Yes, Daddy, give me five minutes.' She calls for me. 'Poppet dear, give Daddy his tea.'

Puzzled, I leave her room. Fifteen minutes later, Mummy emerges, dressed in an off-white chiffon sari stamped with large roses. Her lipstick is a light glossy pink; her hair is brushed back to show her lovely face, a tangy, expensive perfume hovers about her. I can't believe she is the same woman who lay so miserably in bed an hour ago. No matter how sorry I feel for Mummy, she's been loved by Daddy, who drove hundreds of miles across India for her. Burrimummy had the man who fell off his horse and asked for her hand. Mummy and Burrimummy had troubled times, but they didn't have to do the dishes.

Daddy buys our uniforms and books and occasionally studies our textbooks so he can teach us. But it's just like India. Due to lack of space, I'm in an advanced class and find French and Spanish incomprehensible and the other subjects difficult. I come last, as usual. Angel, placed in a class of her own age, on the opposite side of the hall, thrives with the order of the school. Winky is one class from above me, and his classroom is next to mine. Winky protects me in school. He was nearly expelled for pummelling a boy in his class for me on our first day.

I only knew it was him when my entire class rushed next door to his class to a collective, astonished 'Oooooooooo'.

'Say that again, say that again.'

Pinioned by Winky's knees, the boy, turning away from Winky's fists, gasps out, 'Poppet don't fuck!'

'Damn right she doesn't. Don't *ever* take my sister's name.'

Winky got sent to the principal, who tells Winky, Daddy and me, 'We are a peaceful people. Students don't brawl like this in our schools. This may be acceptable in India, but it is not our way.' Daddy and Winky dismiss the headmaster, and Winky can do as he wishes out of school.

He and I love one another with the fierceness of drowning siblings. My abiding feeling towards him is frozen on that rainy day in Simla when a school bus overturned in the mountains, and I'd feared losing him. I look after everyone else. He looks after me. Angel remains reserved; this intrigues boys, who try to get her to speak, looking delighted when she rewards them with a rare bright smile.

I struggle to get Angel and myself dressed and to school. I wash our uniforms, rub the white paste on our school shoes and after the children in school begin snickering at our creased clothes we learn to do the ironing too. 'What happen? You never see ah iron in India or what?' We take turns ironing deep into the night, listening to *Saturday Night Fever* and *Grease* tapes.

We never bring a lunchbox to school like the other children as I've been packing slices of bread for lunch until the girl next to me asks if I have never heard of sandwiches. The next day I pack peanut butter sandwiches and boxes of frozen orange juice for Angel, Winky and me and an extra jam sandwich for tennis lessons. When I lay it out on my desk, the entire class applauds and I realise I must make lunch from now on to show we are all looked after, just as they are. A dimpled boy smiles kindly at me, and the day feels like bursts of marigolds falling from the sun. At home, sitting on the sun-warmed steps of the back veranda, looking at the sunset, eating mango chow with Angel after we've done our chores, the light feels brighter at the thought of the tall, dimpled boy with curly hair.

I don't know if Daddy knows about Winky's afternoons in the garden shed, where I found him heaving up and down on Patsy on his exercise mat, with the bags of disappeared flour from the kitchen next to them. Her thin dark legs are open and spread out like a V. I shut the door quickly and try not to think about what they were doing. Instead of being ashamed, he's full of himself, skiving off school, creating mystery around himself and the girls he meets there.

I think of the dimpled boy all day, during assembly, in class, in my head during our chores and do everything with a daydreaming, giddying joy. With the thought of the boy, his dimples, his shy smiles, I keep cleaning, going out in the rain with the cutlass in my nightie and the gardener's discarded galoshes.

After school on Friday during extra lessons, I see Angel flanked by two boys when the electricity went off as it often did; when the lights come on, Angel is laughing, still flanked by the boys, holding hands behind her chair, each thinking they were holding her hand. One of them is the boy I had a crush on, the boy with dimples and pimples – the one who filled my heart with fields of peaches and marigolds, mountains and snow. I thought he liked me, also that I was Angel's and she mine, and we would know how not to hurt one another. Angel's delighted laughter belongs to those indifferent to a surfeit of adoration, like a rich person indifferent to money, knowing it's multiplying anyway. The more she turns from it, the more desire will follow her, wanting some of what she has. No one will be able to pick Angel apart like a flower to see what's in there; that's how whole and armoured Burrimummy made her.

On Saturday afternoons, after doing our chores and pinning up Indian bedspreads to darken the room from the searing heat, we lay out the Monopoly board and sit on the bed facing one another. I look at Angel's rounded face, light on one slanted cheek, as she reaches for a slice of green mango and dips it in salt. The face Burrimummy loves; the face boys stare at.

'Guess what your name is?' I ask, 'Your initials are FA.'

Angel looks confused.

'Is it Fat Angel, or is it Fuck Angel?'

'Fuck,' she says, the obscenity sounding pure in her mouth.

'Wrong,' I say. 'It stands for Fat Angel. What is it this time? Let's try again.'

'It's Fat Angel.'

'Wrong,' I say, and the game goes on and on.

I push my feet on her face, saying, 'Your cheeks are so soft', wanting to crack her placid sense of self. She is intractable. Nothing can touch her. She lies there, with her long plait and her fat round cheeks, saying, 'Oh God, help me, please help me,' in sweet patient tones, so she doesn't give me the satisfaction of hurting her until I stop, kiss her and say it's a game. I am surprised when she turns away from me and calls me a bully. I do nothing but look after her now Burrimummy is gone.

While rummaging for socks one morning before school, I see a letter from Burrimummy in Angel's diary. It carries the address of one of Angel's friends. Burrimummy writes to Angel as if she is a grownup and not an eight-year-old child.

My Darling Puppa, my father, my Mumma, my Sadrunissa, my two eyes, my liver, my heart. Your mother and father threw me out. I went back to an empty Rest House Road. My piano was gone, my roses dead. Darling, I've lost everyone I've loved. I've had to live without Saied, without Nur, but I can't live without you. Angel, my Puppa, my Jaan, my life, my liver, my eyes, life is intolerable without you. I felt such pain when I came back to this empty house I begged Dr Rao to get a surgeon to remove my left breast. I didn't want to speak or eat, so I had my teeth taken out. Moses hits me. He takes money. I give Asmath, Tahira and people like that money so they can keep me alive until I see you again.

You know, Puppa, the year your mother married your Hindu father, I went to England and sat through a very lonely winter in a flat by myself. I met a few of Mumma's friends, but they were ancient. I came back when Winky was born. I named him Zafar after my own Saied-u-Zafar Khan. When I took you home when you came, my heart was whole after years of being hollowed out. Now it sits empty again. THAT'S why I cut off my breast.

She doesn't mention me. 'Hollowed out', she wrote, that's what this feeling is. Every word is a note of her desolation about life without Angel and without her piano. She is surrounded by strangers and the circling men in the servants' quarters who take her things and are a silent threat.

I ask Angel about the letter in the kitchen garden while pulling out thick weeds from between the okras, resentful she has kept it from me.

Winky says, 'She wrote back to me, too.'

'What did she say?' I'm sour, left out.

He says, 'You mean, what did I say? I said, "Burrimummy, I love you very much, but I love my mother more, and I want to see her happy. Could you make amends with her? Do this for my sake? If you can't do this for us, I don't think we should correspond with you."'

Winky is enjoying the shock on our faces. He says, 'Burrimummy wrote back and said she never wanted to see me again. She showed the letter to her brother, the Nawab of Savanur, told him her grandson hated her.'

'How do you know?' I ask.

He says, 'Mummy told me.'

Angel remains wordless and becomes increasingly impenetrable. She deals with the chaos she finds in Tobago by remembering the order of 17 Rest House Road and by not squandering her words, annihilating those who could wound her by denying their existence. She gathers snugly into herself, enters the time capsule of her first eight years with Burrimummy in Bangalore and finds safety knowing she's the centre of that world. She doesn't budge.

I want to evict Burrimummy from my head, but she persists like the outline of an ache that fills up and becomes part of my fog. I say nothing. Desperate to belong somewhere, I align with my parents, assuaged by their extravagant words of love, the cries of Poppet Polly and Quarter Pint, before they are distracted. It doesn't take much to empty me out. Daddy mentions my poor marks in school, Mummy flicks me away impatiently, and I understand that she sees me as something apart from herself, and I am deprived of oxygen. I'm not me; I'm someone else, in a fog in Simla in the winter of my own.

CHAPTER TEN

St. Lucia, 2016

Fuck it. I've blown it already. It can't get any worse. If Sigrid finds the broken glass, there's nothing I can do. I open the door, eyes briefly stung by the light as the sun rushes in through branches, landing and fading in globes on the grass. I will stay; wait this out.

I understand Derek Walcott's preoccupation with the light. How quickly it changes here on the shifting shapes of water, like shards of glass on the pool, bands of cyan and teal in the ocean, so like his fading eyes. I look across at the house, my manuscript on his coffee table, with its commanding view of the bay. Next to it, just in, new copies of his collected poems.

He was overjoyed when the box arrived last night, watching Sigrid heave it onto the table. He waited impatiently while she opened it with a knife, with the expression of a child avid for cake. He picked up a copy and held it up to the light.

'Do you see that?' The cover showed a view of his house: the green garden, the pool, the cliff edge, the sea below.

'Sigrid!' he shouted. She came rushing over.

'We did it! It's lovely, Derek,' Sigrid said.

Twenty-four years back, I accompanied my editor, journalist Raoul Pantin, to the Trinidad Theatre Workshop, where Derek directed a play he intended to take to Boston. I stayed in the shadows long after the interview was over, and the light faded to a molasses dark.

I could have sat there near the window all night, looking down at shadows of lamp-lit branches sweeping across the street, watching Derek drumming, his profile in shadow, back-lit by the stage lights, accompanying his musicians, directing his actors as if this was all there is. Could this be the way to get through our brief lives: creating form, beauty, redemption out of menace and chaos? I came to realise that this demands distance, a rigorous, unforgiving, relentless craft that skins you as it replenishes you.

Eleven o'clock. I have swept up the shards of glass and have gone back to considering packing my bags, getting a taxi to the airport, leaving the scene of my crime.

But I stay and wait. I sit, my hand on the bedspread where great dead poets have lain, hoping for some transfer by osmosis. I go outside barefoot on the wet grass and get the hammock between two sturdy trees to swing the way I like it.

Derek waves at me from the veranda. Gestures. I cross the lawn to him. It's that easy. In that instant, I feel elation – the sort he writes about – turning my face to the sun's warmth, the rush of breeze through the trees.

'Derek, I had to try out that hammock.'

He ignores that, gestures to a chair opposite him. 'Sit down. That bit about the decaying brocade curtains and the light coming in as you left India was moving.'

I sit as commanded.

He continues as if speaking to himself.

'I've read what you sent me. You had terrible ancestors, terrible relatives. Your grandmother was a spoilt woman who ill-treated you. Your family was on the side of the colonials but treated you like a native. I imagine you spent your childhood wanting to belong to these terrible people. At least the British had an appearance of being fair. Your people were openly racist; cruel to everyone. Thought themselves better than their colonisers, better than all of India. Calling you black. What precisely are you trying to say here?'

I speak slowly, thinking as I go along.

'I've been thinking of your Nobel essay, something about breaking a vase, that the love that reassembles its fragments makes it stronger than when it was whole.'

'What about it?'

'When I read it, I applied it not to this region or colonialism, but to myself.'

'It applies to people. Look, colonialism is deeply wounding. When I was younger, I accepted it. This idea that pigmentation is inferior. Will you trust a black man with your money? We inherited that, swallowed it and perpetuated it in ourselves. Is it forgivable? The whole question of good hair or lighter skin still stirs in families in the Caribbean as it did in India.'

The broken glass in the room. What will I do?

I look around, spot hummingbirds hovering in midair, whirring like miniature fans. Exquisite creatures, they drink sugar water, need food every hour, die in six years. What are their rapid wing-flapping rates: twelve beats a second or eighty? They live hard amidst beauty, die before the sweetness runs out. The wages of beauty.

'Why do you write?' he asks. He asks me twice until the bird flies off.

'I don't know. I asked a Trinidadian creative writing tutor the same thing. He said, to understand why everything is a joke for us. For instance, he came across an accident, a dead man on the street, his body crushed and divided under two tyres of a car. A laughing passer-by took a video of this mutilated man on his phone, saying the corpse looked like "scrambled eggs." This drew laughter from the gathering crowd. Imagine that. I don't know why violence is so comical to people here. It's theatre for most people. As unreal as Carnival. It's the same in the cinema. People laugh at tender scenes: an older woman removing her clothes after her husband's death; a gay couple being shamed; people in so much distress and they don't respond with empathy.'

He doesn't like this.

'Sure, but you are not writing about this. Why go back to those awful people, a grandmother who colluded with the British. Why not write of the now, of the new world?'

The 'now' is too immediate, too raw. Like that man beneath the car, I feel trapped beneath two tyres: the past and the present. The sun is now higher, and there is no wind. Apart from the wingbeat of hummingbirds somewhere, it is still.

I'm writing to fill the ache of Poppet as a child, waiting for her turn. Desire didn't do it for me. Nor love. I say something grownup and plausible instead.

'I know there are worse things than a privileged grandmother. Writing helps me forget I live in a country with the highest murder rates in a non-warring state. Life here is as cheap as a scrap of paper. There is no such thing as an innocent walk in the park or an angry exchange. I've been infected by that poison. I write to survive it. It wasn't all bad, you know. I loved something of those people. I loved the dark days,' I say, resentfully realising afterwards it's a line from a poem of his. I want him to collude with me. I'm not telling him the whole truth, I know.

He says nothing. The air is heavy with humidity, and I feel prickly heat under my arms, on my chest. I rush in to fill the void, reckless, not knowing if I'm doing this right. Too earnest? Pedestrian? Not writerly. I don't know how to do breezy, careless. That takes confidence.

'One can be killed for disagreeing with builders, for giving someone a bad drive, denying them a cigarette. The boys on the hill "spray" bullets from the hill at taxis for fun because they can. A workman slits the throat of a woman who questions him about his shoddy work. Women are murdered after they get injunctions against violent men.'

'What do you make of the violence?'

This is a test.

'We are starting from slavery and indentureship,' I reply. 'Unsaved by the wealth of oil and gas. Tempers catch like fire on tinder. Gangsters are sure of the bullet to their heads before they hit thirty. They book their own funerals in advance with gold-rimmed, glass-topped coffins; they buy the white suits, shades, and the gold chains they want to be buried in. The Indians left a country that demeaned and excluded them and arrived in a new world where they were recolonised and shoved out of the centre.

That's why they are in perpetual flight or fight, settling scores with cutlasses and poison, numbing pain with rum and the rituals of India that you paid homage to in your Nobel lecture. The Ram Leela. They don't understand or speak the Hindi and Sanskrit they use to pray or sing. It must feel like half an identity. They feel it yet don't know why they are not part of it. That must create a void in some way similar to that felt by Holocaust survivors. All that history cut away.'

'You're saying they disassociate like you did. You cut out part of yourself?'

'Yes,' I say, afraid of what the silence would bring, nervously tumbling over words, only seeing what they are as they come. I want to talk about how someone always pays for the brutality around us; I'm not ready to reveal how I personally paid for it. I remember Mummy saying, 'There's no such thing as a free lunch.'

I say instead, 'Beulah taught Burrimummy some lessons.'

He looks thoughtful, staring out at the sunlight now blazing through the trees, the bleached sea and sky. 'Beulah is accurately drawn if somewhat of a stereotype. Slavery truncated her from Africa, took language, history, heritage, stripped her down. Now that slavery is in the past, she is not easily cowed like your grandmothers' servants. She is free here. She has no memory of a feudal past and no fear of a current Massa. Beulah's atavistic memory of her African ancestors is intact. That's why she could speak to your grandmother like that.'

I say, gathering confidence at the look of interest on his face,

'But Beulah also didn't inhabit herself fully. Once, she slipped and fell on wet tiles outside the house, looked down at her grazed knee, shivering slabs of flesh on the floor, and laughed and laughed, punctuating her hilarity with groans of pain.

'I helped her haul her three-hundred-pound self-up and asked her why she was laughing. She said, "Falling is funny. I don't feel upset when I fall because I don't expect anyone to help me get up, so I do what they do, laugh harder than anyone else. That way, they can't make fun of me because I am making fun of me. You get it?" I did. The only other time I heard her laugh was after humiliating Burrimummy, putting the old lady in her place. The only other response available to her was a violent outrage. She didn't expect anyone to pick her up. She'd abandoned the part of herself that felt pain or expected empathy. She would rather die than use the mannered language of the masters. I think she associated "please", "thank you", and "sorry" with a hidden exploitative agenda.'

'But did you have a place in India? Does anybody? You shifted allegiances to survive, putting on costumes like ole mas here. Your mother and grandmother are situated politically and socially in warrior Afghanistan and Uzbekistan in Pakistan and India. Your father was in the nationalistic and

Hindu dominated army. And even in the army, officers speak English amongst themselves because it's the only common language among all the states from which they are commissioned. And your grandmother – she absorbed Europe too, didn't she? She colonised the music. So what does it mean to be Indian?'

'I don't know what you mean.' I'm playing for time. 'It's not as easy as you think to belong amidst everyday casual brutality. Five hundred murders a year, among them women killed by partners and husbands; lawlessness unleashed when the amnesty was granted to insurgents after the attempted coup. No one is held accountable. You know it.'

He laughs. 'And you found safety in India? You, a half-Muslim, half-Hindu woman, found safety with Modi?'

Oh God, yes the Gujarat pogrom, Hindu nationalists, under Modi in 2002, going on a rampage, slaughtering two thousand Muslims – no one believed the official number of eight hundred – raping women, destroying hundreds of mosques and dargahs while Indian police looked away, but I didn't want to admit it. It would mean letting go of every idea of India I had. It was a response to Muslim extremists burning a train, killing fifty-eight pundits, but the brute force against innocent Muslims was state permitted violence, official bigotry.

I concede, 'No, there is no such thing as a generic Indian. Recently, my father took us to Kashmir, occupied by over seven hundred thousand Indian soldiers, four times the entire population of St Lucia. While he spoke of the killing of the Kashmiri pundits, my mother spoke of the occupation. The thread that holds India, with many of its states and union territories agitating for freedom, is tenuous, and it's held together today with brute force.'

'So your place is here.'

I say, 'I was an unintentional émigré at twelve. I belong here now in this place of transplanted people more than I will anywhere.' It isn't enough for him.

He laughs. I'm aware I sound like a Ted talk. 'Transplanted people.' He does a belly heave as if it's a joke. Yet, he speaks as he writes, chooses his words as if he expects to be recorded. 'Rubbish. Your family, who call themselves royal, are trapped people who are stuck in a time capsule. You mustn't be part of that. It's not always about claiming places but claiming yourself.' I know I'm resisting something. He changes tack.

'You have children?'

'Yes. They are grown. A girl and a boy in their early twenties. The boy is in Edinburgh, reading politics; my girl is reading law in Bristol.'

I get a flash of the glass shattered by the stove. They will never invite me back.

Derek calls for water. 'Sigrid. Sigrid.'

'I suppose they will get that solid colonial education like I did. I also considered myself brought up in a benign colonial situation. I felt very much a part of things. I knew people would ask, "How can you talk like that when the background of that is slavery, exploitation?" It's not my experience. My parents were African, Dutch and English. Anyway, my experience in this is immaterial. My father… well, never mind. What's important is what I do to help restore the new world from ruin.'

Abruptly, Derek turns away from me and rifles through his own book of poetry as if I'm not there. Is he consoling the bereft toddler he was when his father died by remembering his father? That bereft toddler lives in him.

Sigrid brings us water, and he drinks deeply, looking out at the sea. I don't know what I'm supposed to do. His father is always present in his head. He makes up poetry to replace that absence. We all go back and back.

Derek's gift to the Caribbean is the poetry, the re-imagined landscape, the healthy embracing of his people as if to say, *The colonials couldn't strip you entirely. Here, hold this. I give you who you are: a ferment and an amalgam of all the continents gathered in these tiny islands* – his way of defining himself. Derek speaks of the light, but I think that if we close our eyes to the brutality, we allow it to swell beneath the surface.

I glimpse Sigrid walking to the dining room with plates, returning with cutlery, looking our way. She must be wondering, as I am, what I'm doing here.

He catches me looking at him and says, 'I asked you to come here because I've been reading your writing on the human condition – rejection, discontent,' he says. 'But I want you to do more than chafe at the human condition.'

It's humid, and I'm thirsty. I came here, thinking he was washed out, but he is all there. He's willing me out of this state of discontent into primal innocence and all for the work.

'Tell me a joke,' he says.

'When I returned to England from India, I met an important Parsee woman called Zerbanoo Gifford. She was the first Indian councillor in Harrow for the Liberal Party. She said she knew of my family in India. "You are absolutely royal," she said. "I will find you a match." She called me up and said, "I want you to go to tea with the queen. I have just the man to take you to one of her garden parties."

'I spent a week's salary on a skirt, hat and stockings I couldn't afford, on shoes I couldn't wear for more than five minutes, excitedly wondering what Burrimummy would say. I was asked to meet him at Hampstead tube station on the appointed day. I vaguely thought this was too far from Buckingham Palace, but I trusted men who looked commanding, as this one did, with stubble on his face, his expensive white shirt rumpled as if he was too important to care about such things.

'He took my arm and guided me down a cobbled street into a dark pub and into a large room decorated with shiny cheap tablecloths, garish crimson satin curtains and plastic roses. It was a themed party.'

Derek doesn't laugh. He sees my embarrassment. 'I get it. You feel you are not the real deal, that you don't belong. You don't need to be locked in that place. Move on.'

Abruptly he waves me off. 'I'll see you at lunch.'

As I get up to leave, he leans forward. 'Did you like *White Egrets?*'

He asks me this in the same tone Burrimummy used to ask my children, when they were small, if they would come to see her grave, if they would remember her. I respond as I did with Burrimummy, like a child carefully carrying delicate china for an adult, a repository for their glory days, waiting, like a mendicant with outstretched palms, for love.

He thinks India should be left behind, but I can only bear Trinidad if I remember India, or more accurately, the only person who made me feel I belonged somewhere. Angel never had that problem. She went as far from all that nostalgia as she could, shedding India, shedding Burrimummy's past, painting all the rooms she lives in white, tidying nonstop as if a fastidious cleaning – the sort Burrimummy taught us, with four towels on our bodies – would wipe out the chaos of never belonging to her parents, and being uprooted from the one person she loved.

ELEVEN

London/India, 1989

On the plane to London, on my thirteenth birthday, I am woken to an urgent call by the air hostess for a doctor. I wake to see the seat next to me empty. Daddy is lying across from me, over three seats.

'He has had a heart attack,' the doctor says.

I feel the plane rock and look at Daddy's handsome face, the grey stubble. I clutch his hand and sit with his legs on my lap for six hours, terrified he might die. I wake him up every five minutes with a question to make sure he's not gone until he starts to look disturbed. After that, I go to the doctor and write down his instructions in my diary. 'Don't let him carry anything. Only boiled fruit and vegetables, and then he needs to have another test before he can travel again.'

People help me haul our suitcases on and off the train. At Victoria Station, Daddy pulls out an address from his pocket, and the cabbie drops us on the wrong side of the street, so I carry both our suitcases, first one and then go back for the other. After we check in at the bedsit, I take him to the doctor in a taxi and count out the change carefully. In the week we were meant to see London, I look after Daddy, shop in the local shops for vegetables and fish, cook for him in the bedsit and give him his medication. We decide not to call home, as we know Mummy will worry. She was against Daddy wasting money on boarding school, and agreed to let me go reluctantly. She equipped me with a copy of Jane Austen's *Emma* with the inscription 'Be good sweet maid and let your beauty shine.' Winky and Angel had become another generation of beautiful people in my family; they were too busy enjoying their popularity to notice my departure. There was no point calling home.

After his second visit to the doctor and a day before he is due to fly home, we take the train from London to the school in Buckinghamshire, where we go straight to the principal's office. While waiting to see the principal, we look over the gravelly driveway, the neat gardens, the tennis courts, the girls swinging by in green, pleated uniforms. He says to me, 'I want you to know I have dreamt of this moment since I was a boy of twelve. I always visualised you: a beautiful daughter I would educate in England. Remember, no one could be as loved as you are, even before you were conceived.'

I take his hand, larger, but shaped like mine, then cover my wet eyes with mine. He's not strong enough to look after my tears now.

After a few minutes in the headmistress' office, where he urges me to study hard, follow the rules and be respectful – to the approval of the headmistress, a large woman with small, round spectacles – he leaves. I watch him in his shabby, old-fashioned jacket as he collects the suitcase he has left at the door and walks out through the majestic iron gates to the street. A soldier still with his big briefcase, he will walk straight-backed to the coach station in Beaconsfield, after which he will take another to Heathrow. Hotels, long-distance phone calls and taxis are all luxuries so he can pay for me to be here. As he goes past the gates, I feel part of me turn ghostly and walk out with him.

After supper, I follow the head girl to the sixth-form common room. On seeing me, a voluptuous red-haired girl says, 'Well, well, what do we have here – a brown fairy?' It stings. But I remember who I've come from. Mummy. Burrimummy. Mumma. Sadrunissa.

'At least I'm not a pink ginger pig,' I retort. I don't know where I got that from. I learnt early in Tobago, after a girl called me a coolie, that she was just testing to see how far she could take it, that people pounce on weakness. I see a quick acceptance in the girl's eyes, and the girls in the room make space for me to watch *Top of the Pops* with them on TV.

Daddy doesn't realise that it's an expensive finishing school. It's not for public servants like him who pinch pennies and don't own a home. The girls here won't ever need to work. But they think I'm too stuck up, too strange, and on my second night, they take all my clothes away from the bathroom. When I come into the dormitory in my towel, four girls surround me, say they will rape me, and pull my towel away, leaving me naked on the floor. I pretend I am not me until they go away, and one girl throws a towel back at me.

American and English history lessons, literature, and economics blow my world open. I want to read on and on, but I want to belong more, so I behave like the girls with money and squander time, drifting from school dances to midnight feasts and walks on long rainy days in the woods. Sitting on damp logs amidst sodden yellowed leaves, I learn how to smoke from a Persian girl who shows me how to blow out smoke through a pouting mouth in a way that attracts men. Soon I am taking drags from the girl who will die of anorexia before I leave, and the redhead who called me a brown fairy takes me to parties in town in houses held by grownup people where we dance with grown men. I am good at being an outsider.

Burrimummy sends me aerogramme letters, giving me news in snippets.

My darling Poppet, England must be so pleasant now. Please send me the address of your guardian. Mumma was the ward of Lord and Lady Linlithgow, and they looked after her. Khaja and Rita are still stealing like hell.

India is a mess. You would have thought the Indians would have known better than to elect Mrs Gandhi as prime minister again, but the fools have done that. I thought it couldn't get worse, but it has, with that Morarji Desai prime minister who drinks his own urine for his health.

They are changing the names, so Bombay is Mumbai, removing the Mughals from history books. Last week, some gundas bludgeoned a Muslim butcher for selling beef. India is no longer safe for Muslims. I'm glad you're not here, my darling.

She sounds herself for most of the letter, which does not mention the breast she commanded her surgeon to remove. Yet her yearning is there. She wants to know how the woods smell in autumn, wants photos, says that sometimes she gets lonely thinking of her two eyes.

From the other side of the world, I get news from Daddy's weekly letter of Angel and Mummy, of the latest maid, of Angel's graduation.

Mummy's letters contain little news. A few words take up most of the page in her large, broad handwriting. She ends each note with, '*I hope you are eating well and not too cold. Please look after yourself, Pet. Your Devoted Mother.*'

Angel rarely writes. We are relieved not to have the burden of each other. We remind one another of loss and Burrimummy. I hear from Daddy that she excels in school, is very tidy and makes perfect round chapatis for their guests.

Burrimummy's letters carry increasingly distressing news, so I stop opening them until months later, and find this.

My Belovedest,
I can't say it was not upsetting leaving my two eyes in Tobago because it was. However, my beloved child, I want you and Angel to love each other so that there is no need for explanations. It's the only way to live. I never had that

There is a gap. The ink changes to the bright green of a felt-tip pen.

I had to discontinue my letter because I had a fall. For no reason at all, Rita pulled my chair when I was about to sit down to write again. I fell flat on the floor and could not get up. Khaja got a man from outside to lift me on the bed. Dr Rao prescribed tablets and an ointment. Moses said the tablets were not available, but I found some balm.

Another gap. The ink is red.

After three days, I am better, but walking is painful – however, it will pass off soon, by God's Grace. Allah was always kind to me. I might have broken my spine… That I am parted from those whom I love and adore is the will of Allah. Your great-grandmother was only allowed to stay in Eastbourne till she was sixteen, and then she had to get married. She was a brilliant woman you know. She would have made a good doctor. The only wealth you will ever have is what is in your brain. Your father may be a Hindu but he understands that. When you write to them, give Col and Mrs Nath my best regards.

I don't want to think of Burrimummy in Rest House Road on her own. She still occupies the house that she's sold and reclaimed many times, that is by right Mummy's inheritance. There is a tangle of litigation around it. Each new lawyer is corrupted by its huge worth and her vulnerability. Each aerogramme from Trinidad and India tugs at me and makes me feel a part of something that is broken.

Daddy's letters are full of dreams for me: Oxford, a profession in law, and advice for life taken from the Gita.

Do your duty without being attached to the fruit of your actions. You are only on this earth to do good. If you fail in your duty, you are a parasite. Don't let your ego overpower you. We are all insignificant. We are all ants.

I have been failing in my duty. I spend so much time fitting in – dancing to the *Top of the Pops*, imitating Kate Bush's raccoon eyeliner, mooning after Bryan Ferry – I pick up only enough information from the classes to have pretentious conversations about the counter-reformation and Chaucer.

'Mummy and I are willing to sacrifice so you can be independent. Owning a home is nothing to your future. All men are bastards. I know because I am a man.'

Yes, yes, all men are bastards. Still, my A Level results are mediocre. I've let everyone down, including myself, with only bastards to save me. Two years in boarding school in Buckinghamshire and I fail at academia, but I have learned how to smoke a cigarette so a man will look at me and how to put on skintight jeans in the toilet of a moving train – careless use of my time in England bought with Daddy's precious pounds.

I have achieved something I've longed for. Approbation. The gentle English light, the rain, meals of potato butties, and Granny Smith apples cooked in butter and sugar have filled me out, put roses in my cheeks. My mouth now has something of Mummy, and my hair has grown thick and long. Older men I meet in London at friends' houses ask me to parties. I am called a 'beauty' for the first time.

After I fail to get anywhere near Oxford University, Daddy looks to Canada, fills in the application forms for a business degree. Wracked with guilt, undeserving of his grand dreams for me, deficient as I am in direction and agency, the old feeling of not occupying my own body returns.

I am seventeen when Daddy accompanies me to Trent University in Peterborough, an Ontario university town, a quiet lazy place, with a lake and tall firs, a campus modelled after Cambridge. At least Daddy will see that, I think, when the graduate student shows us around. Daddy settles me in, buys me a kettle, a warm coat, scarf, gloves. I dread the heart-wrenching moment when he gets on the bus in the same shabby jacket he wore the day he took me to boarding school.

In Peterborough, I live in a house with a boy I think I love, chiselled like a Greek god, a chaste Catholic history major. He has deep-set blue eyes, shoulder-length blonde hair, powerful ice-hockey thighs; he even wears lumberjack shirts. He takes me walking and never makes a move, seemingly content to have me by his side. Bizarrely, for a fancy-dress party we attend together, he wears a Nazi costume, and I, in a red silk kurta, dress like a 'Paki', content with the hit we are as a couple and how pretty I feel – a prelapsarian happiness so searing it's beatific. Another day, on a walk in a whipping wind, as he pulls me up snowy slopes, with the moon high, trees skeletal with icicles like diamonds, there's the ache of unrequited love mingled with timorous hope. Years later, when I read F. Scott Fitzgerald's novella *The Diamond as Big as the Ritz*, I had the same feeling.

Three years go by in a snowy haze of dope, joining a reggae band, playing a triangle, touring around Canada's many lakes in the cold, sleeping in a truck on road trips, arguing existential questions, hanging out in the rooms of boys I don't sleep with, while moping over the one who withholds himself. I graduate in liberal arts, virginal still but already weary of love.

Back in Tobago, at twenty-one, I ease into life like a returned village celebrity, strangely popular with boys who never looked at me before. I use every moment of Daddy's absence at work to go to the beach, to sneak out for moonlight parties and picnics. Winky, studying engineering in Plymouth, England, is no longer there to push me around. Daddy has taken Angel to Canada to a boarding school, and I enjoy being my parents' only child. Angel and I remain separate as if by mutual consent, but she is never absent from me. One night I dream of us holding hands and jumping into the ocean together, shaving the skin off our bodies on the cliff as we go down, holding one another to come up.

Six months later, Daddy announces that I am to be a journalist. He has applied, and I have been accepted onto a master's degree course in international journalism in London. I sulk. I am happy in Tobago, and I don't want to leave, content with my job as a clerk in the magistrates court.

'You must do something that pays. You can't depend on either philosophy or a man to pay the bills. You need to have a profession to support yourself.'

Before our departure to London, I break my ankle while racing to answer the phone. Looking at the large cast and the hateful cane, I think that at least I don't have to go away. 'Look, you must do this,' Daddy insists, 'so you can look after yourself. How many times must I tell you men are bastards?'

Daddy takes me to London, rents a small apartment and drives me to and from City University for three weeks until my cast comes off. At night, he cooks for me. At the weekends, he shows me around the museums and art galleries. But I'm impatient to meet the faces from around the world in my class, many of them seasoned journalists from Nigeria, South Africa, Australia, Germany, Pakistan, Indian, Sudan. I long for him to be quick about leaving me, though each day that goes by, I miss him as if he has already gone. This is the blueprint of my parents – this seesaw of love.

Before leaving, after the cast on my leg is off, Daddy settles me in a residence hall near the Barbican. When he drops me off at school on the day of his departure, I don't look back, suddenly furious at the sadness I associate with him. He leaves and leaves and leaves.

My mind explodes that year on the international journalism programme with people from twenty-five countries as my classmates, learning about wars and politics, upheavals, the price colonies pay for Empire. I meet politicians, attend a press conference with Margaret Thatcher, past sniffer dogs, and hear racism couched as immigration policy.

After I graduate, like everyone else, I start looking for a place but I don't have the money, and I know Winky will not help as he is Daddy's mouthpiece in England. All I know is, I don't want to go back to Tobago, to sneak around with boys and drive to the beach stoned. I am not that girl anymore.

Daddy sends me a ticket home. I send it back, and Daddy gives me an ultimatum: 'Come home to Trinidad or support yourself. It's not right, a young girl living by herself.'

I call up a friend and spend some nights on her floor. A Jewish South African student invites me to a party with his Oxford pals. At the party, in a smart Notting Hill flat where the film was shot, I use Burrimummy's stories as currency to engage with people who never have to think about money, relay her stories of boar hunts, meeting Mohammed Ali Jinnah, Sadrunissa attending the Delhi Durbar, Puppa getting the entire court-room to come to the railway station in 1947 because he'd taken an oath never to step into Savanur again, of the Maharanis reduced to poverty in crumbled palaces after the ending of the privy purse. I had gone, channelling Jean Rhys, putting on make-up in a cracked mirror, borrowing a sweater, fluffing out my hair, determined not to show my poverty. The host tells me he's going to Harvard for a year; I could look after his flat in Notting Hill Gate.

I see fields of marigolds again in this posh place.

I get by with three low-paying jobs: sweeping at a hairdresser in Chelsea; serving drinks at a pub in Islington; subbing articles for the *Jewish Chronicle* in Golders Green, but I am collecting interesting people and having suppers in Notting Hill cooked by pretty Oxford boys.

I didn't inherit my mother's or my grandmother's beauty, but I must have inherited something men liked. There was always some man who had his eye on me. Among them a gym trainer with a council flat in Mile End; a handsome banker who frightens me with unspeakably banal ambitions, boring conversation and the promise of a house in suburbia; a Jewish boy from Canada whose history is rich with stories of the Holocaust; a math major with large biceps (and a fiancée I didn't know about until I dumped him) who hoists me on a kitchen table, closes my eyes and asks me to imagine what it would feel like to have a published book in a bookshop. It remains a virginal play for me, about dates and outings. None get me to go to bed with them. They retreat, sometimes with accusations that I am a tease. I don't care. I belong to two worlds, and I'm not taking chances with either.

I fall in love, finally, with a Jewish man who understands everything South Asian and Middle Eastern about me, who throws open for me the England I was coming to love.

Jacob, who read PPE at Oxford and grew up in South Africa, shows me London, just like Moses did for his girl in Sam Selvon's *The Lonely Londoners*; a London of concerts at churches; bookshops and lectures in Hampstead; the National Portrait Gallery; the proms; the V&A; fringe theatre; jazz clubs; Ethiopian and Korean restaurants. I walk and walk, sometimes alone, often with Jacob, loving how London feels like an ocean with churning surprises, the centuries piled on top of one another. Once we see a man sitting on a bench near St James Park, and Jacob stops and says, 'Look, that's Harold Wilson.' He takes me to the Chelsea Flower Show, and we leave with armfuls of over-bloomed roses thrust at me by a gardener who has no use for them, and they cover the seat of the bus and petals trail behind me all the way home. For the entire year I feel flushed with wine and expectation. I know this is it. When Jacob and I attend a Gujarati wedding together, in that large hall in Wimbledon, amidst shiny saris and bright 24-carat gold, incongruous in this cold, dark place, I feel suffocated, get palpitations, so we have to leave before the four-hour ceremony is over. I'd rather be a spinster than have any part of it. This is what I tell Mummy on a rare phone call home. 'This is what happens when our girls get too westernised, dear.' She sighs, distant and resigned.

Jacob's London is my world, and I can make a life here. I don't know where his sentences stop and mine begin, but we start to fight, with increasing intensity, on every London corner. I want him to marry me, to save me from being an 'alien' to the Home Office because I have exhausted my visa extensions. He refuses and doesn't say why, but I find out when his cultured doctor mother takes me aside one day and says, 'It's best you stay in your beautiful Islamic culture, and he stays in his. I'm sure your mother would agree.' Mummy does and refuses to speak to Jacob on the phone when I try to introduce them. The Jewish and Muslim mothers break it up. This coincides with the return of the smart Notting Hill flat homeowner from Harvard, accompanied by a girl wearing a Laura Ashley dress, carrying a basket of flowers.

They don't have to say anything. I know they will need the flat and I have to leave. Once again homeless, I find a room in Wembley with a Gujarati family where I must be in by 10:00 pm, sleep in a tiny bed, watch a rat scurry across my room and wait for the family to finish eating their dinner before I can gnaw on a piece of cheese and stale pitta bread. I get another gig churning out press releases on cash-and-carries for *Garavi Gujarat*, a free publication in English and Gujarati targeting the corner shops; a deaf and mute man translates them into Gujarati, and women in saris do the typesetting.

Every morning I go to the sooty building through the Waterloo tunnel, past scurrying rats in the Elephant and Castle underground. I am illegal; the last to leave the office, paid seventy-five pounds a week, and after I pay the rent and buy a railcard, I have barely enough to eat, but I refuse to ask my father for money. I know he will say, 'Come home', but I'd rather starve.

When the Indian landlady gives me notice, I recall an older face, a handsome face, a former professor of journalism from my university in the Barbican, and his casual kindness to me. I remember he lived in India in an ambulance in the sixties for two years; that he named his daughter Misha, the same as my father's sister; and he was briefly thrown into jail in Uganda in the sixties with Rajat Neogy, the founder and first editor of *Transition* magazine, the repository of Ugandan intellectual life in the sixties. He seemed safe.

Over a coffee in a tiny shop in Islington, I tell him I don't want to return to Trinidad, that I have no job, nowhere to live.

'I'm going to Nigeria to teach development journalism,' Hugh says. I could sleep in his bed till I found something. I sleep on his mattress, listen to his Bob Dylan records and tentatively make friends with his son and daughter, his ex-wife and her boyfriend. They each have their own corners of food and congregate in the kitchen for ironic conversations about the arts, the Labour Party or a dictator in Africa. The daughter produces window boxes, gives massages, teaches aerobics. His son takes serious arty photographs and always has an impossibly beautiful woman with him. They give me no indication of their childhood in India until I ask about their daughter's Indian name. Perhaps, they need a lifetime of England to forget India's heat and over-stimulation – it's too bright days, of going from city to city amongst babbles of languages and beggars and lepers, who would have crowded around a white family assuming there was money to be had.

No one is in charge in this liberal English household, and everyone is allowed to be who they want. The lack of a patriarch is astonishing, as is the organic family they have where no one owes anyone anything; there are no guilt trips, and they meet and part with the ease of casual friends.

When Hugh returns, slipping into bed with me after a long flight, I find the acceptance I craved. He is twenty-one years older than me, so even I know it's Daddy issues I have. When I answer his questioning eyes with a 'yes' and say I'm a virgin, he says, 'It's a big responsibility,' but takes me and it on with gusto and tenderness. On my birthday, Hugh comes home early, carrying a supersize garbage bag, like a tall, sharp-featured, brown-eyed Santa Claus. He takes out every published Virgina Woolf novel, each wrapped in newspaper, erotic inscriptions in all of them. Socks. Shampoo. Underwear from Marks and Spencer. A warm wool sweater. Woogies. Hairbands. M&M's. Presents for a child. For a time, I belong.

Hugh wakes every morning and goes for a swim with his ex-girlfriend; he lives an ordered day. I spend a lot of time waiting for him, and on freezing nights he covers my body with his oversized winter jacket on the street, hurries me into Chinatown for soup and takes me home to bed.

When I get an eye infection, he takes me to the hospital on the tube, like a father, and then dresses my eyes daily until they heal. He looks after me as if parenting for the second time, takes me to the theatre and introduces me to his family, so I meet his parents, who changed their Jewish surname after the war. I can understand why Hugh is wary. His father is a command-ing man, with Hugh's impressive Middle Eastern nose and a look of set cruelty that Hugh lacks, and his mother is clearly a socialite; both are in their nineties. He is everything they are not.

Too soon, I am hungry again, eviscerated. Hugh has days when he needs to go away from me, brood silently in his study, see people while I wonder what I did wrong. And days when he comes bearing gifts. I had chosen a familiar pattern.

Burrimummy writes again.

Go and see the first mosque built in Northern Europe. It was commissioned in 1889 by your great-great-grandmother, Nawab Sultan Jehan Begum. She was the Begum of Bhopal from 1844-1901, the last in a line of four women who ruled Bhopal for over a century. She ruled in strict purdah. She spoke to heads of state in full burka through a latticed screen. All her cars had curtains.

She was at the coronation of the King-Emperor George V and Queen-Empress.

In 1926, she abdicated in favour of her youngest son, Hamidullah Khan (your mother's granduncle), instead of her eldest son, General Obaidullah (your mother's grandfather). She went off to England to speak to the king, George V, to get your great granduncle installed as the Nawab. This was not only unheard of but was illegal in princely states.

Face to face with the king, she ripped off her burka. She said: 'I have never shown any strange man my face. I removed my burka because I am your sister, and you are my brother. I don't want Obaidullah, who has a hot temper, to be Nawab. I am abdicating for Hamid Ullah. The only reason I, a woman, am the ruler of Bhopal is that Queen Victoria supported me.'

The king protested that this was unprecedented, and he could not allow it. She wept, fainted, made such a scene that he saw the only way to get rid of her was to agree. If she hadn't made a scene, and George V hadn't agreed, your grandfather would have been the Nawab of Bhopal.

Darling, our lives are intertwined with the British dominion over India between 1858 and 1947. It's no coincidence you are there now. Sultan Jehan Begum would have loved you. She believed in educating girls and women. She was the first chancellor of the Muslim University of Aligarh – your father's university.

Your great-great-grandmother's mosque is in Woking, Oriental Road, thirty miles southwest of London. She created her own walled mini city, naming it Ahmadabad after her late husband, and built several palaces.

I went to see it with my bloody husband on our way to our honeymoon. Tell me if it has been kept up.

Your Devoted Old Bag

Burrimummy was still telling me stories, filling my untethered self with a vanished past, allowing me occupation there. I think sharing this is another way to impress Hugh, to make him see I was more than a waif, to make him want me forever. He takes me to Woking by train. My heart expands at the Mughal green and gold dome walls, green minarets, fountain and lawns; it's as if a piece of my history was brought to me when Burrimummy thought I needed it.

On our return journey on the train, as Hugh retreats into himself, I look out at the bland countryside through a smudged window and let the tears fall, remembering the list of visiting dignitaries to the mosque – from the King of Saudi Arabia and the founder of Pakistan, Muhammad Ali Jinnah, to Emperor Haile Selassie of Ethiopia and the Shah of Iran. Sultan Jehan Begum did all this, that woman ancestor of mine, so why shouldn't I scrub toilets if it helps to make my own mark? I will find my own way in the world. The Burrimummy way.

I had been in London for two years. My visa had run out. As I take the train to the Home Office, I hope Hugh chooses me so I can stay. He is Mummy and Daddy wrapped in one package, affectionate, reliable, and detached. Like a child, I jump through hoops to be deserving. I show him my three-month stamp; he turns cold and quiet, as if even that is too long. I am too young for him, he says. Twenty-one years difference was too much. He has already achieved everything I hope for: children, a life of adventure, possibility. He likes the settled days, old friends, coffees, the steady buzz of his typewriter. Early one morning, he says in bed, 'Women are only interesting after they have children', and he leaves for his regular morning swim with his ex-girlfriend. The men who burn for you withdraw when you ask them to fill up the spaces you have long abandoned. No one can do that for anyone. Not that they can't love, but they can't take responsibility for your defection from yourself. If I want anything from love, I must not ask too much of it.

I ask him, sadly, two weeks before my time runs out, what he thinks I should do. 'I could marry you,' he says, over dim sum in Chinatown. He looks so miserable that I do not press the issue, but I need somewhere to live.

TWELVE

India, 1989

While it's ending with Hugh, Daddy writes to me, as if on cue. He's coming with Mummy to London en route to India to attend a wedding and would like me to accompany them. Winky is busy with his new job in Reading; and Angel is studying in Bradford. They ask me if I've seen Angel, if she's well and I say yes to both. Guiltily, I invite her to London, arrange a party and ask Hugh to move to the study so she could sleep in our room. We would go to the Portrait Gallery and then to a concert in a church to hear Gregorian chants, and I know the perfect place for a Peking duck in Chinatown.

She arrives at Victoria on an early train, looks around the bedroom and says, 'Let's get you sorted first.' She doesn't comment on Hugh's things but moves efficiently around them, spends hours sorting out my books, pulling out all my clothes from drawers and asks me to direct her to the nearest launderette where we sit, watching the washer and dryer. After she folds everything away, I say the gallery has closed, but we could catch the concert at St Martin-in-the-Fields in Trafalgar Square if we hurry, and after that, people are coming for drinks. She says I have misunderstood; she can't spend the night; her boyfriend is waiting in Bradford. I had seen photos of Andy, a tall, blue-eyed boy from Nottingham. 'He never raises his voice and makes me laugh,' she says, as if that should explain it.

All the way to the tube station to the Angel and on the tube to Victoria, I try to talk her into staying. She resists with silence, a smile and a firm dash for the train with plenty of time to spare. It's as if her survival depends on drawing firm lines, keeping things tidy and contained within them. Beyond that, nothing matters. She had inherited Burrimummy's pride and her grandiose self-belief. That saves her too.

I prepare for my parents' arrival while Hugh is out, removing his sweaters, shaving cream, books on Africa. I let them in to the only place in the house which I can claim, our bedroom. I'm wearing floral balloon pyjamas made in India that I'd bought from a charity shop, and Mummy looks at me, at the beanbags, my hippie trousers, the Bob Dylan albums near the record player, as if seeing me for the first time. It is Hugh's large shoes and dressing gown peeping under the closet that makes her cry noisily and mercifully briefly.

'This is not the life I wanted for you,' Mummy says, eying the mattress on the floor, as if she knows every shameful act I have done on it.

So when Daddy says that his duty towards me as a Hindu father will only be complete when I am settled, and to do that, I must accompany him to India to find a suitable match, I agree, numb to the idea of love. I wonder, though, why he wants me to marry if all men are bastards.

'Leave everything here,' Mummy says. 'We will get everything in India.'

On the flight, I hear her telling Daddy, 'She's becoming a hippie. It's your fault for introducing her to hippies in Simla, giving her all that freedom in that alien culture, sending her away so young. No wonder she didn't know what to do with it.'

In the officers' mess quarters in Delhi, Daddy lays out a plan. He has asked his relatives to look for a prospective groom for me. They put ads in *The Hindu*, saying I was all that I was not – a slim, tall, fair, beautiful Hindu girl, with long hair, charming, quietly over-accomplished, excelling at academia and expert in the kitchen.

I am a slightly depressed, carelessly dressed Hindu-Muslim woman who speaks more Urdu than Hindi, both haltingly – a clash of *namaste* and *salaam*. I am a young woman of failed domesticity with a distaste for the kitchen, with intellectual pretensions and the atheist philosophy of Nietzsche as my world view.

Mummy and I go shopping. She gets me elegant silk saris, lightly embroidered kurta pyjamas, elegant sandals, a lipstick. She takes me to the spa for a day, gets my hair done, my nails varnished, and smooths out the London grit from my face with expensive creams.

The first man we meet, at a plush apartment complex in Delhi, is a divorcee, working in banking and living in American suburbia. His name is Vikram, but he goes by Vik, and he doesn't meet my eyes. I note the gold chains around the rolls on his neck.

'No need to work,' his mother says – just make two chapatis a day for her simple son. Daddy looks eager. I am outraged that a divorcee would be among my first suitors. I say nothing and do nothing, which is precisely what is expected of me. Two hours later, I get an offer of marriage that I decline. On the way back, I ask Daddy, fighting against a sense of enormous betrayal, that if the best he could do for me was a divorcee, why had he educated me if he wanted me married off to someone who would prevent me from working?

'I'm trying to give you the life of a princess after spending all my money to educate you. And now you're complaining?'

Mummy disapproves of the whole thing because she doesn't have a say and hates the idea of my looking at Hindu men, but doesn't want me to be a spinster, so she's removed herself from the equation with her usual accommodating equanimity.

I am prepared for the second man, a Sid, short for Siddhartha. He is an

Indian Englishman stinking of cigarettes – heroin chic with deep purple eye-sockets, thin legs and deep grooves on either side of the mouth of his ruined face. He says proudly, 'I own many corner shops.' I have swallowed two pegs of Daddy's whisky before we go to Sid's parents' home in a leafy Delhi district.

His mother, a heavily made up and bejewelled woman in a rainbow coloured sari, says – thankfully not noticing Mummy's frank amazement at her frightful clash of colours – 'You won't have to worry about money. What can you cook?'

I say, 'I'm a terrible cook,' envisaging a bleak, grey, cooped-up life on an ugly street in London's suburbia where garbage is regularly blown into the grey sky. 'I drink.'

Sid says, 'I can cook. I don't mind you drinking. We can go down to the pub together.'

I remember how I vomited after waitressing in my university pub, after the bleary students left and pools of vomit had to be cleaned up, and recognising its dried smell on the tube.

I look him in the eye and ask what he reads. He wants to speak to me alone. We walk away from the group at the table towards a large jamun tree. I pick two grape-sized jamun berries from the grass, tasting their sharp, tangy sweetness. We both look at my palm, stained a deep pink, and he says he understands, that I don't need to go to such lengths to show I'm not interested. He is here to fulfil his responsibilities to his parents, repay the debts of their sacrifice, but if I can possibly get away from this, I should.

I want to buckle at his kindness and want to say yes but remember the small dark corner shops in London on winter days and say, 'Thank you.' I am tired, but not enough to box myself anywhere. I know India has three thousand castes and twenty-five thousand sub-castes, and many kinds of Muslims, from many communities, and already I know none of them will fit, but my parents need to know it too.

The hunt continues. I meet no one I like – not the London-born Punjabi with thin lips or the grinning, empty-eyed, wet-lipped businessman I meet in a restaurant thick with mutton smells, whose mother, a diamond on each finger, speaks broken English and looks at me as if I wouldn't do.

We meet the parents of an Indian boy working in computers in Vienna. The parents, both professors, live in grey rooms with bright neon lights with stacks of untidy files and thick mottled books in a respectable but modest apartment. I meet the 'boy', Ajay, in a coffee shop in Connaught Place, a popular shopping complex in Delhi where many middle-class marriages are sealed. Intrigued by his parents' books, I ask him about himself. He says he loathes those mottled books and would like to live simply without too much fuss. His hobbies include sleeping and drinking milk. He touches a ring on his right hand nervously. I ask him the name of his Viennese girlfriend. He sobs and snorts into his coffee about his parent's expectations, and I get up, leaving him to ruminate on his double fate. He will marry a girl from India, I know, and keep the white girlfriend.

The final meeting shakes me up. We drive out of Delhi to the sprawling suburb of Gurgaon (now Gurugram) to meet this suitor. The taxi driver goes past Gurgaon, peering at the address. As we pull into a farmhouse, I think about Hugh, how the love between two people flares, and when it dies, it eviscerates one of those people. We park the car on the dry, overgrown grass in the fenced compound and step into the blistering heat.

A woman, dressed in a thin cotton sari tied traditionally, with material going straight up her legs, rushes outside, her silver anklets creating a frenzy. An ayah, I think.

'Welcome,' she says, looking me up and down. 'You came from abroad, beti?'

Burrimummy would have given her hell for being this familiar. She moves closer and embraces me, smelling of stale cooking. 'My son is coming now.'

Daddy must have got it wrong. When I hear the human barking, guttural and menacing, I wait for him to say, 'Let's go.' A man emerges from the shadows of the house into the bright outdoors. He is barking. Bared teeth are yellow against his dark, pitted skin. Three white lines on his forehead, like a priest, suggest temple attendance. He terrifies me.

Mummy and I back away. My heart thuds against my ribs. I begin to sweat, leaving large wet rings on the silk tunic I have been made to wear.

'Let's go, Daddy,' I say.

'Why?' says Daddy, with mild surprise. I'm wondering if he's being deliberately obtuse, but no, he is sober, if tired; he wants to get rid of me; he hasn't noticed the barking, only the three lines on the man's face. What he sees is a Hindu in India, and he wants to lodge me there.

Daddy hates Muslims, but strangely is very much at home with Urdu, the poetry, the food, conversation, and the women – he always said he married the most beautiful Muslim woman the world had seen. He'd felt helpless against Pakistani bombs dropped from the air, which sent his jeep careening under a tree and killed his colleagues; he'd hated Nehru and Gandhi for chopping his beloved country into pieces – Pakistan and now Bangladesh; he resents the Hindu Kashmiris being forced out of that state by Muslims – and Mummy's refusal to convert baffles and defeats him.

Daddy believes he will have done his duty if I marry a Hindu man. He doesn't care if I end up with a barking one.

'Let's leave, Daddy.'

Mummy tugs at him. We leave. Daddy looks disappointed on the bumpy ride back to the hotel.

I am wordless. This is the same father who used up his salary to send me to an English boarding school, who wept as he walked away, loves me best, whose moon and star I am. Without whom I cannot imagine a life.

Back in the residential quarters of the Madras Engineers Group officers' mess, my parents get dressed to go to the club. Nothing has changed: the swimming pool, the garden, officers in uniform walking smartly with their wives, swishing in silk, heading for an evening of dancing; entering the stately building and its vast rooms crammed with elephant tusks, trophies, arms, portraits, long dining-room tables, and on into the ballroom with its polished wooden floor where there's a live band.

While waiting for Mummy, Daddy says, 'I'm sorry you had to face that barking mad man. After my heart attack, I wanted to see you settled but not at any price. I've done my bit now, and you can look after yourself.' He repeats an anecdote. In 1965, when my parents were holidaying in Srinagar on a houseboat, Daddy was recalled to duty in Punjab for the Indo-Pak war. He had to build a bridge and lay down land mines. He lived a lifetime in those thirteen days. His jeep was fired on by Pakistani aircraft; his commander and members of his battalion were killed by shell fire; he dragged a dead colleague out of a river; drove his wounded driver to safety; then had to go through the pockets of the dead bodies of Pakistani soldiers for information filled with prayers from their mothers. I had heard him say many times: 'You do your duty, knowing you could be drinking whiskey with a friend, and an hour later, find parts of his dead body strewn over a field.' Even a good soldier wants safety at any cost for those he protects.

This is another failed exam. Mummy never knew where she would be, from month to month, when she lived with Burrimummy. I see now why my parents live so lightly. When brutality has been normalised, it is passed on, like a legacy, like DNA. It's why I could go dressed as a Paki to a fancy-dress party with a man dressed like a Nazi and think nothing of it.

THIRTEEN

On the flight from Delhi to Bangalore – the original purpose of the trip – Mummy tells us her uncle, the Nawab of Savanur, has made an excellent match for his youngest daughter, Simran. She is to marry, at barely seventeen, the son of the Nawab of X – one of India's wealthiest states and one which continues to wield political power.

Leaving Mummy and Daddy at the officers' mess, not expecting Mummy to come along, I take an autorickshaw to 17 Rest House Road. I notice with a pang that the house appears to have shrunk. The 'Mrs S. Baig' sign is lopsided; the sagging green gate offers no barrier. The pillars of her garage are chipped, and the wood roses are mottled, stripped of silver paint. I walk past thin young men with hungry eyes who come out to stare from the servants' quarters.

It has been ten years. Yet here's Khaja running towards me, diminutive but inimitably herself. I put my fingers on my lips, and she accompanies me through the front door, laughing, touching me. The house is strangely bare without the piano. Burrimummy is on the bed chewing paan in her silk dressing gown, which is stained with tobacco that the *dhobi* hadn't been able to wash out.

I run to her, revelling in her shouts of joy, her holding onto my face, crying, 'My baby, my baby, is it really you?' I kiss her soft cheeks, immerse myself in her sandalwood and paan fragrance, and sit on her bed, trying not to notice the outline of her ribs, her thinness, that her gingham sheets, once Madras bright, are almost white and threadbare.

'Bring juice for Baby, send for Moses,' she orders Khaja.

In the bed, I put my arms around her, breathe her in, glimpse through the green latticed window to see her roses have gone wild among a bramble of weeds but are still growing.

She orders Moses to fetch soup from the market. He looks at her straight in the face, with reddened eyes, smelling of alcohol.

'Last time, you didn't give me enough money.' He leans in while Burrimummy takes some cash out from under her pillowcase.

'Don't be impertinent,' she says without authority.

He obeys with the swagger of a full-blown alcoholic, doing just enough to keep her dependent and tolerant of abuse. He leaves, nodding at me knowingly, with menace. This is new.

Rita brings the soup on a trolley. Burrimummy barely touches hers while watching me eat. It is nourishing, with mutton and vegetables. 'You're thin, my baby.' She watches me as I eat from a bowl with a tiny crack she can't see.

We never ate in the bedroom. Now there is a plastic tray on her bed, and here I am, half-turned towards her, suddenly noticing the collapsed breast, a cavity bordered by shell-shaped grooves, like a poorly crocheted doily.

'You've been to Europe, Palestine?' Her voice is wheedling, curious, parched. 'What did you see, my Jaan, my life?'

I tell her, leaving nothing out.

'You stayed in a cold tent in Florence, chose between food and tickets to go to art galleries, and lived in a convent in Rome,' she cries, delighted. 'You climbed the Masada and swam in the Dead Sea – Masha Allah, may God be praised! You saw the Dome of the Rock. You saw where the Jews were taken in Auschwitz. You know, belovedest, Allah has blessed you with something no one can take away – Taaleem, knowledge, wonder.'

She touches her pepper-white hair. 'They can grab money, shares, homes, jewels, but they can *never* take what's in your brain, what you've seen, what you've studied, who you are. Now go to sleep,' she says, closing her eyes, and I obey, once again the ten-year-old.

Hearing rain, I get up, look out at the soaked mango tree, the swaying battered roses, remembering when I was a child here, lying in bed, with the thermometer in my mouth; the gasps at the high numbers; the chicken soup fed lovingly, the warm brandy and milk; order, safety; the walks home from school beside rain-drenched Cubbon Park when the combined scents of fruit and earth and the deep wet greens were so intense that I had wanted to lie down and roll myself in it.

While Burrimummy sleeps, loose-jawed and open-mouthed, I go out. The absences strike me – the gap in the music room where piano once was; the line of books Burrimummy still locked up in the glass cupboard, stolen by her from Majid Castle, also look gap-toothed. I am again recalcitrant child, walking out quickly, shaking off the servants' muddy, snotty, naked children, and think I see the cook's daughter, my secret playmate, Mary, with a baby in her arms, following me with her eyes.

Cubbon Park is the same. Soaking in the fine needles of rain in the wind, the scent of frangipani, jamun, bitter leaves, and earth mingling with autorickshaw fumes, I sit under a gnarled tamarind tree on a root, watching couples embracing in the grass with a remembered longing and the fresh shame of the unloved.

The other houses in this neighbourhood seem as soggy with the weight of the past as when I was a child: the sounds of the harmonium for an evening of classical ghazals, men in crisp white kurtas, women in cotton saris, spread out on sheets on the grass, taking cold lime juice, jugs of beer from the uniformed bearer with a silver tray. It's still here, just. Pashmina shawls are spread carelessly on chairs, but in gardens that grow wildly. The old bearers still know just how the *memsaab* wants her gin and tonic, but the old India is disappearing so fast I know it won't be here, or at best will be a parody of itself, when I return. Most of these houses have already been sold, cemented over to make way for ugly multimillion-rupee high-rises – the fate awaiting 17 Rest House Road.

The rain is pelting thick drops, and I run back, soaked, to No. 17. I hear Burrimummy shouting at the ayah. She sits on my cot with a notebook, pointing her pencil at a broad-faced man with a flaring white lungi, on his haunches on the floor, spinning around to arrange clothes in mounds: white sheets, multicoloured cotton, underwear, T-shirts and jeans. She had sorted out my suitcase.

'Now, bring back Baby's clothes first. She's going to America…' – that's code for abroad. 'Oh God, darling, your hair is wet, your clothes. Come on, come on, put on a nightie. Let me dry your hair. Fetch the hairdryer,' she says and gets it herself from her dressing table. She would have to shout a lot longer for any servants to appear. She moves with urgency.

I am still 'Baby' to the servants, two of whom are new and younger than me. 'Bring hot milk for Baby. Warm up more soup. Where is Baby's sweater?' She begins blow-drying my hair after chastising me for going out in the rain. 'Do you *want* to get sick? You've journeyed so far for this grand wedding. *Please*, darling, be sensible.'

Her voice is low, loving. It sounds how hot chocolate feels when it melts in your mouth. 'Now,' she says, 'drink up your Horlicks, darling.'

A television has arrived at 17 Rest House Road. The dryer's warmth spreads over me; we watch a Hindi broadcast announcing a memorial fund for Indira Gandhi, assassinated back in 1984.

'Good thing she's dead, damn woman. Bloody dictator, imposing a state of emergency in 1975 so she could do all the rot she wanted – abolishing the privy purse. I hope she rots in hell going to war with Pakistan in '71 for no good reason; sending the army to the temple to kill the Sikhs in her bloody operation Blue Star.'

She gives me a key. 'Pick out one or two of the books.'

She is letting me into the locked shelves of books she stole from Majid Castle. In the music room, I am eagerly turning pages of old English novels marked by rivulets made by termites, looking at the faded Majid Castle emblem, 'In God I Trust', when there is a thundering crash.

I run to the bedroom and find her standing on a stool holding up the dangerously tilting steel cupboard, its doors open. Something must have dislodged and brought things tumbling down. She is bleeding from a gash on the head; a curl of blood slowly makes its way down to one eye. I help her to push the cupboard back in place.

'Take my hand, Burri. Here, come down.'

She doesn't take my hand and, still precarious, looks at the floor. I follow her gaze to a low, solid silver, extravagantly filigreed table with intricately carved paws spattered with drops of her blood. On and around it are scattered gold bracelets, red velvet jewel cases, a sealed envelope marked 'Fixed deposits' and bundles of letters. My beloved Burrimummy opened this cupboard for me and hurt herself.

'*Please* go, Poppet. *Please* let me clean this up.' She looks more distressed at my presence than the blood pouring down her forehead.

When she's standing safely on the floor, I leave the room as instructed.

Later, when we are getting ready to go to Savanur House for the mehndi, the pre-wedding celebrations, she shows me her wedding gift for Simran.

'Come here, Poppet. Look at this. Is it all right? Is it good enough?'

Burrimummy carefully wraps the solid silver table and silver slippers belonging to Sir Afsar in velvet. She never gave me anything like that. She won't ever; I see that now. She summons Moses to take it to the car. She says with satisfaction, 'She's marrying a Nawab's son.'

Standing in front of the same three-way mirror, where I'd stood so many times as a child having my hair oiled and plaited, I feel the same as I did in Savanur House, where I was first called a little black girl. I am Nur's black child. I am Hindu because you can't be half-Muslim. I could never be worthy of Burrimummy's gift.

The wedding is my first glimpse of the dregs of the Raj. I soon realise I am overdressed in one of Mummy's south Indian saris. It is too yellow, too thick, too middle-aged for me. Burrimummy is dressed in taupe silk, with the pearls her father gave her when she was eighteen; Mummy is in elegant navy.

The pre-wedding celebrations begin as relatives and dignitaries arrive throughout the day. A heavy Mughal lunch is laid out on long, black dining tables, unending whiskies and cocktails are served on the veranda, on and on till the chilly dusk, when the racket of crickets goes head-on with the frantic chirruping of birds. The story of the proposal is told and retold: how it came on a silver tray from the grand state of X; how the groom's family said all they wanted was Simran herself.

Burrimummy says to Mummy, 'You know, Rasheed had to sell the piano and the full-length portrait of Mumma to match the opulence of the Nawab and Begum of X.'

Once again, a select few women are allowed into the drawing room and the door is bolted rapidly behind them. *The little black girl is back*. But when I go to the door with Burrimummy, feeling like a thief, they let me in.

Savanur House's mirrors are picking up shattered reflections. I see the mark on the wall where Mumma's portrait, side-saddled on a horse, which I remember seeing as a child, once hung. Stripped of Mumma's painting and the grand piano, the room is now a museum to display Simran's dowry, what she has received and her trousseau: dozens of sets of jewellery, emeralds, pearls, rubies, gold – some many centuries old, some new; clothes interwoven with threads of finely-webbed gold and silver; miniature and life-sized paintings. I spot Burrimummy's silver table and silver bathroom shoes, for the groom.

The following day, the bridal party is moved to a whole floor of a five-star hotel. Guests arriving in Bentleys, Rolls-Royces and Jaguars are greeted by the Nawab and Begum of Savanur.

Mummy has overwhelmed me in a shining, buttercup-coloured South Indian silk sari with a shocking pink border. Her cousin, Sweetie Pasha, the eldest daughter of the Nawab of Savanur, takes one imperious look at me and declares I won't do. Sweetie is a statuesque woman whom everyone says resembles Mumma the most.

'Take that frightful gaudy sari off, Poppet. We are not bloody South Indians,' Sweetie says, flinging the nine yards of yellow silk into a corner. She shoots an exasperated look at Mummy, digs into her own suitcase, then calls the hairdresser to blow-dry my hair, so it falls softly around my face. She gives me a gold tissue sari, clouds of material, a tailored blouse, and a dupatta that she gracefully wraps around from the back to fall in neat pleats. She finishes me off with an emerald necklace and diamond earrings, delivering this kindness without ceremony.

They were stunned by my transformation – as was I. Burrimummy tells me that I am beautiful. She has already told Shaheen that I am very educated, living in London and travelling in Europe. She's scoring off her sister, trying to make up for Nur's disgraceful marriage.

Burrimummy says Shaheen never acknowledges Angel, whose framed photographs I have seen carefully placed between Burrimummy's books. They are of Angel in her private boarding school in Canada, looking as European as Mumma. With her narrow, almond cat-eyes, kohl-rimmed, framed with waves of long hair, her beauty has grown as the baby fat has been chiselled from her face. 'It would kill her to say something good about my Angel,' Burrimummy says. Then, bafflingly, she adds, as if she switched sides when I wasn't looking, 'But my God, Shaheen played tennis well. Puppa didn't allow her to wear tennis skirts, so she played for India in a white sari and walloped Pakistan, but sadly Puppa thought no proposal good enough for her, so that's why she lives with Rasheed, poor man.'

Shaheen catches me alone for a minute; drops of chewed betel nut land on my face as she speaks. 'Now, these things are costly, do you hear, Poppet? Sweetie has been very generous to lend them to you. The minute the wedding is over, take them off. Do you understand?'

'Yes, I do, Mummy Darling.' All her nieces call her this. She is none of these things to me.

I try complaining to Mummy, but she says, 'How dare you speak against her? She is more of a mother to me than my own mother. Aunt Shaheen was just stating the obvious. We can't keep things belonging to other people.'

As guests mill about, drinking champagne and sherbet, the hotel assumes the look of a *durbar* hall during the Raj. Swathes of roses cover doorways and the stage. My granduncle, Rasheed, Burrimummy's eldest brother, the Nawab of Savanur, sits taking gulps of whisky, complaining about the cost. In emeralds, his wife, Farha, replies, 'Please, Rasheed, not now.'

I stand in the hotel corridor for a while with the servant girls, looking awed at me. This once, I would be an insider.

Seventeen-year-old Simran is being dressed in one of the hotel suites, but minutes after she is brought out for the wedding, she faints. 'It's the weight of her wedding clothes,' I hear Aunt Shaheen saying. The outfit is three hundred years old. It has been worn by brides of X state for centuries. It is spun in brocade and covered in emeralds and rubies. Simran is roused from the depths of centuries-old jewels and brocade just in time to say 'yes' to the union.

There are a multitude of swords, *achkans* and turbans, each signifying the importance of a princely state. I get the giggles at a pink turban knocking against a blue one, their owners, in jodhpurs with ropes of pearls and jewels around their necks, nodding to one another, saying, 'Your Highness this' and 'Your Highness that'. There are the usual stories of privilege, of pranks, of Oxford. Someone says Lord Mountbatten told him that he had never seen a woman as beautiful as my granduncle's wife. There are stories of hunts and shoots, elephant fights, harems, pearls spread across balconies, Swiss bank accounts and their time with Dicky.

Some Begum, dressed in an elaborate cloud of voile, her hefty chest covered in pearls, with diamonds on every finger, looks at me and says to Aunt Shaheen, 'Who is that pretty girl? She's Nur's daughter, isn't she?'

'Yes,' Shaheen says sourly. 'She's half-HINDOOO, you know. She is Nur's child.'

The Begum peers at me as if I am an imposter.

I cannot let Aunt Shaheen do this to me again. I say to Burrimummy, 'I would die of boredom here. The men are frightfully backward. They don't read. Spending your entire life in a drawing-room waiting for people to envy you is a useless life.'

Burrimummy laughs and says in a stage whisper. 'Look at them – anyone would think they still run the states of India. Most of them are dim, darling, inbred you know.'

'I can't wait to get out of this costume and into my jeans.'

'Yes, darling, you must go off to London to your job. What a clever girl you are.'

Shaheen turns away.

Burrimummy laughs and says, 'She's madly jealous of the one thing she can't buy with her money. Your education.' She taps her head.

Mummy scolds me for being rude to her favourite aunt. 'She loved me in a way my own mother didn't. Apologise to her.' I apologise, and before I leave, the aunt, who once called me a little black girl, hands me a clock of jade. 'I may be rough, but I love you, you know.' It dawns on me. She's as dark as I am. She suffered. She took it out on me, and she realises it, and I feel something like love for this woman who has looked after my mother in a way Burrimummy could not.

Maybe to be human is to be a mix of shit and silver.

When the guests have departed, and there is just family left, my granduncle, six-foot-six, overweight, fighting gout, wheezing heavily with asthma, says, 'I've had to sell my mother's portrait, I've had to sell stocks, I've had to sell shares. Down to sixteen servants. They say they want nothing, but the bridegroom must have silver shoes and diamonds, and the reception must take place in a five-star hotel.'

I feel sorry for my granduncle, the last recognised Nawab of Savanur. People like him have deified their relics – old portraits, bulky furniture, faded jewels – bewildered at the world that has moved on. Our ancestors hang on the walls, a succession of Nawabs, immigrants from Afghanistan, titled for fighting and killing on behalf of successive Emperors of India.

After the wedding, I accompany Burrimummy to the lawyer's office. She says she wants to reclaim 17 Rest House Road for her 'two eyes, her Angel and Poppet', I sit outside the office and wonder at the futility of it all.

Before my departure, I bury my head in her starched cotton sari and sob. Her big hands knead my arms, a touch once used for lovers, as if to say, 'Homeless, unrooted girl; neither Hindu nor Muslim, neither beautiful nor ugly, neither Trinidadian nor Indian, if you love me enough, if you save me, I'll save you from the world.'

The pact might be broken, but I take what I can, and she must do the same.

Burrimummy has dumped past generations in my lap and said, 'There, that's your road map.' As her repository, I leave Rest House Road under the weight of centuries.

PART THREE

I can give you that historical bird's eye view. But I cannot really explain the mystery of... inheritance. Most of us know the parents or grandparents we come from. But we go back and back, forever; we go back all of us to the very beginning; in our blood and bone and brain, we carry the memories of thousands of beings... We cannot understand all the traits we have inherited. Sometimes we can be strangers to ourselves.'
— V.S. Naipaul

FOURTEEN

St Lucia 2016

Back in the cottage hunger, and something else gnaws at me. Still an hour to lunch. I take the loaf of bread to the bed, lie back and stuff slices of bread in my mouth, but I remain hungry as if nothing could fill me up.

I lie back on the pillows, chewing, looking out of the window at the stunted shadows in the garden, searching for clues from the past that could help me become more than a fragmented thing. My mind settles on a picnic in Simla when I was seven.

*

'Imagine,' said Mummy, 'an entire field of marigolds.'
We had driven in a jeep to get on one of the buses for the officers' picnic expedition. I got on, sat down, then noticed my parents had not boarded. The woman beside me, noting my panic, assured me she'd seen them get on the coach ahead.

The bus hurtled around the mountains, the Himalayas remote in the background, the snow achingly vivid and unreachable. As we wound further up, I could see the rusted carcasses of fallen buses in the valleys. I was hungry. The buses stopped in a clearing surrounded by giant yellow marigolds. We disembarked. Briefly, I forgot my hunger and stared at that field of tall flowers with giant petals.

I smelled peaches. My stomach rumbled. I walked in circles searching for my parents in mounting confusion. I spotted a loaf of white bread near a solitary picnic basket. I grabbed about five or six slices and stuffed one after the other in my mouth, barely taking a breath, as if this would stop the tears in my eyes.

What would I do if I couldn't find them, if their bus had gone over the mountain and nobody knew? Burrimummy wouldn't have the money to keep me. I wanted the comfort of Daddy's hand, to cover my face with Mummy's shawl. Then I saw them.

They were sitting on blankets, surrounded by people, my mother in a blue-grey crush of silk, legs to one side, revealing one white ankle. Some people use their bodies as a utility, to get them somewhere, to create or build something. Mummy moved her body as if it was a shifting tableau, like precious art, wisps of hair brushed off her cheek, a fold of sari adjusted,

so that, seemingly without trying, she got people to look at her as this was
her purpose. What would she do with that mouth, how would she touch
her throat?

Smoking lazily, looking at her, was Daddy, staggeringly handsome,
reckless, who lifted himself out of the middle-class morass of a small town
by fighting three wars, taking piano lessons, studying engineering at the
Aligarh Muslim University (ironically begun by one of Mummy's direct
female ancestors, one of the four Begums of Bhopal), and continually
overreaching, rebelliously marrying a Muslim aristocrat. People gathered
about them; a turbaned Sikh officer, with his eyes fixed on her, kept saying
'Heh heh', as if it was something very clever, as an excuse to be in their
circle. I pushed aside a woman who had her arm on Daddy's shoulder,
offering him a snack. I didn't want to think how Daddy could reach into
other women's hearts. Clutching a ball of bread in my sweaty hand, afraid
they might take it away from me, I got back on the bus and sat there until
it was time to go home.

Hours later, when we got back to the meeting point, they spotted me.
Mummy said, 'Hello, Pet. Where were you? Why do you keep disappearing, my quarter pint?'

I was on the fringes of love. Absence and hunger.

★

Too full of the bread at lunch, I gulp the wine instead. After Derek
pushes his plate away, I avert my eyes as Sigrid wheels him to the porch
and returns to the kitchen. I sit opposite him, and the deepening afternoon
light filters through the sheer curtains, briefly turning Derek's eyes
into eerie, opal cat's eyes.

I try not to look at my marked manuscript before him. He nods at it
before looking up.

'You know, the really great writer – Shakespeare, Joyce – is beyond
prejudice. I like the irony of your great-grandmother not wishing people
grandeur in her Christmas card. We love grandeur in the Caribbean, so our
poetry is performative. We live for flourish and style. Maybe that's why
Beulah laughed. Your grandmother liked that too, didn't she? But wasn't
hers a performance of imitation? The piano. English songs. How is that
better than the mimicry of people here? Is educated mimicry anything less
than mimicry? Your ancestor, Sir Afsar, who fought for the British in
China, forgot how his father died in the mutiny humiliating his own
people, killing them. He became one of them: Sir this and Sir that. Your
grandmother was so proud of it. I suspect you are too.

'Your father brought you and your racist grandmother to Tobago from
post-colonial India. I went to Lagos. It was like going to market in Saint
Lucia. It was so recognisable, I felt I hadn't left home for over 365 years. Yet
I feel entitled to reject Africa. I don't have to be told, "This is your heritage".'

'You want me to reject India?'

'No. Your family bought into a phoney ideal of the Raj and the Victorian Empire. Don't you see your responsibility to yourself? To debunk that. You can do that here – restore the essence of your humanity, separate from what India thinks you are. It is unconnected to whether your family thinks you are dark or adulterated Hindu-Muslim blood and therefore inferior.'

'The trouble is,' I say, emboldened by the wine, 'I can't inhabit it – this new world preoccupation with entertainment, carnival, music. It precludes introspection, creates a mindless enervation. This perpetual need to be entertained, as if the noise could shut out everything we feel, it eventually shuts down entire thought engines. Fatal in this heat. Naipaul saw it.'

Derek says nothing.

'I interviewed Naipaul once at the airport,' I continue. 'He had come home on the invitation of the university. His answers were dripping with contempt and provided enough material for another journalist to write a column on my admittedly naïve questions.'

Derek laughs, jocular, his belly aquiver. Encouraged, I carry on, more relaxed than I've been for the entire visit.

'What did you ask him?' He's curious.

'I asked him if he had grown more bitter or mellow. I'd created a trap for myself. He asked me to clarify. Was the question that he was "mellowly bitter or bitterly mellow?" I asked him his opinion on Trinidad politics, the then looming possibility of an East Indian prime minister. He said the politics of a country of 1.2 million people did not interest him, adding, "Indians, I don't know any. Do you?"

'I said, "I'm Indian." He looked blank and said, "Are you?" It was deeply humiliating – and hilarious if I could have separated myself from his contempt. But I had rattled him. He followed his supercilious remarks with "What do they mean, what do they mean?", before dismissing me.

'That must have been his disappointment in Trinidad. He was right on fundamentalism, too. His novel, *Guerrillas*, could be a guide to Trinidad today. It sums up the brutality in the islands. And he was right with *Mimic Men*, too. Stripped of language and history, the insurgents put Islam on like a cloak without understanding the theology, language or meaning of the suras they recited, the gestures of namaaz. The guns and beards and shouts of Allahu Akbar were nothing like Burrimummy's prayer – it was just another Carnival costume, a jihadi 'look' that created respect around disaffection. They didn't believe in anything but enjoyed the power they felt with their AK47s.'

Derek's face is closed. Perhaps he didn't like the comparison with Naipaul or preferred his own lyrical version of New World reinvention; maybe I'm goading him. It's inescapable: two men, from the same part of the world, both Nobel Laureates for literature within a decade. Naipaul is known as one of the finest living writers in English – Derek, *the* poet.

I remind Derek of his poem about Naipaul, 'The Mongoose': 'I have been bitten; I must avoid infection.' And his derisive poem about a character in Naipaul's recent novel: 'A prick called Willy. Hilarious!'

Derek laughs, briefly, like Burrimummy, from a quivering belly, eyes disappearing, teeth appearing and abruptly disappearing. He looks down at the newly arrived book of his collected poems, turning pages. Maybe he's done with me. Momentarily I feel vertigo, disoriented.

Unsure, I get up, hover between sitting and standing, staying and going. A hummingbird fans crazily around a purple honeycreeper.

'Why aren't you sitting?' he asks, as if just noticing my discomfiture. I sit. He turns to me and reaches for my hand; I look down at his, broad, firm and weathered against mine. 'Why did your father do this to you? He was progressive. Sending you abroad to study and then wanting you off his hands with anyone?'

'It wasn't like that. My father adores me. I'm unworthy of my father's sacrifice, a civil servant sending me abroad instead of buying a home. I disappointed him by not choosing a career that would make me independent, and then again by marrying against his wishes.'

'You don't have to dissemble around me. I'm not your father,' says Derek.

I dissemble anyway.

'I was always testing Daddy. In Simla, days after my tenth birthday, I said, "You can do anything, Daddy. I bet you can take me to meet the prime minister of India." Two days later, we were on a train from Simla to the foothills of Kalka to catch a plane to Delhi, where an army van took us to the officers' mess. We spent the evening at the Gymkhana Club, where Mummy was rude to an Anglo-Indian pianist, remembering when she came here as a girl with her grandfather, who was given entry as a state's ruler, but there were signs "No dogs and Indians".'

Derek grins, briefly looking like his old photos. 'Did you meet Mrs Gandhi?'

I tell him how, on the drive to meet Indira Gandhi, I noticed Daddy wasn't wearing his army uniform but was in mufti with a cravat, as if he had something to hide. Mummy wore a navy-bordered ivory silk sari, pearls and dark shades, looking like a movie star. Winky was in school uniform and I was in my blue, going-out dress. On the way, Daddy pointed out Mahatma Gandhi's house. 'He created Pakistan.'

The driver couldn't pull up at No. 1 Safdarjung Road because the place was surrounded by a throng, twelve feet deep, chanting in Hindi, 'Indira Gandhi is good; whatever she says she will do, she does.'

Daddy told the driver to stop in front of another bungalow, saying that another man who had ripped India apart lived there.

'Was he Indira Gandhi's father?' I asked. Daddy got angry and said, 'Don't they teach you anything in school? Nehru was her father. They all ripped India to pieces, so Nehru could be prime minister.'

Daddy had a word with the security guard at the gate. Two minutes later, Indira Gandhi's guards came to get us. The crowd parted as officials cleared a path for us through the gates and into the garden where she stood, her hair slick in black and white stripes, telling her gardener something about pruning the roses.

'Say namaste,' she spoke to a little boy with a round face, cherry-red with the day's heat, standing next to her. 'Greet our guests,' she repeated in a quiet voice, as commanding as Burrimummy's but deadlier. 'Rahul, my grandson,' she said, placing her hand on his head. Obediently the boy put his hands together in namaste.

We all sat on garden chairs, and she chatted with Mummy and Daddy as if the throngs at the gate didn't exist. She smiled at Winky and then at me with a half-smile, as if we didn't deserve all her teeth.

A photographer was summoned. After that, we were dismissed.

That uninterested look again.

I say, 'I called my father a king that day. Mummy was annoyed and unimpressed by the whole thing. "Such nonsense talk from a young girl. I didn't know you brought us here just because Poppet asked. What a thing to do, to pander to a child like that. You're ruining her."'

I pause. 'My father set up my expectations of men.'

'Your father. He reads me?'

'My father's real interest is in military biography. He was in the army.'

'Your father is important to you? Why don't you write more about him?'

'I don't know.'

'Why not?' He plucks at something inside me that I have failed to look at. When I think of Daddy, I think of departures. He's leaving to go to war, leaving me with Burrimummy, leaving me in boarding school in England, leaving me in Canada.

Derek sits back, rattles ice, drinks. He breaks the silence. 'Your husband, is he like your father?'

'Yes, yes, he is.'

'Did he make you dislike Trinidad? Something did. Write about that, what happened to you. Get that monkey off your back. Write it. Then this will be restored.'

We hear the sea rumbling in regular beats in the near distance, taste the brine on our mouths until it's time for him to be wheeled to his room. 'See you this evening at dinner, dear,' Sigrid says.

The sea is history to you, but not yet to me, I think as, obediently, I go back to the cottage. I don't know when I will tell them about the broken glass, the stove. This evening perhaps.

FIFTEEN

After I fail to marry a suitable boy, I return to London, where Winky meets us to announce he has a job in an engineering firm. Daddy buys a flat in Clapham Junction, putting Winky in charge of the mortgage and of me. Working for the Gujarati paper for seventy-five pounds a week, I am often way behind with my share, which Winky tops up.

We make do on little money, and Winky's wife, Aanya, with a child's sweetness and unbelievably non-transactional nature, cleans my room, darns my stockings and makes one chicken stretch for two days by adding lots of potatoes. Their child, Pixie, with large eyes and Mummy's face restores something in us all, making our drab flat a cocoon for her butterfly movements, her constant surprise. People stop us when we take her out in her pram to say, 'Oh my, what a beautiful child! We've never seen a baby like that.' There is no division between Winky and me; our unspoken childhood pact – strong from the moment of relief that he didn't die in a bus accident – is frozen in its love, so it never occurs to me that in the flat I am the outsider.

As Daddy's stand-in as a gatekeeper for my virtue, Winky is strict. I am not allowed to bring home any boyfriends. Once, I came home late with a man I thought lovely. Winky asked the man if he didn't have a home, marched him to the door and slammed the door on his shocked face. After a week's silence between us over the now vanished man, Winky looks so devastated that I answer his slow, sweet smile – so sexy to women and so loving to me – with a hug, accepting his judgement that the man was a bastard. But then I shout at Daddy on the phone: you knew what you were doing when you forced me to stay with Winky. You knew.

Often, we are like one person in two bodies, each carrying bits of India within us, so when he plays ghazals in the kitchen on a tape recorder or fries mushrooms on rainy days, we are children again, in the winter in Sagar, or in 17 Rest House Road, wrestling one another over the chessboard. We take turns parenting, to give each other time to be reckless and unrestrained. Winky pays my share of the mortgage, flings twenty quid at me when I most need it, buys me warm gloves, cooks me something I love. I get him press tickets for a football game, look after Pixie as if she's part of me, and in his generosity he makes me feel it true.

We do our talking at the laundromat where we spend hours together, ribbing one another. We were drying clothes once, giggling at how women gravitate towards him when a persistent female with a Mohican haircut began chatting him up. Desperate for escape, he walked through the glass window of the laundromat like the hulk, leaving the indent of his body in the shattered pane. He kept walking, waiting for me by the corner where we held on to each other and laughed till our bellies hurt.

But it seems he may have walked straight out of his body when he walked through that glass. I come home to find him, all six-foot-one of him, curled on the small sofa in the corner of the kitchen, sobbing, his handsome face contorted. 'Poppet, I just want to go home. I want to go home.'

He packs and takes off for Trinidad, where Mummy and Daddy now live, and before a week has passed, Daddy calls to say that Winky has collapsed in the gym and lost the use of his legs. Angel and I fly home to find Mummy in bewildered shock and Daddy ready to battle to save his son. We hear that he has sent Aanya away, unable to bear her seeing him in his state of need.

We go straight to the bedroom, where we find Winky on a mattress on the floor, his legs, already thinner, sticking out of a bed so crumpled it's clearly the space where he spends all his time. His eyes are frightened, with deep circles under them, but his face seems to have gotten younger with pain. Mummy is exhausted from taking care of him, so Angel and I fall into a routine right away, taking turns to cook, feed and bathe him. When he needs a bath, we get him onto the wheelchair and into the shower. He stands in his trunks, puts his hands on my shoulders while the water pours over us, and I soap him.

I'm not sure how I feel about being at home, watching Winky get so thin, his limbs turning into long useless bones, his rages intensifying with his frustration at having to depend on Mummy for everything. Sometimes he is quiet, collapsed into himself, his hair still thick and black and curly, his face strangely luminescent and handsome.

Before the week is out, Angel and I are both working. She with a dentist and me as a journalist on a radio station. I work there as if it's a temporary gig, grieve for Hugh, waiting for his phone calls. Hugh, in fact, has sent me letter after letter and receiving no reply, he starts to number them. We figure out that Mummy has been throwing most of them away. She doesn't give me options, but she knows what she doesn't want for me.

No doctor in Trinidad has been able to diagnose why Winky can't walk, and Daddy takes him to Venezuela for a second opinion, returning with a diagnosis – it's polyarthritis, when the immune system attacks itself, and the prognosis is not good.

I am six months into my job at the radio station when Ella, a colleague, says, 'Come out for a drink with me. There is someone I want you to meet. It's time you stopped living in England in your head, time you stopped rereading *The End of the Affair*. Also, that checked skirt is a no-no.'

I agree, reluctantly.

Ella and I walk into Veni Mange, a once-grand colonial home that the owners, enterprising sisters who rocked London in the sixties, had converted into a popular restaurant. We join a man blowing smoke rings into the air.

'This is my friend, Sadiq,' she says.

He frightens me. He looks wealthy in his beige turtleneck and khaki trousers, a cigarette dangling out of his mouth and tapping another on the table looking strangely like my granduncle Wahid. A darker, shorter version, but a prototype of men who are careless with women. He will not be interested in books and certainly not in me.

He glances at the copy of *The Lighthouse*, given to me by Hugh, and the newspaper I am carrying. I think there is nothing he could say that would interest me.

'Does Virginia Woolf get on well with the *Guardian Weekly*?'

'Yes,' I say, surprised. 'The two go everywhere together.' *What a prat*.

I ignore Sadiq, looking out through the white shutters and fretwork doors, wanting to get away. I sit through small talk. I give him short answers. Eventually I say, 'I have a younger sister. I have to go babysit.'

'Not so fast,' says Ella. 'We've just arrived.'

'You have an English accent,' Sadiq says, 'but I hear other things, Indian, and something else.'

'I was born in India. My father sent me to boarding school in England, followed by a university in Canada and finally back to London.'

I repeat that I want to go home. Ella asks Sadiq to drop me home.

I give him directions but say nothing else on the drive home. At the gate, I fumble in my bag. I have forgotten my keys and gate opener.

I run around the locked house, shouting, 'Angel, Angel, Angel!' unaware that he is standing on the roof of his van looking into our bungalow and at me. I didn't know that it was polite in these islands for a man to make sure the woman he'd dropped home was safely indoors.

Just then, Angel pulls into the yard. She parks her car neatly and gets out, slim and neat, walking at a clip in her high heels, black skirt-suit and carrying a briefcase. 'Poppet,' she says in a sharp voice, 'you've locked yourself out again.' As a dentist, her paycheck is fatter than mine.

Sadiq called me the next day and every day after that for six months.

On our first date, driving to Maracas beach through the rainforest, he stops on a mountain plateau. In the distance, the ocean is slate grey with breaking whitecaps. On the beach, we're flanked by stalls with vendors selling stewed plums, tamarind balls, packets of green mangoes in vinegar and salt.

As we watch the sun come up, he sings slowly, carelessly, 'Yankee gone, and Sparrow take over town' – a calypso about American soldiers and Trinidadian prostitutes. He tells me how the Americans built a lookout here to track German submarines during World War II and Churchill gave America access to bases throughout the empire in return for oil, which the British needed for their tanks. 'I'm a fount of endless facts about Trinidad,' he adds.

'I've noticed,' I say.

He shows me how to dive deep beneath the sea and surf the waves to drive to the shore on my stomach. We walk out of the ocean, exhilarated, salty, wet, sun-warmed, already familiar, head towards the cabanas, where a vendor neatly slices off the top of a coconut. After we drink its sweet water, he cracks it into four pieces, opening it like a lotus for the coconut jelly. As the sun gets high, he brings shark and coconut bread covered with sauces, chadon beni, mint and pepper, which we eat under the shade of an almond tree.

I examine his silky, chocolate back. 'Your tattoo covers your entire back.'

'It's a map of Trinidad and Tobago.'

I place my index finger on his back.

'That's where I live,' he says, like a man with eyes at the back of his head. 'Now shift your finger to the right and take it higher – no, you've gone too far. Left and lower. That's it – this is where we are. The Maracas Valley. I had it done one icy winter in Manchester.'

'Why?'

'I missed Trinidad. I took the tattoo artist a map of Trinidad with all the districts. I'd intended to fill it all in, but it was too painful.'

There was a cross over the 'o' of Tobago.

'They spelt it wrong,' he said, 'I had it fixed. But then my cousin died in a diving accident. Jumped into the sea with a spear and disappeared. And I hated my course. I couldn't stay in England.'

He tells me how, in Manchester, he lay in a tub filled with cold water and shaved his legs, arms and torso. Then the hair on his toes and, finally, his eyebrows.

'You were thinking of your cousin?' I say.

He doesn't respond. We lie with our eyes half-closed, salt on our lips; his feet touch mine in the warm sand.

I say, 'This is faded gold. Tobago's sand is white, crushed corals.'

We drink rum. Sadiq tells me about the Tobago mermaids. They swim amongst the swirling currents just where the Caribbean meets the Atlantic Ocean, wedged between St Giles and Misty Marble Island, past Anse Gouleme and Anse Basant, towards the Bird of Paradise Island down the coast, past Speyside to Fat Hot Bay.

'How do you know all this?'

'I used to dive there, Tobago girl.'

We drive back into the rainforest, stopping to wash our salty bodies in a waterfall, eat watermelon slices in the car, the pink flesh coming off warm and sweet like candy floss. I look at his smooth muscular arms on the wheel, think of them gripping me underwater, guiding me through the waves. The next time his thigh brushes against mine, I swallow the flesh of the watermelon and spit black seeds at him. He spits some back as if we are conducting some animal mating ritual.

'I'd better take you home to shower.'

He lives next to the Spanish Embassy, along a boulevard with guard booths, high gates and gardens like the ones on Rest House Road. In his male bedroom, with the dark bed and the bathroom smelling of cologne, he lends me soft pyjamas, dries me, rubs cream on my sunburnt back. To my astonishment, he doesn't jump on me. He strokes my hair as if to make up for every hurt and puts me to sleep as if I were a child, his arms around me crooning creole songs in my ear – Dodo, Petit Popo. I sleep heavily and wake when it's dark.

We end the day in the library of his luxurious home. His parents are away in Europe, he says. Out in the garden, I see a gardener pulling weeds. In the house, a maid is rushing around with a fresh pile of laundry. Sadiq guides me to complete collections of Shakespeare and the metaphysical poets – all the classics. He shows me V.S. Naipaul and C.L.R. James; essays by Dr Eric Williams, poetry by Paul Keens Douglas, novels by Earl Lovelace, Sam Selvon. I pass my hand over them, lovingly, as if reading them in braille. He has claimed his West Indian identity, absent of any nostalgia for India.

Sadiq piles them up on a chair.

'Borrow them, take them,' he says. 'It's not often I meet a woman on these islands who reads.'

In his library, his profile dark, South Indian – yes, same lips as my granduncle, Wahid – he stands with the confidence of a man who expects life to be as good to him as it has always been.

I keep digging, wanting more. His childhood was perfect, he says; he doesn't remember most of it. Hadn't there been times when he, like me, had pretended to be someone else? No, he says, no.

Sadiq didn't know where his family came from in India, just that he was the descendant of indentured labourers. His parents grew up in poverty, each with a dozen siblings, his father in a village in central Trinidad, his mother in a crowded government apartment in Port of Spain. His father walked barefoot and had to change his name to Roger to study in a Catholic school.

Sadiq looks Tamil, but who knows? He doesn't speak any Indian languages. He was just part of this place, and, with him, I could belong too.

'What is your first memory?' I ask.

'I don't remember any of it. It was perfect.'

He pulls out the *Collected Poems* of Derek Walcott and starts reciting, 'So much rain, so much life...'

I think I could reinvent myself in this island nation inhabited by descendants of Indian indentured labourers and enslaved Africans, European, Chinese and Arab traders, people from all continents; I could be anything, everything.

'But I am learning slowly, to love the dark days, the steaming hills...'

The room dims until I can see a crescent moon in an ink-splashed sky through the windows.

Sadiq takes me home. Daddy is waiting for me, furious.

'Out with a man all day, whoring around, disgracing us,' he says.

Mummy says, 'Oh God, you're practically naked. Is this how you dress in public in full view of men?'

I go to Winky's room, but he shouts and turns away, 'Whoring, and that too with a Muslim!' Winky switches religions to suit his case. He says Allah Allah when he's in pain and speaks of bloody Pakistanis if he wants to score points with Daddy.

I hear them as if I am still underwater, tasting watermelon and rum. With every continuing, defying infraction, theirs and India's hold over me loosens.

I tell Sadiq he isn't allowed to phone me at home. Visiting is out of the question. 'No problem,' he says. His secretary calls every morning at ten minutes past nine, after the newscast, and I shed the accumulated burdens of the night before onto him. He is parked up outside the station in the afternoons before I go home, and I slip into his car for a few minutes before I head home. On Fridays, he picks me up after work, aerobics or a writing workshop in the evening, and joins me during late assignments. There are moonlit night sails on Ella's and her husband's boat, *Sweet Love*, where there are just the stars, the dark ocean wide around us, his grinning face.

He takes me to the steelband yards on the hills to watch bands practice for Carnival, telling me to listen for the bass, the low and high notes, explains how the instrument, the only one invented in this century, was made from oil drums, how the music was once associated with fighting gangs, and now produces the nuances of a Beethoven sonata, with its semitones, all twelve to an octave, and all the notes of the classical Indian raga, twenty-two intervals with seven natural notes and five sharp/flat notes and turns; how it can even transform the bawdiest calypso into something lyrical.

He tells me how, before the money came, his parents' sold tickets to pan and costume and calypso shows on the Savannah, and how he slept nearby in the grass, covered by blankets, to the sound of the Carnival. Before he slept, he wandered the pan yards, listening to musicians – Indian, European, Arab, Chinese, and African – the echo of continents.

His parents worked their way up in the public service as clerks, and eventually, from the money they made from a grocery, they began a soft drinks company that now employs over two hundred factory workers. He remembers the new money, the Mercedes, the blue one-hundred dollar bills and worldwide travel, moving from what was already a big house in Valsayn to one of the most coveted addresses in Port of Spain.

With Sadiq, there are discoveries of these twin islands, a 'courtship' that feels like a love letter to Trinidad.. We have our sun-blanched days driving through the mountains, sitting in the sand in freshwater pools, lying on hot beaches. Sadiq's first present is four tyres for my second-hand car. He returns the vehicle with those tyres after a thorough checkup and conditioning. 'I want you to be safe,' he says. With him, there are no unpleasant triggers. No sudden abandonments. No need for longing.

Meantime, Daddy shouts at me almost every night. 'If you keep this up, nobody will marry you.' Mostly, I am silent. Sometimes I say, 'Well, you hardly brought a prince on a horse for me.'

'No, but there were sons of generals.'

'Yeah, well, no generals' sons here,' I mutter.

One evening, after a full day, cricket at the Oval, and a boat on the river at sunset to see the scarlet ibis settle like ripe red fruit in the trees in the Caroni swamp, I get home a little drunk on being this chosen. I encounter Winky in his wheelchair. He is livid. 'This is the time you come back? Daddy told me you were gadding about with that Muslim.'

I rush into my bedroom and lock myself in. But Winky punches at the glass, makes a hole and lets himself in, shouting, not noticing the shards of glass on the floor or the blood on his hand.

Something between us ends, and we stop speaking. I feel, though, that I have abandoned Winky, betrayed him. Ours was the first pact. He has always treated his relationships lightly, as if our first promise was to get one another through life. I spot *The Mill on the Floss* turned upside down on his bedside. I know he feels abandoned, but the need to save myself overpowers everything else.

Sadiq takes me for a drive back to Maracas. The sea is like a slab of crushed black diamonds beneath the full moon. He is looking at me when he nearly overshoots the cliff edge, protected only by a flimsy fence. His four-wheel-drive teeters on the edge, the sea far below us. We laugh as he fiddles with his gears. The front wheels of his van rev and spin in the air. With a cigarette still hanging out of his mouth, he gets out and tells me to sit in the driver's seat. 'Reverse when I say,' he shouts. He pushes and I reverse and land safely with a thud. He gets in the passenger seat, hugging himself, breathing deeply. It was a near miss. We could be dead. We could have gone clean over the mountain in his van and I understand why I am drawn to him – we share the ability to be somewhere else when there is danger to the body. It reminds me, too, of my own father's handsome recklessness. He may not be as safe as I thought when he replaced the tyres of my car. We look at one another quietly. I like the danger of him, the suspense. Seven months of this, and he hasn't made a move. Sadiq jokes, looking straight ahead at the dark arc of the hills, 'It makin' cold, eh.'

I say, 'It isn't the Himalayas, is it?' I lean in and kiss him on the mouth.

The next afternoon, I encounter Daddy as I head to the front door. He says, 'This man is ruining your chances with a decent family.'

'You mean a family from India? They seem decent enough.'

Mummy says, 'You may end up a spinster. Why buy the cow when you can get the milk for free. I don't understand these western ways, dear.'

I tell Sadiq of my distress at home.

'My father wants me to settle down,' I say miserably.

'Why would I want to marry?' he says. 'I have a comfortable home and my clothes and food are sorted out by a housekeeper. My parents ask no questions.'

'Okay,' I say. 'It's over then.'

'It's not over for me,' he says.

I stop taking his calls.

'He's not our sort of people,' I tell Angel.

She lays into me. 'Why do you feel better than anyone else? Do you want to be left on the shelf in this godforsaken country? What would you do then? Now, go back to him and tell him that you don't care if he doesn't want to marry you. Take a chance.'

I decide to leave it alone, feeling curiously free.

Six months after his first collapse, Winky gets off his wheelchair and starts to walk, his feet, which he can't feel, flopping like flippers. 'Baba,' says Daddy, 'You are walking, you are walking.' Mummy cries, 'Allah's will, my sweet child, Allah's will. I prayed for this day.' Like children following the pied piper, laughing, clapping, we pursue him around the ramshackle colonial house, and around the dining room, in a rare moment of family love, all pain forgotten.

Winky goes back to work part-time with a driver, unfeeling feet in a brace. He takes on a failing company for no salary but a share in the profits if he succeeds. He does. Within months he turns it around, and the company makes him a partner, and he's flush again. He rents a flat and another for Pixie and Aanya, resumes his life, ruefully shaking his head over his ability to attract every woman he encounters, of every race and religion, married, young, old, taken and single. He calls his inherited charm from Saied Uz Zafar, 'a curse'.

He flies to Costa Rica to learn Spanish, and returns with a young bride called Laura, with a tiny waist and pitted skin. This is something we marvel at given he is still legally married to Aanya. He shows us photos of the wedding in a Catholic Church. She is dressed in white, and he's in a business suit. Mummy dislikes Laura, and Winky soon tires of her. He exchanges his car and savings again for freedom and sends her back to Costa Rica.

Winky files for divorce, gives Aanya a lump sum and he's a free man. The money comes rolling in as he fixes company after company. A few months later, he falls in love online and goes to India to marry the daughter of a general, a former colleague of Daddy's, an attractive, highly educated, independent working woman who won't put out without marriage. The wedding takes place with much grace on the Delhi officers' mess lawns. Within a week of returning to Trinidad, he encourages his new Indian wife to migrate to Canada, claiming she burped throughout the night, which was intolerable.

I ask, 'So you spent almost a hundred thousand dollars to go to India, marry her, have a wedding at the officers' mess, pay her off, all for a fuck?' He laughs uproariously, as if I've paid him the compliment of his life.

Winky's example, how he guns for what he wants, makes it easier to think about going out with Sadiq again. But I must find out one last thing. If Winky could get what he wants, so could I. I plan to fly to Europe to meet Hugh. I give myself a week for the mission, enduring the usual abuse from Daddy.

But Hugh, despite the loving letters, presented with my availability, is once again intractable and closed when we meet in Florence in a small dark room, where we lie uncomfortably together, waiting for the hours to pass before we can head back to the airport.

On my last night in London, Sadiq calls me at midnight, drunk, just to say hi. I know then that it's over with Hugh. On the flight back, I decide to call Sadiq but know that if I want this thing between us to last, I could not abandon myself to him as I'd done with Hugh. I could not risk heartbreak or abandonment. But I also sense that something has happened to him to break the idea of 'love', that he, too, does not expect it. He isn't inclined to speak of it, and I harbour no curiosity about his history. I like being around his family; there are no sudden explosions or fights. He does as he pleases. He accepts his parents and they him, no questions asked.

I call Sadiq and say I'm willing to date again, no strings attached, but I'm lying, longing to be rid of home, rid of the detritus of what I thought was love. The nightly round of dates resumes.

Sadiq can send a stone skidding across a vast tract of water with ease. He is an unbeliever, a quiet man with restrained movement but given to operatic gestures, like buying cheesecake and champagne as the only nourishment for a four-day sailing trip to Grenada. There, he crashes village weddings and goes on deep dives as if it's just a swim. He comes with no damage. I call him my pool of peace, safety. I sleep in his bed, curled into him.

On 27th July 1990, he calls me up at the radio station. 'Can you come to my office? Bunk off for the afternoon?'

I pop my head into the studio and get permission from my supervisor, not knowing that in a few hours he would be barricading the doors of the station from insurgents involved in an attempted coup.

Sadiq sends his Mercedes around with a driver. I am ushered into a three-storey building with giant billboards advertising soft drinks. An electronic gate closes behind me. His secretary takes me up the stairs through an open-plan office to the third floor – a vast space with only one room. I knock and go in. Sadiq is swivelling on a chair behind a large, curved desk, wearing a suit with big shoulder pads. His teeth are very white against his dark face and thick dark curls. He gets up, comes over to me, shakes my hand and settles back into his chair.

'Nice office.'

'It's my dad's,' he says, putting his feet on the table. He pushes a cold Coke towards me. 'Got this for you.'

We pass the bottle back and forth, having a good look at one another. I can't see Sadiq sacrificing for his parents, who look more like his siblings; I can't see him getting up early to wash dishes or handing over his salary to them. They are as shiny as he is, with big toothy smiles in framed photographs in front of the Taj Mahal, the Eiffel Tower, with a Bollywood megastar. This is a guilt-free zone.

'What are you doing next August?'

'I don't know. I don't even know what I am doing in twenty minutes.'

'Want to get married or what?'

I am taken aback. I want to give myself time to think.

'On your knees,' I say.

He gets down on one knee, unable to keep a serious look. 'Will you marry me? Is that okay?'

'Umm, yes, but I want to tell my children that you were romantic. Can you please ask again, without asking, "Is that okay?"'

'Want to get married?'

'Yes.' I laugh.

'Okay,' he says. 'Let's go tell my parents.'

It doesn't occur to me that I should ring my parents.

We drive to his house, a sprawling, white bungalow surrounded by a garden splashed with the sun, covered in the shade of fruit trees. I am elated. He leans over and kisses me, and I feel more relief than love. I've never seen such a smile.

As we drive into driveway, we hear shots, see bullets flying through the trees towards the police station next door.

'Shit,' he says.

Inside the house, the television is on. Two armed insurgents stand over the news anchor. A huge man dressed as an Arab in a white tunic is saying with a deep voice, 'This is a coup.' Then, 'Don't loot.' Then, 'Stay calm.'

Sadiq's parents say I must spend the night. His mother, Yasmin, is overwhelmed and excited at our announcement. She gives me a towel, clean pyjamas, and pointedly puts it in Sadiq's room. Lucky Sadiq.

I call home. I blurt out to Daddy: 'Sadiq just proposed.' There is silence, and I can hear Mummy pick up.

'Hello… hello.'

I tell her. She says nothing, but I feel her joy.

I tell them about the shooting, the attempted coup, that I'm not coming home tonight. 'Don't use this as an excuse to spend the night with a man.' Daddy is furious. Mummy says those insurgents know damn all about Islam. I feel as if I've wet my bed.

In the days after the state of emergency following the Muslimeen's attempted coup, Daddy says Sadiq needs to ask him properly for my hand. Sadiq makes contact Daddy he is permanently unavailable, too busy for lunch, too busy for a drink, too busy for dinner. Eventually, Daddy agrees to meet Sadiq at the Savannah, for coconut water.

'Your father asked,' Sadiq told me later, '"Why do you want to marry her? She's untidy. She's got a temper." Then he said, "If you must marry her, there are conditions. She will remain a Nath. You will take the Nath name. Your children will be Naths. You will convert to Hinduism. Your children will be Hindus."'

Sadiq agrees to everything. Daddy had become even more religious with time; unable to sway Mummy, his distaste for Islam had increased. Mummy says that though she never knew her father, and her mother had robbed her of community and inheritance, nothing will rob her of Allah. Even after agreeing to the marriage, Daddy looks pained at any mention of Sadiq. 'You're making a name for yourself. A bad name.' He puts his head in his hands. 'I failed,' he says, 'I failed in my duty to marry you to our own people, someone who shares our world view, our values.' He threatens, begs, cajoles and rages. 'Not him, not a Trinidadian, not a Muslim.'

Three months after the attempted coup, with Sadiq and me not having spent one night together, we get our chance. Daddy is away on a work trip. My boss says I must go to Tobago to cover for a colleague who has taken study leave.

I tell Sadiq I'm leaving in the morning.

'I'll look into flights,' he says.

'I still don't know if you're gay or frigid,' I say, laughing. We've never slept together.

'See you tonight, Tobago girl.'

I fly to Tobago and straight to the radio station. The building overlooks a leafy, abandoned cocoa estate which I remembered walking through as a

child. There is a storm warning. All flights from Trinidad to Tobago have
been cancelled. I return to the hotel in the rain to see Sadiq, sopping wet,
walking towards me in a suit as if it were a sunny day. A bottle of champagne
in an ice bucket is his only baggage.

'How did you get here?'

'I hired a small plane.'

I think of how Daddy rode five hundred miles on his motorbike to
celebrate Mummy's birthday.

Sadiq and I don't sleep that night. I will never forget his face in the wind-
needled rain, his skin smooth like molasses. I tell myself I could learn to
love this man and be happy with him. Sadiq wants us to marry in October,
just three months after his proposal.

Daddy repeats his conditions to Sadiq's parents, adding there must be
only one wedding – a Hindu wedding. They agree to everything.

The week of the wedding, Sadiq says to me, 'You know there has to be
a civil ceremony the day before the actual wedding? It's just a paper thing.
The real ceremony will be Hindu, as he wishes.'

I tell Daddy about it that evening. 'It's just an official thing, Dad, for the
government. Sadiq and his parents would like you and Mummy to be
there.'

Daddy looks grim. 'In that case, there will be no wedding. They are not
to be trusted.'

I think of the barking man.

'Well, you didn't get me a Prince Charming, Baba.'

'Poppet, I'm warning you, I won't have anything to do with you. They
are nothing like us, not our kind. They will make mincemeat out of you,
see your politeness as weakness.'

'Not Hindu, you mean? Okay,' I say.

'They will teach you the lessons I can't.' Daddy looks helpless.

I speak to Mummy in private.

'Mummy, will you come at least?'

'Darling, I'm so happy you are marrying a Muslim. You know that I can't
say it out loud as my happiness will send your father into a rage. Marry him,
but don't put your head on a block for him. Make sure you save, keep
working.'

'Sadiq is lovely, Mummy.'

'He is, dear, but don't depend on any man, or any human for that matter,
for your happiness.'

This is territory I had long wanted to explore.

'Would you have done this all over again, Mummy – married Daddy if
you'd known what your life would be?'

'I lost everything. If I'd had a normal mother; if she had let me go to
university as I'd wished... I wanted to teach, you know, small children in

a Montessori. If she had explained that I would be losing her, I might have listened.'

'Don't you love Daddy?'

'He is everything beloved to me, mother and father. But love isn't everything, dear, and we've had tumultuous times before we got to this point. He must have wanted a Hindu wife, so I practised my Islam on my own, came to be a Sufi after being isolated from my people. Ved changed after the war in '71 against Pakistan. He returned from a meeting with his general to find his entire battalion blown up. He still wakes up shouting at night, dreaming of men he's shot, bombs that missed him. He sees Islam only as the dogma of its radicals, its suicide bombers, but I grew up with the beauty of it, the lyrical language of Arabic. You need your family's blessing, need to be part of a community that cherishes you.'

I say, 'This is not the business of the community.'

Mummy continues. 'When your father asked me to marry him, I begged your Burrimummy to agree to my marriage, but she refused, cataloguing the sacrifices she'd made for me. She said I, a princess on two sides, from Muslim states that spanned the entirety of Mughal rule, would cease to be a Muslim, that I should not cast away my past and my future. She didn't change my mind. While I was packing my things, she tried to make me feel sorry for her. "You're all I have," she cried. I just said, "I'm going." When she saw I was serious, she began shouting, "*Munakhif*" – someone who accepts then turns away from the oneness of God. She pulled down her Quran and pointed to passages. "Look, it's here, anyone who marries outside is expelled from Islam."

'I told her it was not up to her to decide who was a believer and who was not, and she said, "If you go without my blessing, you will go empty-handed," and she ordered me to give her my bangles.

'I put my hands out, and she stripped the gold bangles from both arms. She took my emerald, diamond and pearl jhumka earrings. She asked for the keys to my bank deposit box, and told me to put every piece of jewellery she had ever given me on my dressing table. She called a lawyer and within an hour, she had made me sign away my rights to any of her property. She said I had to return every penny she had ever spent on me. "I will," I said and signed away what little I had saved from my father's money. I just gave it away. It was hers, and it wasn't in my destiny. Burrimummy roamed the house, roaring like a tigress, beating her chest, saying she loved me, loved my father, and we had both betrayed her. Allah would punish me.

'With the help of old family friends, Mrs Mangal, a Gujarati lady, I got a plane ticket the following day. I showed it to Mother just before I left for the airport. I said, "I'm going, Amma." We both wept. "No, Nur," she cried as I phoned for the taxi. "Infidel," she shouted as I got in and drove off. I left with maybe five rupees in my bag to pay for the taxi. She didn't give me a teaspoon from that day to this.'

'When was that, Mummy?' I ask.

'It was 22nd August 1960.'

'You remember so clearly?'

'You'd remember, too, if you had a mother like mine. She never took the trouble to teach me or say why it was wrong. She didn't explain that marrying Ved was not possible, not only because he is a Hindu but also because I would be utterly dependent on one man's goodwill – which could turn against me at any time. She didn't tell me there was no security in the marriage if his family did not accept me.'

'But you went out. You had a good time. You had servants.'

'Yes, dear.'

Yet they clung together like children who never had safety.

'So, you do love Daddy?'

'We've had some good times.'

'I'm confused. Now I don't know if you are happy or not.'

'Happiness doesn't come into it. Don't depend on a man or any human for happiness, dear. They will let you down, every one of them.'

'You think I should NOT marry Sadiq?'

'You must do what you think best, dear. I will say marriage is hard enough without having cultural differences. Everyone looks charming at first, but under pressure, people reveal themselves.'

I go to Winky's apartment and hand him an invitation.

'I won't be coming,' he says. 'I don't approve of you marrying a Muslim coolie.'

I drive home upset, but not for long, as I contemplate a life that's all my own, even if love hadn't entered my mind, only freedom.

A day before the Hindu ceremony, I get dressed for the civil service wearing the checked skirt I'd worn when Sadiq and I first met, and a white blouse. I'd taken care of my make-up.

Daddy shouts, 'You are not my daughter. I agreed only to a Hindu marriage. If they break that promise, they will break others.'

But I am in deep. Sadiq's brother had been to America and brought me back things I would never have spent money on – cosmetics, shoes, trousers. His mother had taken me for a fitting for a dozen work suits. I feel cherished.

'You're really doing this?' Daddy asks as I make my way to my car.

'I am,' I say.

'You're not my daughter,' he shouts as I leave.

I drive away in my little car to Port of Spain and meet Sadiq in the Red House for the ceremony. We exchange rings and sign a register. Only his parents and Angel are present. I knew that Angel was helping me escape, that, unlike Winky or Daddy, she wanted me to be free and live in a grand house in a leafy neighbourhood.

'You're doing the right thing,' she whispers.

Afterwards, in the rain, Sadiq drops me to work. The downpour turns torrential, and I can't cross the road. I sit in a dark rum shop opposite the radio station with old men soaked in a lifetime of rum.

'I got married today,' I say, sitting in a corner with wet hair.

'Now what you went and did that for?' one says, shaking his head. Another gallantly finds an umbrella he holds over me while I cross the road to work.

I only find out that Daddy has decided to go ahead with the Hindu ceremony, despite the civil wedding, when he and Angel set out to finalise things at the hotel. 'He's invited people, the pundit and ministers and whatnot. He won't humiliate himself,' Angel says.

My mother-in-law Yasmin's wedding gift – twelve work-suits and a wedding skirt and lace top – is laid out on my bed. She's having five hundred guests at the Country Club and wants to know what I will be wearing.

'I'll wear one of Mummy's saris,' I say.

'You must have a wedding dress,' she says, picking out the lacy white material.

A woman arrives to do henna designs for me, a gesture from one of the aunties from the Indian community, thinking we would have a mehndi ceremony with women.

'You do it, dear. I can't bear sticky hands,' Mummy says. The woman looks at me pityingly.

Roses, in colours from lurid to baby pink, and deeply fragrant lilies, streaked with pink, arrive in such abundance the delivery man has to contort himself to get them to fit through my bedroom door. I crouch on the floor, dangling the phone on my arm, my fingers spread out to dry the henna design.

I call Sadiq. 'Thank you for the roses.'

'Do you like them?'

'So extravagant,' I say, breathing them in.

Mummy comes into my bedroom, holding a silver tray with eight silver goblets and several velvet jewellery pouches.

'For you, my quarter pint.' She holds up the diamond and ruby earrings. I remember her wearing them when I was a child. She shows me the long diamond earrings, which I recognise from a photograph of Burrimummy when she was young, and she puts them on me. Finally, there is a diamond star belonging to Sir Afsar.

'This is all that remained, Darling. Dregs. Still, whatever I have is yours.'

Mummy looks at the white wedding outfit on my bed. 'Darling, I won't let you wear that at your wedding. White is for widows. Do you think your mother is such an idiot that you must depend on these people? Come here. Don't let the mehndi smudge.'

I follow her to the drawing-room. A fuchsia *lehenga* with green and gold paisley designs is spread across the sofa. A pile of brocade and chiffon saris is on another chair in all the shades – peacock blue and silver, salmon pink, olive green and gold. I feel like a bride, finally.

'Angel brought these for you, Darling, on her last trip to India after Sadiq proposed. I gave her a list to give Daddy's brother. He's done plenty for his nieces and nephews, and it was time they did something for you.' Angel had brought all these things home in a suitcase without letting me know.

Now that it is happening, I panic. I call Sadiq.

'I like you. I don't love you,' I say.

'Same here,' he replies carefully, and keeps me on the phone for a long time. I ask to speak to his mother and say I have a wedding lehenga. She sends for the white skirt and top she had made for me. These mummy hands over with relief to her driver.

Angel comes home at 2:00 am. All the arrangements have been made. I know she has helped pay for the reception.

'I'm sorry, my Puppa, my Sadrunissa, my Angel Child, for all the times I hurt you,' I say.

'You took care of me too, remember – washing my hair, packing lunch, cleaning my shoes. Remember how you always caught me when I cleaned around things instead of under them. You were like my mother.'

A year later, I would do the same for Angel when she decides to marry the boy from university. She and I are living parallel lives, like Andrew Marvell's parallel lines that never meet, but we mother one another when the other is in danger of sinking for good.

At the wedding, I am surprised to see my mother-in-law in the wedding outfit. 'I had it let out', she says. Winky doesn't attend the wedding or the reception at the Country Club and makes himself scarce as if I have wounded him irretrievably. I'm sad about losing him but my need for freedom from his grip is stronger. I take off happily for my honeymoon, leaving our bedroom strewn with rose petals from the reception.

SIXTEEN

On our European honeymoon, I take Sadiq to meet Hugh in a coffee shop. We sit, the three of us, as if nothing has happened, no break-up, no marriage, no loss, no gain, speaking of the latest exhibition at the Saatchi gallery. We talk about the horror of the miniature Ron Mueck painting of his dead father. It's my way of telling both those men I have options or had them. Be careful of how you treat me. The yo-yo-ing of giving and withholding love goes both ways, and revenge sometimes hits the powerful when they least expect it. It's how the victimised are taught cruelty.

'What a lot of pretentious shit,' Sadiq says about a one-woman Virgina Woolf play in Hampstead.

Hugh looks startled, but he's lost his chance to have an opinion over my life.

At the hotel, I say angrily to Sadiq, remembering what Mummy said about everyone being nice until they had you in the bag, 'You are an upstart.'

'At least I don't read one book by Virgina Woolf repeatedly and call myself well-read.'

Stung, I call him 'soulless'.

I want him to enter my world. I don't like five-star hotels. He thinks the pubs I went to when I was a student are dumps. I am nervous, think I can never belong with him. I dress purposely badly to go to the theatre.

I call a friend in Oxford whom I knew from my Notting Hill Gate years. Emma studied classics, and her parents are in art restoration. A grandparent was once an official in India during the years of the Raj.

'Come to lunch. With your husband.'

'I want to dress up,' I say. Sadiq is game, as if it was time I entered his world. He helps me pick out a dress at Harrods and tall, stylish, mahogany leather boots. I get my hair done. I am desperate to show that I am tethered. They know of my desperate days, the humiliating treks to the Home Office, standing in the line for 'Aliens' for extensions to my visa.

Emma lives on a street where women wobble by on bicycles with flowers in their baskets. She greets us at the door in a floral dress and a jumper with holes at the elbows and ushers us into a room with a worn sofa, sagging bookshelves, with Vivaldi's *Four Seasons* on a bad music system. Nervy and cold, I keep my jacket on, as does Sadiq. She introduces us to Patrick, a shambling academic dressed in corduroy trousers, autumnal colours all the way up to his rust-coloured hair. Neither seems to feel the October chill. We sit at a tiny table where we can see weeping willows by the river. Patrick opens the wine while I help Emma set the table.

'It's probably nowhere as good as the real thing, but I tried,' she says, heaping dal, rice, lamb, curried vegetables onto our plates. Everyone picks up knives and forks except Sadiq. To my shock he plunges his hands in the hot rice, scoops up dal, mixes it up and shoves a large morsel in his mouth. Our hosts are looking down on their plates. She is set to marry someone of her own kind.

'What do you do?' asks Emma.

Sadiq warbles with a full mouth. 'Drinks.'

'Drinks?'

I wait for him to clarify this and say he means he's the general manager of soft drinks company.

'That's right,' he says, his mouth full again.

'Oh,' she says, trying not to look at the dal and yoghurt running down his hands as if she's just figured it out. 'Bartender!'

'Yep.' He helps himself to more yoghurt from a dish. 'This looks like Royal Doulton.'

'Yes,' says Emma. They nod as if eager to find a point of contact.

He says, 'I went into a place selling fine china when I was a student. They looked at me as if I was a criminal, so I told them, "Pack up the lot, the twenty-piece Royal Doulton dinner set, the side plates, the serving dishes, the lot." Paid for it and told them to ship it to Trinidad. They changed then, ran around, offering me tea and coffee.' He laughs uproariously.

'Oh, we don't bother with all that,' says Emma, 'we get our mismatched things from the charity shop.'

What you think is class isn't class, I want to scream at him.

He laughs. 'When I was in Manchester, old ladies and children crossed the street on seeing me. This black man dressed in black.'

I move to help her clear the table. 'Oh, don't bother with that. Are you late for your train?'

Her partner closes the door firmly with what I feel is a relieved click.

I feel disgraced.

On the train back, he says, 'Bloody snobbish shits. I don't care if they think I'm a bartender.'

Walking home in the rain, he is shivering and sweating, and I put newspaper inside his shirt not knowing how else to warm him up.

Back in our rooms, Sadiq says, 'You think I don't have a soul just because I don't want to dress in rags like your friends with holes in their sweaters?'

'I don't know,' I say, turning away from him, wanting him to overwhelm me with love. I hear abandonment. I see the retreating figure of my father in a strange cold village in England.

'Why did you marry me then if you think my friends are pretentious?'
'Breeding up,' he laughs.

I am terrified that he will leave me; I go quiet that night. Wanting to be reassured, I say, 'You will leave. This is a joke for you.' He turns away. I see myself small, alone in a bus clattering up a hill in Simla.

In the morning, still sweating and shivering he calls a cab that takes us to the Dorchester. 'Get a doctor,' he says weakly. 'Pneumonia' the doctor says. The days go by in a dark cold haze.

We return to Trinidad a day before Eid, our honeymoon cut short by a month. He has lost twenty pounds. I have lost five.

'Well, boy, it look like your wife don't feed you,' his mother says at the airport.

Back in Trinidad, in an apartment set up by my thoughtful in-laws, who had got rid of the wedding rose petals we had strewn everywhere on the night of our wedding, I wake up with my mouth on Sadiq's neck, breathe him in, sweet and rancid, and rush to the bathroom to throw up.

I call Angel, panicked, thinking my very body is rejecting him.

'I need to talk to you. I've made a mistake.'

'How?'

'Sadiq is not the right man for me. He makes me physically ill. I wake every morning feeling sick when I breathe him in, and again at night when we are in bed.'

'Have you seen a doctor?' Angel asks. She is brisk, busy preparing for her wedding to Andy and her departure to England.

I say no, not yet.

When the gynaecologist confirms the pregnancy, I remember how I fell upon a big bright bottle of olives on display in an Italian food place in London, walking in and drinking the brine in great gulps on the sidewalk.

At Angel's wedding reception, my mother-in-law announces that she feels like the child I'm carrying is hers. She says, 'I have been throwing up.' Mummy and Angel exchange a look, but I don't collude with them. At least I'm safe.

On Eid day, we spend the holiday the way he has all his life: early prayers at the Mosque – where the women sit at the back – and then visiting his family all day long.

As the day progresses, I grow more bewildered. No one is welcomed, invited to sit or eat. Sadiq ignores me, going from person to person, kissing indifferent cheeks. I follow him. I kiss cracked old faces and babies, women in clothes Khaja would consider gaudy. His people look through me as if I am not there. I begin to doubt if I exist. I wonder if I'm too ugly to look at. There are rows of people of all ages sitting on tin chairs and long tables made of boards of wood. This is how they would have eaten 170 years ago. Sadiq speaks Creole, a language I don't understand.

'How?' says an aunt. She doesn't need to say anything else. She means, *How are you?* 'You lookin' nice,' he replies and moves on. 'Eh, I nearly pass you by… I was in town the other day…' 'Next time,' Sadiq says and walks on. Conversation seems extraneous.

When we leave, I search out the host, his uncle, and thank him for lunch. He doesn't know what to say. Sadiq's father laughs. 'You don't have to say thank you. He is our family.' His mother says, 'You could relax, you know. You don't have to talk proper all the time.'

'Nobody spoke to me,' I complain to Sadiq on our way home. I'm popping pills for a migraine.

'That's because you look like a snob,' he says.

'But I speak to them; I ask them about themselves, your aunts, your uncles.'

'It's how you speak.'

'It's rude. I would never treat one of your friends like that.'

'I never needed friends,' Sadiq says. 'I have sixty cousins, three hundred people in my family. They sense you don't love them. If you love me, you must love all my family, all three hundred of them.'

'I need to get to know people before loving them. I barely know how I feel about the handful of people I love.'

'You could leave,' he suggests when we get home.

I go to the small back garden, looking at the fragrant vines strangling a tree, wondering where to go, when he comes to find me.

'I'm sorry,' I say, 'I will try to love them all.'

It will take me time to understand that the individual has no place here. Survival is about being an unquestioning clan member with no private face, identity or needs. It is the opposite of my experience. My mother, grandmother and great-grandmother survived by doing it alone.

Besides Sadiq's little abandonments, we cohabit with great tenderness. Sadiq reclaims me each time, tenderly washing and drying my clothes, holding me till I sleep, going with me to each Lamaze class, outfitting our home for the new baby, taking me for a trip to London where he buys me slick trousers that expand with my belly.

I'm grateful that, finally, things are tidied, there is order, that someone is in charge in my life. My closet is rearranged and colour coordinated. Wedding presents that cluttered the kitchen disappear. Baskets of food appear. A chicken lands in my oven. I wonder if I'm seeing things, going crazy, until Sadiq says he's given away things we don't need, his parents have keys, drop in food, while we sleep. He organised my closet when I was at work. I understand that I'm not competent, which is why I am getting this help. I keep working as my feet swell, and my belly grows. I'm covering the news, anchoring the weekend television newscasts. It's all crime.

The aftermath of the 1990 coup attempt brings more bloodshed. The

114 men freed by the courts, with access to guns from Gaddafi's Libya, and more drugs and guns from Latin America, unleash terror – turf wars, five hundred murders a year. Trinidad is the third most murderous country in the world in a state not at war.

I go out on police boats to see where the drugs and guns are dropped off on our shores on moonlit nights. On the abandoned beaches, the police say it's financed by untouchables in big businesses and allowed in by 'certain police'. There is an inevitability about violence as a tool of survival. A group of grieving mothers whose sons have been gunned down in gang wars tell me gang leaders have taken the place of absent fathers.

In the studio, I read the news about decapitated heads in the forest from kidnappings gone wrong, the slit throats of two middle-class women in a quiet residential neighbourhood while a toddler looked on.

Funeral homes do a brisk business. Port of Spain – the place Derek says is percolating with a new world culture created by people from every continent – is in a state of freefalling anarchy, with twenty-five thousand men in gangs running the underworld. Gangsters are buried with gold chains hanging from their necks to their stomachs.

Terror in the world around us penetrates the home, seeps into arguments. Over fifty women a year are murdered by their common-law husbands, many after leaving home or seeking an injunction against a violent partner. I write a column composed of the names of dead women and run out of space.

I wake one morning to see the bars in my windows wrenched apart. Sadiq has already left, gone to work at dawn to open the factory. I get up slowly, check my dressing table. The jewel box is empty, my wedding rings gone. Burrimummy's emerald ring is gone; I also bought a leather briefcase in Florence on my final trip with Hugh, and that, too, has gone. I phone Sadiq's parents. I weep. 'The robber could have killed me. He would have killed the baby and me if I had woken.'

'You're not dead yet,' Sadiq's father says. 'You mustn't be so sensitive,' his mother adds.

One blazing afternoon I fling off my work suit after an assignment in the sun, relieved to be in the cool house, thinking I was home alone. Someone says 'Hello' when I'm down to a bra and panty. I look up to see my brother-in-law is sitting on the stairs watching me. When he laughs, I laugh. I hear Burrimummy's voice saying 'monkeys' and am overcome with shame. When my in-laws find it funny, I remember what Daddy said about them not being like us.

I am now entirely dependent on my in-laws, who have surprised us with a home, a place they have helped us buy and arrange, down to the fabric of the furniture in our drawing-room. They have keys to our house and our cars, look after us and check up on the housekeeper while we are at work.

We make no decisions without consulting them, and I am grateful for their kindness. I have gratefully joined their safe space.

To show my gratitude, I keep my promise and try to love Sadiq's family. On Christmas Day, I join him going from house to house in his father's village of Tunapuna. He is not ashamed of them or their 'gardens', that are vegetable patches. Their living rooms are arranged simply, plastic flowers and 3D wall hangings, and they speak Creole English, but their children go to the best schools, and they don't expect anything of me. There are no dramas, none of the snobbery of Rest House Road. They smile and welcome Sadiq, and I sit there quietly, not getting references to the old days, not understanding their dialect. I am tired, nauseous, just grateful they don't expect anything of me, barely notice I'm there.

But over long hot days, my gratitude turns into discomfort. I would like to be asked how I am, to be seen, to decide on things. The arguments begin slowly and escalate repetitively. I rebel over spending all day with his family, at being invisible. 'It would be nice to be greeted, to be asked how I am.'

'Stop that formal Indian shit. This is how we've always done it,' he says.

I'm furious. I ask him to stop the car to let me out into the searing heat of the highway, wanting him to understand my resistance to being absorbed into nothingness. I wait for him to persuade me to stay in the car, to tell me I mean more than them. He does not. He hears rejection. I don't recognise I'm threatening his safety, that to puncture the group security with my individuality is fatal to community survival. I get out, my flimsy sandals sinking into the steaming black pitch. He drives off, leaving me standing there, rolls of sweat running down my back, my breasts heavy and my eyes stinging with the endless salt running through them. But just as Daddy did, when I was late getting into the car for school, he returns, saying he found a pomerac tree that has stained the ground purple and he knows how much I love picking and eating the tangy fruit. And he's right, the tree is carpeted with brilliant colour – Mountbatten pink and intense purple. We pretend nothing has happened

In February, when I am four months pregnant, he persuades me to wear a bikini costume for Carnival. I baulk, hearing Burrimummy's voice saying 'dancing girl', and Daddy saying 'whore'. But it's him, my Sadiq and I cling to him on the street, marvelling how women sway their bellies, move groins with easy abandonment, eyes closed as if in an ecstasy of a private orgasm, marvelling at how unjudged and unjudging everyone is. But the old-world voices are loud, and they win. I pull away from his groin, his thrusting super-lewd dancing. My face must have revealed some Burrimummy-like distaste as his reaction is immediate: he disappears into the crowd, races off, his body taut, oiled, muscular, unyielding. I know I will never find him amidst the denseness of the drunken crowd jumping in unison, as if in a trance. Clutching my belly, feeling naked on the street, unprotected, a whore in red lipstick, not comforted by the ribald, near naked crowds, I am a loose woman attracting the gaze of men who call out to me. I stumble to my parents' home, where Mummy covers me with a shawl, turns on a hot shower, wipes off my make-up with Ponds, lays out a tunic and pyjamas – still scented with sandalwood from a Delhi shop that reminds me of Burrimummy – brings me cool lime juice, draws the curtains and makes me lie down. She absorbs and absolves my shame.

We both have barriers to each another, but we let one another in when we get knocks. Lately, it's as if I've returned to the comfort of her womb. We understand one another in uncanny ways. She calls me when I have a migraine. I know when she's distressed. By applying balm over the other, we apply it on ourselves. It must have begun when she saw me in London, the hippie gipsy. She'd never had stability herself, but she tries to make everything bearable for me. Her beauty has softened, and her self-consolation is now the wisdom she shares with me. 'I don't take it on when people try to hurt me. I expect to be hurt. I know humans are unreliable, needy, self-interested, weak, vain and will betray anyone to save themselves. I've never depended on them.' Mummy speaks of humans as if we are all aliens.

Pale, slender long fingers on my arm, she says, 'Sleep my quarter pint.' I half-close my eyes and absorb the sunshine through the sapodilla tree. I could be in Rest House Road, except instead of autorickshaws, I sleep to the thudding of the music trucks.

Hours later, Sadiq shows up at my parents' home, his arms full of half-ripe Julie mangoes from the country. On the drive home, he says I was the most desirable girl, that I looked great in a bikini, and he could never lose me. Where he sees desire and beauty, I see shame. We are continents apart.

I seek other authority figures. 'Mom, Sadiq is moody.' My mother-in-law dismisses my complaints.

'Get around him,' she tells me. 'Act like nothing happened.' Without missing a beat, she produces a present for me that she'd been saving up – a leather thong for me from their Brazilian holiday. 'Make him happy,' she says.

The baby is late. Labour must be induced. The day before I am due to give birth, Sadiq takes me for a drive in the country.

'Where are we going?'

'To pick up my aunt. She is moving in.'

'Why?'

'You've never looked after a baby. She looked after me. She did a great job.'

His aunt has her bag packed. I get out of the car and say, 'No. Just no. Leave me here in the fields.' I feel aggrieved yet have the urge to laugh when Sadiq says I'm speaking like a tragic Bollywood actress.

His aunt goes back into her house. 'Go,' she says. 'I go come after.'

On the drive home, I begin to doubt my decision. What if I can't look after the baby? Living in here is a crash course in survival. What if I am the only person like me on the island? What if I have to fend off groupthink? What do I need to do to keep myself me if everyone else is different?

'You don't know how to live in Trinidad,' he says. He's right.

I am admitted to the hospital with contractions. Sadiq sends in his brother to time them. I swear at him, and I swear at Sadiq and the doctor who takes his time with the episiotomy. I tell Mummy, who doesn't seem to understand my pain, to leave the room.

Two days later, back home, with painful nipples, unsure of how long it would take for my milk to flow, I say to my mother-in-law, 'Mom, I want to stop work and look after this baby. I want to heal from the episiotomy.'

My mother-in-law's nausea stopped after I gave birth. 'If you stop working, Sadiq might do the same. How will you live? Don't worry. We will look after the baby.'

Three days after giving birth, breast milk soggy on my clothes, I'm back in the studio reading the news. My milk dries up. I try to escape from the tensions at home by adding to my TV workload – a column, a radio show – while my mother-in-law and housekeeper look after my son. I leave home at four o'clock in the morning to host a morning show and sometimes work till two o'clock the following day to edit segments for television. I rush out of the house to read the news.

Over the next few years, we do the very things we feared for ourselves. Abandon one another, keep the other off balance.

At our first dinner party at home, he says, shouting over the din of young couples at the table, 'I describe my marriage like the Chinese curse. We live in interesting times. She infuriates me and puzzles me, but I am never ever bored. It's why I don't buy a TV. I have sixteen channels, and I don't know which I will get when I wake up.'

I remember from my childhood the army couples dancing with one another's spouses and how unsafe that was for my parents. I feel for Sadiq something so close to craziness that I'd even probably kill for him. I'd burst past all feminist ideals, law and dignity for him; I'd beg him to stay. I know my feminist women friends won't understand, so I keep that to myself, the way he's like Daddy and my handsome granduncle who died smoking as heavily as Sadiq smokes. He's every bloody thing, and that's why I can't let him know. When Burrimummy read *Arabian Nights* to us, we learnt how the queen must keep her king on tenterhooks to stay alive. I keep him off-balance, refuse to blend our books, 'just in case we don't work out'. I take off at a Carnival fete to sit some ways away and smoke cigarettes to worry him. He does the same – goes on bike rides around Tobago without telling me, leaves my carefully cooked meals untouched.

One night we watch a film where the husband gaslights his wife, flickering the lights, so she thinks she's mad. We recognise one another in it; we tell each other to grow up. But our wildness doesn't abate after our first or even second anniversary. He strips off his clothes and goes skinny-dipping after a Pavarotti concert in Barbados; I make him stop his van and climb it to steal sugar apples from people's gardens in a posh neighbourhood after a party. We say terrible things to one another: 'Trini coolie', 'Indian hypocrite', 'liar'; the language of family and strangers, of people continents apart. It's the strangeness and the intimacy that binds us. Idyllic days would not suit either of us. I dress badly to go to a cocktail party with his colleagues and spend a long time talking to a man, knowing that will make him want to go home. Even as I look at his thunderous face, I'm grateful he never looks at other women. 'I like shoes,' he says. 'I'm not allowed to look at the women wearing them.' He says it with a kind of pride. At nights, after another row, we lie down on opposite sides of the bed and wake wrapped around one another, but we know we are close to combusting. We never speak of this seriously enough. But the jabs at one another are adding up. Much more, and I know we will not be able to live either by ourselves or with one another. I use the usual tools to survive: sleeping tablets, pain meds and anti-anxiety medications.

The years pass. Another pregnancy. A girl. Once again, after giving birth, I am back on TV reading the news, my breasts heavy and painful with milk. I smother my baby with kisses when I see her, but she doesn't see me enough. When she's older, she's passionate, with swift, hot, angry tears and kisses that are almost desperate, 'Why are you so cute, Mummy?' she asks when I put her to bed, 'Why do I love you so much?' And I say to her all the words Burrimummy said to Angel, 'You are my Seraph brought to earth on a chariot carried by six angels, the most beloved child on earth.' She sleeps on my stomach, feels a part of me, but I know I've missed her first steps, her falls, the day she stopped drinking from a bottle. She must have had as many bereft moments as I did. Mummy spends time with us, loves her granddaughter to such an extreme that she fears carrying her down the stairs. Sometimes if we love, we stay away so we can do no harm. That's how Mummy, I and Pia fit into one another, untouching Russian dolls, close yet apart.

Hugh writes a chatty letter reminding me about my old life, the days in coffee shops, racing for buses, closing my umbrella before entering the restaurant, the cold sprinkle of water and warm soup. He asks if I liked the roses he sent on my wedding day. He made sure to include lilies and freesias. I sit at my computer and write to him.

Hugh,
I loved the roses. Sadiq said they were his but I knew you sent them. I made a

mistake with this man. I wish it were you. It's always been you. I don't understand
him, his family, the harshness of their language, their customs. These people are
strangers to me. I would have had more in common with a Tobago man, a black man.
Their quick rage, refusal to say please, sorry and thank you, scares me; there's an
undertow of the brutality Naipaul writes about. I see so many dead women. I don't
know how to leave.

The children, three-year-old Pia and five-year-old Tej are in their pyjamas,
colouring with crayons, and I am researching a news story when he comes
up behind me in the silent way he sometimes does, startling me.

'I read the email you wrote to your lover. Have I ever hurt you? I haven't.
You think I'm a peasant? Beneath you?'

He slams my computer shut. I wonder about my work.

I say, 'You lied about the roses.'

He says, 'You are still in touch with the man who sent them. What's
worse?'

He is so hot with rage that I imagine fire coming from his ears and can't
resist the urge to giggle. The children, quiet, look at us, me still laughing.

'You think your family is so great. Really?' He takes the photographs off
the wall and piles them on the dining table: the ones from 17 Rest House
Road; Burrimummy at eighteen; Sadrunissa at the Delhi Durbar; Mumma
in Savanur leaning on the urn with the Christmas card in 1914; Puppa in
London in full regalia. One by one, he flings them on the floor. 'You live
here now. Not there.'

I am speaking to the children, trying to sound reasonable. 'Go to bed,
darlings. Mummy will be up soon for our bedtime story.'

Sadiq says, 'Do you want some tea?'

I hear Pia crying. Sadiq's parents walk in.

Now I am relieved at their arrival. Sadiq's mother will see the splinters
and support me.

'Your son,' I weep bitterly, 'is a brute. He is messing with my computer.
Look, he broke the frames of the photographs of my family.'

'How do I know,' my mother-in-law says calmly, 'that you didn't
threaten him with a knife?'

This woman, who struggled and fought her way up in the world, cannot
and will not protect me. She says, 'I hope you know you can't take the
children if you leave.'

I can't believe she thinks my children belong to her. I say, 'I should have
listened to my father and never married into this family.'

'You must not be so negative; you can't get a better family, eh. You have
all your family pictures around you. But where de money, eh? Where it?'

'Your computer is fine,' says Sadiq, who had left the room to check. 'You
should get these reframed anyway. They were looking tattered.' He hands

me a cup of tea and never mentions the letter to Hugh again. And we sit there, half an hour later, drinking tea, while the children leapt about in a sugar-high from the candy I gave them to keep them quiet.

I take the family photographs with smashed glass on their faces to the frame shop and the girl picks out the glass. All these daughters of my ancestor, Sir Afsar, did his bidding. I think how they hated and adored their husbands, and how deep that inheritance goes. Alongside those pictures are others, of Sadiq and me, some glossy; others are clippings from newspapers, at the homes of diplomats, Carnival parties, charity functions.

There is one of Sadiq, the children and me on the beach in the sunset, the afternoon he saved a drowning man's life; another of Sadiq in a smart suit and me in a navy and silver sari titled 'Glamour Maxi'; we were togged up for a party to welcome the Indian prime minister. I was in Mummy's green brocade sari with Sir Afsar's diamond star around my neck. We have turned into Mummy and Daddy. It's either fight or flight, and I want neither now.

SEVENTEEN

St Lucia, 2016

Bolting the door to the cottage, I pick crumbs off the sheets and think of my parents.

Both born in pre-independence India: my father was born in 1933, the third of five children in a crowded home on a busy street in Aligarh. His parents belonged to the staunchly Hindu Nath clan of the Vaishyas, who come after the Brahmins in caste terms. The tribe were scribes, first in Mughal India as ministers and advisers of the emperors, then keepers of public records and accounts, and state administrators. Aged seven, my father's siblings left him alone for being too serious, listening to Gandhi on the radio, agitating every night for self-rule from the British.

Meanwhile, Mummy was sitting on a highchair being spoon-fed by an English nanny in a palace in the Royal Muslim state of Bhopal, the second largest Indian state in India after Hyderabad. She was watching her mother play one of the four baby grands in her house, weep, gallop off in her Asquith riding gear, or pack to go to the farmhouse where her husband's uncle, the Nawab of Bhopal, entertained guests in wild parties with an assortment of British officials, actresses and other members of the elite.

When my father was in a free secondary school in Aligarh, an obedient and wary son to his bridge-obsessed, accountant father, my mother was as alone and bereft as an orphan in an elite boarding school in Karachi. My grandfather on my father's side, Amar Nath, was an authoritarian man, perpetually enraged at losing most of his inheritance through gambling. (This was a family failing. My great-grandfather was a zamindar, a land-owner who gambled away all his villages.) As a widower, my grandfather, Amar Nath, was still served by the women of the household – his clothes washed and ironed just so, his samosas fried hot, his tea brought on time. He inspired fear. My father was mute in front of him and in high school, he spent his evenings studying, desperate for another life. He fled to the army after qualifying as an engineer.

If I go back far enough, I can see our parents were not responsible for the fissures when things broke for us. Both suffered from authoritarian parenting and defected from their families. They turned to one another like children for consolation and made up for lost playtime.

Marrying my mother was a conquest for my father, like Naipaul's marriage to Nadira, a Pakistani journalist who knows who she is – an elite, educated, fair-skinned, well-connected woman with spades of entitlement in a poor country like Pakistan. Perhaps both Naipaul and my father had the urge to crush what rejected them or held them in contempt. Perhaps Naipaul hoped that propinquity to this Aryan South Asian woman would help him get over the shame he seems to have felt about his antecedents. Why else was he so livid with his mother for describing her native village in India to reporters in Trinidad as a place of poverty, ignorance and filth? It seems to have made him detest himself. He tried writing himself out of that self-hate with his brilliant, supercilious observations, but it didn't work. I saw that same mother in President's House on the day V.S. received The Trinity Cross from the President. She was a humble woman wearing a printed dress, her head covered by a plain white shawl, a woman who would have been invisible amongst India's poor. Yet, unlike my grandmother, Naipaul's mother created her own independence, managed construction sites, wearing hard hats after her husband's death. The new world had allowed for change, turned everyone into chameleons to survive.

My own poor paternal grandmother died unnoticed of a massive heart attack. Docile and quiet, never giving anyone any trouble, she died in the kitchen while peeling potatoes for dinner a day before she was due to come to Guwahati for my birth. My father worshipped her, followed her in his devotion to Lord Shiva. I suspect she accepted him unconditionally, yet my father wanted bigger challenges. He never looked for that approbation in the woman he wanted to be with. Instead, he went for beauty, for a woman who herself needed mothering, my mother who blew up kitchens, for whom the matter of marriage was never settled. He had to guard her and woo her simultaneously, perpetually. He works hard at love.

The light has faded. I shower, put on a dress covered in tiny daisies, paint on light-pink lipstick and arrive ten minutes early for dinner.

Dinner is in the formal dining room facing the ocean, smelled in the brine brought in the breeze through the billowing ghostly curtains.

It's a careful, healthy meal of fish and vegetables and coconut ice cream, all prepared and served by Sigrid, who is unfailingly courteous. If she feels impatience over another acolyte, she never shows it.

After dinner, Sigrid wheels him to his usual spot on the veranda facing the sea, and when we are alone, he says, 'Okay, so you don't marry in India. You marry in Trinidad. What's the difference?'

'I would have been closer to my culture if I'd married a middle-class black man. The Trinidad Indian is a creature unto himself. I see a country of 1.3 billion people, four hundred cities, snowy Himalayan mountainscapes, desert, rain forest, people who are blue-eyed and coal-black, who speak over 450 languages, reduced to the motifs of flags, prayers by rote and a few vegetarian dishes, and clothes worn like costumes for festivals. I would admire that preservation if it wasn't accompanied by the undercurrent of rage.'

'There is a contempt there you must vanquish. I'm not saying you must idealise it – poverty or illiteracy. Capture that. The culture mingling, the ferment of that in a tiny space like Port of Spain.'

'It's not contempt. It's frustration. Why don't people who've done so well in the new world shed their rage, take on some of the bottled philosophy of equanimity for which India is famous? Update their idea of India?'

I tell Derek about interviewing a surviving former indentured labourer brought here by boat from Bihar. Avid for details of why he left India, where he was from, what it was like working on the sugar fields, I threw him questions. He responded with grunts and words like 'dis, dat' – unsatisfying sentences. He had forgotten his original language and not acquired a new one. I say, 'There was a profound loneliness in his face, frustration in his eyes. The frequent use of violence, the cutlass to resolve pain in rural Trinidad made sense. Without access to words, he found it impossible to access himself. It was tragic.'

I am aware of how this connects to my periodic recoil from my husband and his people (themselves descendants of indentured labourers), not because of any poverty, but because I associated them with a brutality that marked the end of my own innocence.

'It's about the brutality the men pass on to the women, and the women to one another.'

He interrupts me. 'It happened in India with your family too, didn't it? I've read your newspaper columns. You endorse V.S. Naipaul's opinion that we are half-formed, the idea that Africa and India and China are somewhat bastardised.' Then he returns to my work. He says, 'So what are you hoping to achieve with this?'

'I'm hoping it will get the boulder of my grandmother off my back.'

He says patiently, 'If you stay in the past, you are as stagnant as pond water. How did these terrible people affect your present? We talked about this.'

I say, 'I was reading Naipaul's *A Way in the World*. I read it so often I know it by heart. But we go back and back, all of us, to the very beginning… That's why I went back to my grandmother. I'm fearful of what the marriage has done to me. I know far worse things happen to people, and they survive. I'm hoping to find something salvageable in the ruins.'

Derek picks up my manuscript from the table and looks at me. 'What colours would you name this first section? I would say, crimson and khaki.'

Silence. We hear the ocean agitating at the cliff's edge, distant thunder.

'The landscape got to you too, eh?' he says. 'If you choose this life, it must be as an athlete. You must train up. Look after yourself. It's a long game.'

I don't look at the wheelchair.

I know Derek stopped drinking and smoking after a health scare. But in all the early photographs, he is smoking, with a drink in his hand, giving the photographer a cocky smile, as if this luck would go on forever, the world permanently filled with low-hanging fruit.

'Sigrid,' he shouts.

My time is up.

Sigrid emerges from the yard, follows me back to the cottage and speaks to me as if she knows what I want. 'You know, dear, in the end, he can't help you with agents or anything else. You've got to do it on your own. Everyone does it on their own.'

The words sound harsh, but I see great kindness in them.

When she's turned away, I go outside to look at Derek's white house glowing by the light of the milky moon. I feel a bit crazy. Here I am at the home of a man who reportedly hurt some women. His love for the truth encourages me to write about how I was hurt by men like him. But the truth is this: the men may have taken the subjugation of women as their birth right, but it's the generations of women, battling for the morsel of leftover pie, for the dregs of power, who perpetuate the damage by hurting their daughters.

We turn to others to fill the spaces our parents leave in us, not knowing those spaces are ours to fill. I take my laptop outside, where the moonlight throws concentric webbed threads into the night.

There is either truth or nothing.

CHAPTER EIGHTEEN

Angel writes to me from Daventry where she has bought a home, an old vicarage, with a garden. She drives daily to the nearest city, Nottingham, Andy's city, where she works at a job she loves, doing dentistry. He works for the Ford Company, and a local nursery takes care of their toddler son, Rahul. Angel's letters are packed with the joy of an escapee. A trip to Turkey, a pottery course. She has been happy to reinvent her past, create an entirely separate identity from our family.

For a time, Daddy tried to get Angel married to his satisfaction. There were failed liaisons, including a divorcee with a moustache as imposing as Sir Afsar's and other young Indian men who looked as if their parents had stunned them into silence with a lifetime of expectations.

But with his understanding of Angel's intractable nature, Daddy eventually accepted Andy's transatlantic offer to marriage, with caveats, as he did with Sadiq. The ceremony would be Hindu, the children would be Naths and be Hindus. We reflected that we had never been to a temple with Daddy and had received from him little idea of Hinduism apart from the *Gita*, which he said was a philosophical book and not dogmatic like the *Quran*, which encouraged people to kill.

I had done for Angel what she did for me, helping Daddy with the wedding arrangements. While I was adjusting her wedding lehenga, she told me she'd woken to Mummy kneeling and praying by her bed: 'You don't have to do this, Angel, not with an Englishman.'

I asked Mummy later why she had done this. She said, 'I told you, no? I saw the sign "No dogs or Indians" at the Gymkhana club. It's why I refused to curtsy to Queen Elizabeth when she came to Tobago, and Daddy and I were invited to a reception to welcome her. All the women were fawning over her. I shook her hand and said, "How do you do, Ma'am." She seemed quite happy with that.'

Afterwards, Angel fled to England, away from the bewilderment of us, the family she hadn't known when she was a child. She told me at the airport that she'd forgiven Mummy and Daddy for giving her away. 'They did their best and I don't want to carry this burden of abandonment on my back forever, so I've let it go.'

I knew I was part of what she needed to escape.

But there is one family entanglement Angel cannot escape. On her second anniversary, Angel telephones me in alarm.

'Burrimummy wants me to come to India to contest her 17 Rest House Road sale because she's made a mess of it. She was terrified Mummy would get it as the legal heir, so she sold it and then said that sale was illegal because she'd gifted it to me. 17 Rest House Road is worth a lot now, with the construction boom in India, and lots of people are after her, after the house. People from Bangalore are calling me in thick accents I don't understand. They say she's dying, that vultures are trying to take the house from her.'

The next time Angel calls it is from India. I can hear the operator saying we are connected. That we should speak.

'I'm here. I arrived safely.'

'In Rest House Road?'

'No, at the Sita Bhaveja nursing home, with her, on a mattress on the floor.'

A terror grips me as if there is something I'd left undone, something that could hurt someone.

'What happened?'

'She's stable. Don't worry, Aapa.'

I listen, barely daring to breathe in case I miss a word from that long-distance, crackling call.

'When I got to Rest House Road, Asmath and Tahira were lolling on her bed, surrounded by takeaway curries. The servants' children were serving them water, juice, hot samosas. They eyed my suitcase, but I left it anyway. They told me Burrimummy was at a maternity nursing home.'

I can hardly take it in – Tahira, Asmath, toadying once, now lolling on Burrimummy's bed. Angel's voice is high.

'I raced to the hospital, ran up the steps two at a time to the maternity ward and found her in a private room where a Tamil nurse was spoon-feeding her runny dal on a high maternity bed on a soiled sheet. The floor was a wet river of dark yellow urine covered with soggy newspapers. I don't know how long it had been there.

'She was inert, her sheets stained with food. I went racing down again to find a doctor and barged into the director's office, asking how she came to be in this maternity hospital. He said some man wanting to buy her house called them saying she was puffy, breathing unevenly. No one had given her insulin, and she was slipping into a coma. She would have died that night. He brought her to this maternity hospital, where they gave her insulin, put in a catheter, and left her here for weeks. When I arrived, the stench of the mattress was so overpowering I vomited. I got her another room, put her on a chair and gave her first bath in six weeks.'

'Oh my God, Angel. Is she awake now?'

'Yes. Moses pushed her when he was drunk, and she fell, injuring her shoulder and upper thigh and then got too frightened to go to the bathroom in case she fell again. People keep warning me that if I go to Rest House

Road, I will be harmed and killed because of the house. I don't know who to trust, Aapa. They all want the house. Everyone is a vulture in India when it comes to money. The good guys become the bad guys in a flash. Someone told me Burrimummy's lawyer was a crook and was thick with the new buyer who dumped her here. I went to see him, the new lawyer. I asked him for her file, and he got really threatening in his thick Tamil voice, saying I would have to hand over the keys to Rest House Road and sign a power of attorney. The thought of Burrimummy lying there gave me courage, and I grabbed the file and ran as fast as I could... Hello, I have to go.'

'Angel, Angel? I'll call you tomorrow.'

Desperate to hear Burrimummy's voice, I phone the hospital late at night. A nurse says Mrs Baig has been discharged. I call 17 Rest House Road.

'Angel, are you alright? Angel?'

Angel sounds shaky.

'I must get her out of India. Some people want to kill us for this house. They've already emptied it. I arrived, expecting to pack up her house, but as we arrived, Dr Rao appeared and, instead of examining her, said he wanted her dining table. More people arrived until the house filled up. Another man said Burrimummy promised him the dressing table, somebody else the stove. I don't know who told them we were back. She looked frightened, told me not to fight with them, to let them take what they wanted.'

I could hear the tears in Angel's voice.

'They took the silver frames, threw aside the photographs, took her writing desk, and dumped the contents. Within minutes, the mirrors, carpets... everything... had disappeared; the steel and glass cupboards were bare. There is not a single toothbrush, not one pair of slippers, not one nightie left. Everything of hers fits in two plastic bags – photographs and letters.'

'You saved her, Angel, think of that. Don't cry, my darling. What can I do, tell me? Is anyone looking after you both? I can't believe this happened to our beloved Rest House Road.'

'Nothing beloved about it anymore, Poppet. For the past week, we've been in this stinking, rotting house, walking around, protected only by a flimsy chicken-wire door. At night I lock it with the key a fourth buyer has given us.'

'What about her locker in the bank?'

'Burrimummy gave me the locker key that she managed to keep around her neck, even after they stole the gold Allah pendant. The locker was empty; her account was cleaned out. She has been giving one of the "buyers" the cash I sent her monthly. He told me it was all spent on her "expenses" at the hospital. Now she wants to sue the bank.'

Angel and I sigh together.

'I've paid a hefty bill to the nursing home. The doctor who owns this place told me she would die if I moved her, but I can't leave her here. I told her she must come home with me. I've bought her a wheelchair, stocked up with her medication. Her arm is healing. I've taken another two weeks off work, organised her visa, and had money wired for our tickets to England.'

Angel calls me again, from Bombay.

'We are at the Taj.'

'Wow. Must be exorbitant.'

'I was fed up with living like a dog for six weeks, under the cold-water taps of the nursing home and Burrimummy's dark bathroom, and I thought, fuck it, and booked this place. I wanted to get rid of the memory of the stench. I went under the hot shower and scrubbed myself for what felt like hours with fragrant soaps. I left her with housekeeping, had a facial, and got my hair cut.'

'Can I speak to her?'

'Poppet, darling,' Burrimummy says when she comes on the phone, 'we are at the Taj. The food is lovely. I can see the sea, my baby. The sea. I lived here with your mother, Nur, for months.'

'Soon, you will be home with me, Burrimummy, where the sea is everywhere. I love you.'

'Is this Poppet?' she says. 'Hello, hello? Do you remember we stayed here on our way to Trinidad thirteen years ago, Angel?'

The phone goes dead.

Angel calls me from Daventry, whispering, sounding exhausted.

'The flight to London was scary. The catheter leaked. When I got her off at Heathrow, she was a mess; the air hostess helped me to clean her up. Andy was fascinated by her, and as soon as he saw her, he folded his hands together to greet her in what he thought was a traditional Indian way, and she put her right hand out and said, "How do you do?" with her old loud voice. She instantly came alive on the drive to the cottage. She kept exclaiming over the scent of lavender and the fields in Daventry.'

'Oh, how she needed this, Angel.'

The question of where she will stay hovers over our silence.

Angel says, 'Yesterday I ran out to pick up some groceries. I returned to a trail of urine and the baby playing in it. All I do all day is look after her. She is a maniac with cheese and white bread. I'm always on call. Up, down, up, down. No time for our baby. I can't leave the house at all. I am grateful she is safe and alive, but I'm traumatised by it.'

Silence. I can't bear it. Angel allows people to fall into it. I fall.

'Angel,' I say, 'bring her home to me.'

'Are you sure, Aapa?'

'I'm sure.'

'I promise I will come back from England and help you care for her.'

I say, 'I'm here.'

'I've got a week of holiday left.'

'Just bring her.'

Sadiq and I meet Angel, Andy and their baby at the airport, wheeling Burrimummy out. Burrimummy looks shrunken, tiny.

'Sadiq? This is Sadiq? A Mussulman?' Burrimummy is eighty-four. Her stomach is swollen with water. So are her feet. They are hard, big, inert and cold to the touch as I help Sadiq settle her in the back seat of the car. I put her head on my lap.

She sits up. Her mouth is open. She looks at the cane fields, up at the mountain ranges, at the brightly painted wooden shacks, at the sliver of the ocean, the lighthouse, the wharf, a glimpse of the sea. We pass the high-rise towers, the town with its hawkers and Lebanese cloth shops and Chinese takeaways, parks, homeless people lying beneath the samaan trees, the gingerbread houses and the Cricket Oval, the circle Queen's Park Savannah with its seven magnificent colonial buildings. When we pass the Country Club, and just before we turn into our home, I say, 'Burri, it's like the Bangalore Club,' but her expression doesn't change.

Sadiq helps Burrimummy out of the car and into the room I prepared for her in my children's old nursery. She asks for the children. 'They are sleeping upstairs, Burrimummy. My in-laws are with them. I'll show you the bedrooms, library and balcony when you're stronger.' I set up a little area for her to pray with a janamaz. I want her to be happy here.

The house fills up. Mummy and Daddy came and greet Burrimummy as if she'd never left us. 'Hello, My The,' Mummy says affectionately. 'I've made you your favourite: kheer with basmati rice and cream.'

'Thank you, Nur,' Burrimummy says with great formality, like old times, except now she's in dentures with lank hair and not a crisp sari and pearls. Daddy greets her with affection and says, 'As soon as you're better, we'll have a drink together.' She laughs as if remembering something from far away. We all laugh along as if nothing has changed.

My in-laws' troop downstairs; my mother-in-law, in red trousers and an electric blue sweatshirt, comes towards us, shouting excitedly.

'Welcome, welcome to Trinidad and Tobago, to the land of scarlet ibis and steelband, where we have the best KFC in the world. And Brian Lara, you know him? Carnival, too, eh? Just now, we will take you for a jump up.'

I shout in her ear, 'Sadiq's parents, Yasmin and Bilal.'

With her curved back, Burrimummy bows her head in a profound salaam. They look at her, puzzled,

'Hi, hi. How you goin'?'

She says, 'I don't want to go anywhere. I want to lie down, Poppet. I don't understand.'

Before I guide her to her room, I show her my surprise in the drawing room – a second-hand piano. She runs her fingers on it weakly, but the disparaging look is unmistakable. I have made a mistake; she finds it cheap, no Blüthner.

'Maybe later. Keep the keys covered, darling. Get it tuned,' she instructs.

She waves away the basmati rice, lamb and vegetables I made for dinner. She will have 'bread 'n' butter'.

While Mummy and Daddy sit in the drawing-room with Sadiq's parents, I make her a sandwich, my heart full. I have my home now. I will look after her.

The first night is exhausting. She is hot and in pain, scratching herself, bleeding. I call the doctor at dawn, a slim, nervous-looking man in his early forties with darting eyes. He sets his black bag down on the dressing table and looks over the letter from the nursing home in Bangalore.

Coyly, Burrimummy covers her head with her shawl, with the expression of someone expecting deference and admiration. Her caved-in face, thinning grey hair, wrinkled legs, and her one sagging breast is a burlesque echo of her younger self. I remember when she would pull up her petticoat and say, 'Look how white and shapely my legs are.' All of that has gone.

I repeat to the doctor what Angel told me last night about the pus in the toe, the wound on her back that refuses to heal, a deepening crevice gathering more pus.

He holds up cotton wool.

'Is that for my face or my arse?'

'Eh?'

'I said, Doctor Sahib,' she repeats, with a deep musical voice that seems restored for this moment, 'is that for my face or my arse?'

The doctor turns to me.

'I thought you said your grandmother was a sick Indian lady?'

'She is,' I say.

'Wow,' he says, shaking his body as if to rid himself of an unwanted feeling and turning back to examine her and clean her wound.

'What are you doing to me?'

'Burrimummy, the doctor needs you to keep quiet so he can examine you properly.'

'That's right, Doctor Sahib. I can't hear, I can't see. Can you fix that?' Her voice is as cloying, as wheedling as a courtesan's, in an eighty-four-year-old's body.

'We will think of all that when you get your sugar stable.'

We all know there will be no operation to fix her hearing or sight. Her sugar was never stable enough for a procedure. The doctor says aloud, 'The main thing now is to prevent diabetes from harming her organs.'

She tugs at her hearing aid.

The doctor ignores her, expertly unrolling a bandage, wrapping up her wounds without looking up, 'Please change it every day with this sterile bandage.'

She keeps the conversation going as if she were at a party. 'One day in Savanur, my older brother, the late Nawab of Savanur, shot a monkey. Have you seen a monkey, doctor? Are there monkeys in Trinidad?'

She explains to the doctor, as he is looking for a vein, drawing her blood, 'The monkey is a Hindu god. There were many Hindus in my father's state. A big crowd came to the gates at Savanur, outraged that their God had been shot. Father apologised, leading a procession of Hindus to the temple, where they all fell prostrate in front of the statue of Hanuman. Father didn't do that because, as a Muslim, he thought praying to a monkey and a statue blasphemous. But he respected his subjects and stood by humbly while they said their prayers.

'When he returned to Savanur House, he gave his son, my brother Rasheed, the late Nawab of Savanur, a thrashing. Mother tried to stop him, but Father kept asking him, "Why did you shoot the monkey? It's their God." My brother said he did not know. After that day, none of us dared even joke about the Hindu gods again.'

I mouth 'sorry' to the doctor. I ask him if he'd like a cup of tea. To my surprise, he accepts and sits in a small chair near Burrimummy's bed. The doctor looks slightly awed by Burrimummy. He knows the real deal. Never mind that he wouldn't have a place in her world: here he is, a doctor with all the power; she, a dying patient. Still, she unsettles him.

The doctor says, 'I went to India, planning on staying for a month. The sight of people defecating on the train lines sickened me. Being in first class on a train didn't help. I heard there was a slum – Dharavi – with the population of Trinidad, a million people living in inhumane conditions, and just a mile away was the most expensive home in the world owned by industrialists.'

'The Ambanis,' I say.

He nods. 'I couldn't bear the idea that my ancestors might have suffered from this kind of inequality. I went back to Mumbai and remained in the Taj for a week, booked my ticket and came home. I was glad to be home.'

He feels more explanation is required

'My father was one of thirteen children, a poor farmer who spent a lifetime cutting cane. He gave us all Christian names so we could go to schools run by Canadian missionaries and Catholic monks and nuns to learn English and become doctors. But we continued going to the mosque and temple, celebrating Eid and Diwali.'

Burrimummy looks frankly contemptuous, at this mangle of religions, this sense of unbelonging.

I look at the doctor with an affection I didn't expect to feel. He had reinvented himself as I could. I don't need to feel like an outsider to Burrimummy's family. Daddy moving us here allowed us to be everything and nothing. I suddenly pull away from everything I thought I could never be – aristocratic, fair, tall, of a single determined religion, caste or class. Burrimummy has only one window to the world while I can see the world from prisms of multiple identities: Hindu, Muslim, India, Pakistan, Caribbean, Europe.

I say, 'Either I'm nobody, or I'm a nation. Walcott.'

The doctor pretends not to hear me, straightens up after examining her eyes, ears, feeling her pulse, palpating her stomach. He explains Burrimummy's condition to Angel, Sadiq and me as if she were not there or wouldn't understand. 'The report is correct. Her heart is failing,' he says. 'Her kidneys are failing; her diabetes is out of control. I'll send a nurse so that I can update her blood work.'

Burrimummy, no longer deferential, gives him a combative look which he ignores. He hands me the prescription and leaves.

NINETEEN

Some days later, after her sugar is stable, Burrimummy is more herself. My in-laws visit, and we sit out on the porch. Burrimummy goes into the bedroom and reappears outside, covering her head like a begum in a Hyderabadi court, carrying a sari on a silver tray that survived the mess of 17 Rest House Road, to present to my mother-in-law. Yasmin leans back, is bewildered by the courtly gesture and pushes the tray back at Burrimummy. 'But what is this? A sari? For what? I not going to no prayers.' She finds Burrimummy's gesture absurd.

Burrimummy doesn't understand that Yasmin associates saris with religious rituals. Yasmin doesn't get that Burrimummy's gesture belongs to a courtly India, that saleekha, or manners, is her only currency, that a false step, a perceived lack of grace, of reciprocity is fatal. Yasmin's indentured history was unrecorded; she wasn't sure where in India her ancestors had lived. She is Muslim; her forebears were possibly Dalit converts who were escaping the caste system. She didn't read or write Urdu or Arabic. What could Burrimummy – a sick old woman needing care – give Yasmin? Anyway, Yasmin doesn't wear saris, so she refuses the gift, telling the old lady, 'Keep it. You go have more use for it.'

Yasmin doesn't notice Burrimummy's bewilderment as she continues speaking, airily, confidently, loudly. 'How the flight was? I hope you fly in first-class because you could stretch out and sleep. If you know how much we fly. We went all about the world – Japan, Saudi, London, Paris. Everywhere we stay in top five-star hotels, only in first class. When we went to India, we stayed in the Taj and travel on the Orient Express.'

Burrimummy sits there, holding the tray with the sari. She and Yasmin face one another across a chasm of mutual incomprehension.

Yasmin's great-grandparents came on ships sometime in the nineteenth century to work in the sugarcane fields for the British. She said that her great-grandparents didn't know where they were going, were relieved to escape poverty, eager to believe in a promised land. What they found was subhuman barrack housing, often the same that housed the former slaves. Their customs, though permitted, were treated with so much contempt that to survive they had to forget much, over several generations, including their languages.

Burrimummy's father was the nawab of a state bequeathed to her

Afghan warrior ancestors by Aurangzeb, a much-hated emperor of India in 1672. Sadiq says, rightly, that the nawabs were just Afghan thugs, rewarded by the Mughals, who adapted courtly manners after looting India. There is nothing inherently noble about your family, he says.

This insight is immaterial to my mother-in-law, who is affluent, healthy, self-made, with the upper hand on people like Burrimummy, and she knows it. She has no time for the niceties that would have gotten her ancestors nowhere. She grew up in Port of Spain, in government housing, ten people crammed in three rooms near a panyard. With Bhojpuri half-forgotten and having only broken English in its stead, for some there was inchoate pain that was barely numbed with rum and passed on with rage. Embedded in Yasmin's DNA, if not at the forefront now, were crowded ships and an arduous three-month crossing by coolies, as the British called them, from Orissa, Bihar, UP, Madras and Calcutta. Many died of cholera, typhoid, dysentery and measles on the voyage and in the squalor of the sugar estate housing.

What was not forgotten was the pain of marginalisation in bitter rural poverty in Trinidad, the long exclusion from education unless you were prepared to become a Christian convert, and the dismissal of Indian Trinidadian culture as 'foreign' and not part of national culture. These were the experiences of all but a minority of East Indians until the 1950s, and though they were rarely to be dwelt over, they were never to be repeated. It's why Yasmin would rather die than say 'please', 'thank you' or 'sorry', as these words of servitude are traps, vanities of the privileged. On her first date with her husband, Sadiq's father, she had ordered condensed milk from a parlour to show her superiority over him; he'd grown up in rural Trinidad where his father cut cane, a single apple was shared between a household of thirteen and only half his siblings could afford to attend Government school.

On a family vacation to Costa Rica, Yasmin seemed impelled to visit the three restaurants in the resort as if this bounty could be snatched from her at any time. It reminded me of a trip to Jerusalem with a Jewish friend. His Dutch mother had survived the Holocaust with the help of a couple who hid her in the barn with their animals. She was often hungry, covered in straw during the raids. He told me how, after she arrived in Tel Aviv, his mother planned the entire day around food, thinking about the next meal before she'd finished the one she was eating.

I think that Yasmin needs daily reminders of her triumph, her escape from a history of degradation in India and Trinidad. With some accommodations and her business savvy, she had slid into a space of superiority with her Mercedes Benz, substantial bank balance and large home. She scoffs at the soft-mannered modesty of the really privileged and uncovers Burrimummy's head as if stripping her of her vanities, saying, 'What you doing that for? It's hot here, you know. You could come by me. I have air-conditioning.'

'I would love that,' Burrimummy says. 'I remember the heat in Tobago. Unbearable.'

'Yes, I have a big guest room with air-condition.' Yasmin's pride bursts from every pore. She sees Burrimummy as just a bent old lady holding a tray with a piece of cloth.

The continents had faced off, and neither came out looking good. Burrimummy seems as stunned as if she'd been on a long journey and got off at the wrong place, and there is no way back. She gives me a look as if to say, 'Who are these people? What have you done?'

Yasmin wasn't to know that wealth was not Burrimummy's currency; a mannerly grace was what she valued. I wanted to shout at Burrimummy: 'They are good people. The days in Hyderabad, under the Nizam, where women dressed in brocades and pearls, kept slaves, had rose-filled baths, and sent elaborate invitations in poetry to one another in silver trays, are OVER.'

But it was useless; I could tell Burrimummy thought she'd made a mistake when her offering of the silk sari was refused. She had learnt nothing from her experience in Tobago. Her retreat from Trinidad began early. She was too old and wanted to go back, while the rest of us pressed forward. She was alone again.

Sadiq is best in the role of protector and organiser. Like his father, who, unasked, cuts down blossoming branches of trees in our garden to tidy up, who equates a utilitarian order with survival, he maintains control by tidying up Burrimummy.

He picks up her prescriptions, gets her a plastic chair for the bath, installs hand rails, puts in the ad for the nurse who comes twice a day to give her insulin. He thinks of her needs before she can think of them herself. He is better than me at that. He is not squeamish around her. If there is a smell, he says matter-of-factly, 'Come on, then, let's sort you out.'

He walks Burrimummy to the bathroom, his arms around her waist. I try not to think about what he is doing, removing stained clothes, disposing of a dirty diaper. I hear the water. I smell soap. She emerges clean, a towel in her hair, in a clean nightie. By now, she not only respects him as the man of the house, but she also needs him. She sees he does not flinch around her like everyone else. When I go to her soiled bed, she says, 'Sadiq will clean me, Poppet. Come when I am clean.' She is ashamed around me. My contained revulsion embarrasses her.

One afternoon, our golden dog Pushkin saunters in with his head bowed. 'Such a beautiful animal,' Burrimummy says. 'You know Puppa had two Alsatians in Savanur, always by his side. They bit Nur. She stepped on both their tails, the same colour as the carpet.' She laughs, 'Nur was jumpy all that time not just with dogs… Anything set her off, banging doors, thunder, a bell.'

Just like me. I'm jumpy too, and dogs hadn't bitten me.

'Pushkin is sick,' Sadiq says, 'Cancer. She's in pain. I'm having her put down.'

Burrimummy reaches over and holds Sadiq's hands. 'You remind me of my Puppa, you know, Sadiq. I want to show you something.' She goes into her room and comes out ten minutes later. I watch them, wanting them to have their moment. 'This is Puppa's gold cigarette case. He would have wanted you to have it.'

'Thank you, Burrimummy.'

'Will you visit my grave and pray for me?'

'You're going nowhere near a grave,' he says, kissing her forehead and forgetting the cigarette case on the table.

Sadiq tries to get Burrimummy out of the house again. 'Let's take you out, Burrimummy. I want to show you the greatest show on earth.' It's Carnival in Trinidad – two days of costumes, street revelry and calypso competitions.

Our drive is slowed to a halt by the carnival parades. She watches curiously as a river of people of every nationality, dressed as American sailors and Native American Indians, Chinese dragons, Greek goddesses and genies, gyrate, sway and break away.

When we stop in front of a band mostly of women of all sizes and colours in jewel-coloured bikinis, silver boots and plumes in their hair behind a music truck obeying the commands of the DJ to jump, wave, gyrate, Burrimummy reacts with her entire body heaving, widening her eyes battened shut with cataracts.

'Darling, is this the red-light district of your country?'

'No, Burrimummy.'

'Why are there so many prostitutes here?'

'They are in costumes, Burri.'

'But their gaafs are out, darling. They are dancing as if they want men.'

'No, Burri, they are just having fun.'

Sadiq slams on the brakes. Three paint-covered men in loincloths holding forks surround the car. A blue face with mocking eyes and grinning teeth leans onto the windscreen.

The car is rocking. With contemptuous closing thumps on the bumper, they move off, exaggerating the movement of their bums from side to side. They enjoy our faces: Burrimummy's wide-eyed fear, Sadiq's laughter, Pia's laughter, Tej's astonishment, my curiosity.

She doesn't close her mouth for that whole drive. It is open for the rivers of semi-naked people, mostly women, gravely gyrating, eyes closed, lips pursed inward, in the deliberate concentration of circling their groins.

'I want to go home, Jaan.'

But Sadiq is already parking. He takes her hand, leads her to the stands, makes her sit on a wobbling plastic chair.

In the row ahead, a little girl of about seven with a bright pink dress is jumping up and down on her mother's lap, 'Mummy, where de king, where de king?'

Burrimummy smiles at the child. She approves of her tidy hair in ribbons, her crisp pink dress, her shiny, scrubbed face. She turns to me. 'You never told me this is a monarchy, Poppet.' She pronounces it *mon-ake*, which sounds strange after hearing years of it being pronounced *mornaarkee*.

'No, Burri.' I sift through my head to try to explain. In this new world, the burlesque eclipses reality. It's magical realism in a place where artistic genius is ordinary. The calypsonians are self-appointed 'barons', 'lords' and 'ladies'. People with the best costumes are crowned kings and queens and handed cash prizes and cars by the government. People, unrestricted by birth, can be who they want. In the end, I say, 'Burri, it's all made up, part of a street play.'

Her sari is wet. Her face droops. A yellow trickle appears on the stained white plastic chair. Sadiq and I take her home, clean her up, and give her bread, butter and cheese and icy-cold water. I put the fan on and hold her hand till she sleeps.

As Burrimummy's strength returns, the complaints rise to a crescendo, and despite the presence of the day nurse, I have to fill the role of several servants. She finds it hot – we don't have an air-conditioner in our rented house. She dislikes the Creole food Beverly cooks, spits it out.

'What is this? Is there ketchup in the dal? Is there sugar in the chicken? Take it away.'

She complains when I come home from work. 'I'm lonely when you both go to work. I don't understand Beverly's English. I don't understand the nurses. I can't leave the house.'

Burrimummy misses the activity of 17 Rest House Road, the shouting, the servants, the noise of the streets. I urge her to play the piano I bought. She says it needs tuning and never touches it. She lies in bed all day; there is no Asmath, no Tahira, no audience. I thought being with our Tej and Pia after school would be enough, but it isn't. She needs to be in charge, and she can't push our housekeeper around the way she did servants in India. Beverly manages the children who call her aunty, and she is family to us, not a servant. I need her in our fractious lives. I work sixteen-hour days, three jobs in radio, television and newspaper journalism, sleep badly, my eyes often scratchy and tired.

Sadiq installs a buzzer for her. Now, Burrimummy buzzes for me nonstop. She wants cheese; she wants to pee; she wants cleaning up; she wants a bath; she wants a walk; she wants a book.

Everything sours. The rose incense I sprinkle on her clothes turns into a stifling smell, its oil turning in the heat. Her clean nighties give her rashes with the bleach and harsh soap powder Beverly uses in the washing machine. She cries with pain when the rashes become boils and bleed.

We return from a New Year's party, feet aching with dancing, heads throbbing with music, to find a trail of faeces from the front door to the kitchen and her bedroom. I go into her room at the end of the dark house, wake her, and clean her up using baby wipes. I can't bear to think of her sleeping in her own faeces. I don't think I could have done it – pass those wipes over that wrinkled, stinking flesh – if I hadn't drunk so much champagne. She has sucked away everything out of me. I can't look after her, nor can I let her go.

In those long months when Burrimummy stays with us and batters me with her ongoing recriminations, her need as bottomless as the black hole of Calcutta, I think that if, somehow, I manage to keep her clean, I could bring back her past, restore her power to what it was when we were young and in her care.

One evening, Sadiq hands me the invitation to his cousin's wedding.

'I don't want to go,' I say, picturing it.

'A wedding,' Burrimummy says. 'Sadiq, darling, I would love to go.'

Nobody hears my 'No'.

On the appointed day, I bathe and dress her and take out one of her cotton saris. 'No darling, I want to wear silk. It's a wedding.'

'It's not that kind of wedding,' I say, but she's not listening. I spend a long time dressing her, pinning her sari, changing her pampers, putting on her pearls. We pile into the car: Sadiq driving; me in the back with Pia, now five, and Burrimummy; Tej, eight, is in the front. In the car, she brightens at the sight of the green hills three thousand feet high. A line of white birds, egrets, swoop down and then rise up into the sun. Her eyes follow them with her still-intact sense of wonder.

Along the way, Sadiq points to the white-tipped, mint-green stalks to either side of us, swaying in the sunlight as far out as we can see 'That's rice planted on our wetlands. I'll take you to the Caroni swamp one day where the scarlet ibis land in the thousands on the trees at sunset.'

We drive on narrow roads and encounter a sight of terrible beauty. First, we are engulfed in a cloud of black smoke, then watch as ashes softly fall from the sky on us, on the charred fields. 'It'll clear up,' Sadiq says, driving on steadily. 'The farmers started the fire in the cane to cleanse it of terrible things – snakes, cockroaches, rats.'

'All that cane burnt?' asks Burrimummy.

'Fire doesn't touch the cane, only makes it sweeter. My ancestors knew that,' Sadiq says, and points out the crumbling, barrack-type quarters his cane cutting great-grandparents lived in. 'They were poorly ventilated, ten feet by ten feet, with flimsy partitions. They once housed formerly enslaved Africans.' He's not ashamed of who they were, just proud of their escape from India.

'No kitchen?' asks Pia in her baby voice.

'No, they cooked on wooden stoves outside, sometimes on the steps. Each room accommodated either a married couple and their children, or two to four single adults.'

We see houses on stilts, some with limp clusters of flags at the entrance.

'What are those flags, darling?' Burrimummy asks. She's never seen anything like it, never been to an Indian village.

Sadiq replies, 'They are jhandis, coloured pennants, each symbolising prayers to a different deity – Hanuman, Lakshmi, Shiva, Krishna.'

She shudders. 'All those frightful gods.'

'These are Indian villages in a time capsule,' I say.

Burrimummy looks blank. Sadiq is expansive. 'My ancestors came here, Burrimummy, as indentured labourers to work in the cane fields over 160 years ago. I have both Hindu and Muslim ancestors.'

'Oh,' she says. That look of incomprehension again. My heart sinks.

The new highway is packed with Japanese cars and dominated by billboards: Brian Lara advertising mobile phones; Priya's Creation fashions, modelled by Madhuri Dixit, a famous Bollywood star; Nike sneakers; fine dining at a three-star hotel near the airport. We drive past Chaguanas, an expanding city. It's new and brash with brightly coloured shops, American food chains, roti and rum shops, gated communities full of McMansions.

Sadiq detours to a crumbling majestic multi-terraced white house flanked with lions, a thick-leaved ficus tree growing through the foundations – 'The childhood home of V.S. Naipaul,' he says, 'featured in his novel *A House for Mr Biswas*. I wanted to show it to you before it collapses. Our people don't care to preserve the past…'

Burrimummy hasn't read Naipaul's books, although she read every European classic in Puppa's library.

We swing off the highway by the petrochemical estate, Point Lisas, a vast horizon of towers, smoke swirling into the sky from tangles of pipes.

'We are the America of the Caribbean,' Sadiq says proudly. 'We produce oil and gas. In that estate alone, there are over a hundred multinational companies. They mine our oil, gas, ammonia, urea and methanol. There is an Indian company near here, Mittal, with a huge steel plant.'

He stops the car in front of a house on stilts, on a narrow street bumpy with potholes. 'We're here.' We join others walking through the gate to a garage towards a stage where the bride and groom shine in red, gold and white satin. Bollywood music blares from gigantic speakers.

We are carried by the momentum of the crowd to sit on steel chairs.

People who look like Khaja, dressed in cheap, bright sequins, stare at Burrimummy. She stands out, pale and broad, and bowed. Someone puts a sweet drink in front of her on the long table made up of sheets of plywood. There are yellow balloons in the trees. Young boys are laying banana leaves on the table; she wonders aloud what it is. Someone throws something on the banana leaf in front of her, someone she can't see. She turns her head to see men holding pots of mashed, curried pumpkin, pulpy curried green mangoes, curried spinach, boiled curried chickpeas and potatoes. They put a little of each on her leaf. A mound of half-cooked flour rotis is placed in the middle of the table. People grab at them with their hands.

'Oh,' Burrimummy says. She reaches for the doughy bread and starts to chew. She puts more in her mouth.

The woman opposite us says, 'You like de "bus-up-shut" lady?'

I don't try to explain that this means the roti resembles a shirt that has burst, been ripped up.

'I've never had green mango that is curried. I never knew you could eat off a LEAF. What is this?' Burrimummy is poking a finger in the mushy pumpkin.

I see it through her eyes. 'No, no, no, thank you,' I repeat to the server.

'Can I have some more of that fried dough, darling? Lovely,' she says, tasting the mango. 'Such a strange chutney.'

There is a wail and a squawking sound. A group of boys enter the compound, creating a noise that gets louder, more frantic, drowning out all conversation. A woman dressed in shiny satin, in rainbow colours, with long gold earrings in elongated ears, is accompanying them with a nasal folk song, in Bhojpuri Hindi, words I don't understand. The woman performs a crude dance, thrusting her hips at us, grinning.

Burrimummy's mouth opens.

The woman opposite us is watching Burrimummy closely. 'Dat is chutney. How you from India and you don't know that? Dat is de tassa,' she says pointing to the men who are hammering at their drums.

Burrimummy looks frightened; she says, 'I want to go home.'

I whisper, 'We are going home in a bit, Burrimummy.'

She says, looking at the woman wailing in Bhojpuri and the drummers, 'Whose servants are they, darling? Your mother-in-law's?'

I am indignant on behalf of Sadiq, my children, and Trinidadian Indians. She'd got it wrong, just as I once had. These people were dignified and rooted by remembered rituals.

'Burrimummy,' I say, watching the shock on Sadiq's face, 'the bride is Sadiq's cousin, an engineer; the groom is a pharmacist. They are respect-able people, NOT servants.'

'They look like servants,' she says. I beg her not to repeat it in Sadiq's hearing.

'She's tired,' I say to the brightly dressed woman opposite us, listening keenly as we leave.

Another day, I take her to the zoo. She is shocked at the tigers and lions. 'Darling, they are so thin. They are drugged. I shot tigers after Saied-uz-Zafar drugged them. It's not right, you know.'

She paces, talks to herself. 'I was better off in Bangalore. I can't breathe. Why are there bars all around the veranda? Why is the house so shut up? I want to go for a walk. I haven't been outdoors. I want to go to the shops.'

'I can't take you now, Burri.' I always have an excuse. 'I'm working on my newspaper column. I must put the children to bed. I have to serve dinner.'

'I'll go by myself,' she says.

'You can't.'

'Why?'

I can't tell her. A killer is loose on our street, a drug lord called Lizard, who has already shot dead twelve men. Before she came to stay we were broken into twice. Both times we were asleep. Burglars came in while all four of us slept and stole jewellery, US dollars, silver. Thankfully they didn't touch us. We were lucky. Two months back, bogus plumbers brutally raped and killed two sisters in their bathroom, slitting their throats while their toddlers ran about downstairs, unaware of their mothers' blood seeping through the floor. After that, dark with fear, we fully burglar-proofed all six bedrooms.

'It's hot, it's hot. I'm trapped.'

'You can't go out alone, Burri. I'm sorry.'

'Why?'

'It's dangerous.'

'You're making this up, Poppet. To keep me prisoner.'

'Why would I do that?'

I shrink into the walls, wanting the hot days of working as a reporter to stop, the fridge to fill itself, her perpetual need to go away. I explode. 'You're ungrateful; that's what you are. I am the prisoner, Burrimummy. Your prisoner. I haven't had a minute to myself since you came.'

I go upstairs to my bedroom, my heart thudding, already wondering how to apologise. Contrite, I take a dinner tray to Burrimummy's room. She is not there. I rush outside and see the side gate open. Frantic, I get into my car and drive around until I find her sitting down on a chair next to a vegetable vendor.

'This kind lady told me to sit down.'

Terrified, while driving her home I shout at her as if she were one of the children.

'This is not Bangalore! Women are murdered on the streets here!'

Her mouth becomes a tight line.

She says, 'Let me go, Poppet. I need to get my house back.'

'What house? Have you forgotten? You bought and sold Rest House Road three or four times over, each time getting lawyers to declare the last sale void, all because you don't want Mummy to have it. It's so legally mangled that it will be worth nothing for years. It is worth nothing.'

'Never mind, Poppet. It's mine. I want to go back to Bangalore. Please, give me my passport and my locker key. My house. I need to get it. My jewels.'

Angel had given the key to me. She'd told me there was nothing there – just a jumble of legal papers concerning Rest House Road. I don't give it to her, thinking that if I did, she would go back for jewels that aren't there.

'There is nothing there, Burrimummy.'

She nods mysteriously.

Sadiq sits with Burrimummy every evening, a gin and tonic in his hand, making small talk as if they are in an officers' mess. He even gets her to go on the second-hand piano he's had tuned for her, and listens dutifully as she runs swollen yellow fingers across it, failing to play a scale.

Every evening when I get home, it is the same. Burrimummy wants the key; she wants her passport; she wants to go home to India. She wouldn't survive it. The servants would strip her, leave her for dead like they did before. I begin avoiding her.

When I walk through the door after a long day's work, she shouts and cries, 'Give me my key, Poppet. I want to go back to Bangalore.'

I know I need to ride this out until she stops asking to go. I think of her lying in a nursing home in her own filth. She is clean here, cared for. She just needs to get used to us, to Trinidad. I say, repeatedly, 'Where would you go, Burrimummy? Who is there to take care of you?'

She goes still, lying in her bed, not bothering to go to the bathroom anymore, soiling the bed.

'You can't keep me hostage for my things,' she says.

Just when I decide to give her the key, just to keep her quiet, she announces one evening that Sadiq has bought her a ticket back to Bangalore.

I can't believe it.

I shout at Sadiq. 'She's old. She will die if she leaves. I can't understand how you, my husband, could make such a decision; after all, she is my grandmother, not yours.'

He's unapologetic. 'She's a grown woman. She wants to go home. I respect that.'

How could she go behind my back and conspire with my own husband? Why wouldn't she speak to me? It becomes part of a battle between Sadiq and me. A long-standing one. He's scored a point against me by pitting my grandmother against me. I am not so much surprised by his betrayal as by hers. I start crying, saying to Burrimummy, 'You don't trust me.'

She says, 'It's so hot. It's so hot.'

I beg. 'Who will take care of you?'

She is implacable. 'I never knew it would be like this, or I wouldn't have come.'

I say, 'I can't lose you.'

Her reasoning is ineluctable. 'I must go. I have a house. I have to get it for Angel and for you.'

The vultures will rip her to shreds.

Exhausted and disappointed at how ungrateful she is, I lose it, tell her how she'd used me when she was unwell and now that I'd looked after her, made her better, she'd encouraged my husband to deceive me. I call the doctor and say she's raving and ask for help. He writes a letter saying she shouldn't travel. I wave it in her face.

'Burrimummy, you can't travel unaccompanied. I better hold on to that ticket for you until you're better.' I show her the doctor's letter saying she was not fit to travel.

She gives me a bitter little knowing look, as if she's expected this of me. I spend less and less time with her. She stops asking me about the key, but keeps saying, 'I was better off in Bangalore.'

'Burrimummy was not better off in Bangalore,' I whisper to Sadiq in bed, wanting to believe it. This was my chance to restore her and secure a place in her heart, to be her beloved child. For weeks when I go into her room, she turns away from me. Looking at her body, curled towards the wall, I know I've blown it, whether or not she goes back. The nurses and Sadiq are taking care of her. I hear her speaking to Angel on the phone.

Angel and Andy move back to Trinidad permanently. They live with Mummy and Daddy at first. When they buy a home that looks much like Rest House Road, I am grateful for her return, thinking Burrimummy could divide up her time between us. I look after Angel over the next few months, helping her set up her dentistry business, occasionally babysitting her toddler.

Angel visits Burrimummy every evening but can't keep her.

I heap food on Angel. 'You don't eat enough. You're too thin.' We are stuck in our roles. I fret as if she is still an extension of me, not expecting her to be able to look after herself, let alone Burrimummy. She and Andy are working full time. Burrimummy stays with me, getting unhappier, roving the house like a tigress saying, 'I'm trapped, I'm trapped.'

One morning she buzzes for me before I head out to work, and I think she's forgiven me. After I kiss her forehead, she says, 'I don't know why I keep dreaming of snakes. I see them everywhere now. You know, I used to keep Nur's milk locked up next to me so the servants wouldn't steal it.

When I got up one night and unlocked it, a fat coiled snake was drinking it. It had the head of a human. I don't know if I dreamt it, but I'm sure I saw it.'

My skin crawls. All my life, I've feared and been revulsed by snakes, unable to even look at them in photographs or on television – this after an incident when a python slithered into Daddy's dressing room, and his orderly cut it in half with a cutlass, but it kept moving, so Daddy shot at both its separately moving parts till they were still.

Who could that snake be?

'Whose face, Burrimummy?'

'It looked a bit like your mother, and you look like her, don't you, dear, but I didn't realise it then. I didn't know what your mother would be like when she grew up, did I? I got a fright.'

That is Burrimummy: insinuating, cruel, self-serving and compelling. Knowing her defies every premise about mothering and forgiveness. I can't resent Mummy for not taking care of Burrimummy, for leaving it up to me. Mummy's defiance of Burrimummy is her refusal to be crushed or dispossessed.

TWENTY

Port of Spain, 1998

When Burrimummy first came to stay, I hired a day nurse. We installed a buzzer for her, and she started buzzing all night, alarms all equal in urgency – *Check my sugar, bring water, bring tea, press my feet, I can't see, I want bread, I want cheese.* I got a night nurse, too.

But this brought complications. She'd ask the Trinidadian Indian nurses what state they come from, what language they spoke, the religion they follow. She'd ask the Africans what kind of food they ate and if they wore grass skirts at home.

'She's racist,' I tell Sadiq.

'She's old. She doesn't mean it. She's curious.'

When the nurses don't answer, she says they're ashamed of themselves. She snitches on them when they have a sandwich or a shower. She has them going back and forth like tennis balls. Each evening I return to find a nurse outraged by her volley of commands; I mollify the nurse – or make calls for a new one as most stay only for a few days. Burrimummy is always surprised when an offended nurse doesn't pitch up.

One day I find Jaanaki's name and address on a post-it on my desk at work. She is an acid attack survivor. My television editor has assigned me to interview her. It's at a time when I'm frightened at how the violence I cover has permeated me. What if it happens to me? Every year over fifty women are maimed, shot, killed. The murderer is always a man, a husband, a lover, a drug-pusher, a stepson, someone close to the woman. It seems to take so little to set these men off. They are tinder. Sadiq gives me no indication that he would ever hurt me, but I look at him suspiciously, starting when he touches my shoulder. Menace smothers the house like a blanket. This is how societies disintegrate. Daddy says I see snakes where there are ropes, imagining things, that I'm a soldier's daughter, and I must soldier on.

The cameraman and I drive uneasily and stop just short of the hill in Port of Spain controlled by over 250 gangs, where Jaanaki lives. Over five hundred boys have died from one another's bullets, scrabbling over turf. Jaanaki lives in a rundown building, part of the government housing built in the 1970s. We walk up narrow, dirty stairways strewn with old KFC

boxes, bones, used napkins, darting cockroaches, until we find her apartment. I realise this is the area where my mother-in-law grew up, and think
of her with renewed admiration.

Jaanaki opens the door to the light outside. I hope my face is shadowed,
that she can't see my recoil at the sight of her pink nostrils and Dalmatian
pink-and-chocolate-coloured patterned face. Her forehead had receded
deep into her hairline, and her bent fingers are a mottled ham pink. She asks
to sit in the shadows in the front room facing the yard where men are
beating steelpan.

Her parents left Caroni village after the sugarcane factory shut down and
were lucky enough to get this apartment. Few East Indians were awarded
government housing. Her father, an alcoholic, had died years ago; she'd nursed
her arthritic mother for five years till her death the previous year.

She's not in touch with her family; her sisters, who ostensibly reject her
for being creolised, are repulsed by her face. She worked as a clerk in a
government office when her policeman partner accused her of an affair she
was not having and threw acid on her, corroding her face, dissolving bones.

She points at a photo of herself on a cabinet covered with a dirty
crocheted doily. I peer in the dark, and she says, 'That was me.' In the
photograph, she looks like a dark, velvety beauty queen with vivid eyes, a
pretty face and thick hair down to her waist. 'I could have had anyone. But
I went for Stephen, a policeman – like Pa, he was jealous, with an eye for
the women. He would put his gun down on this table here and play with
the lock as a warning when he got jealous of how men looked at me. I
thought it was because he loved me too much. I was flattered.'

After the attack, she had to leave her government job for a long
rehabilitation. She got some compensation money, but it was running out,
and now, even though she was functional, after people saw her face, they
didn't want to give her a job.

'Come work for me,' I say as the cameraman packs up. 'My grandmother
from India needs someone to care for her. You can sleep over some nights.'

Jaanaki agrees and arrives that very evening. I greet her and take too long
to hide a fresh shock at her charred face and receive a knowing bitter smile.
We agree on her salary in the kitchen over a soft drink. I show her where
she is to keep her things or where she could sleep on the nights we go out,
in the children's 'toy room', amidst strewn Lego pieces and stuffed animals.
An extravagant rocking horse that Mummy and Daddy gave to my son on
his sixth birthday dominates the space.

Burrimummy's eyesight is terrible in the dimmed light, and she doesn't
comment on Jaanaki's appearance. I ask Jaanaki to give Burrimummy her
insulin. Jaanaki picks up a cotton ball to disinfect Burrimummy's arm
before injecting her insulin, and Burrimummy makes her usual quip,
asking her if it was for her face or arse. I worry Jaanaki will take offence, but

she smiles, and I am relieved. Later Jaanaki says, 'I thought you say she was a Indian lady, but she is a Venezuelan.'

Jaanaki is surprisingly efficient. She cleans up Burrimummy gently, showers her, organises her medications, takes her for a short walk in the garage, and back into her room.

Soon we hear cries of 'Jaanaki, Jaanaki' all day and sometimes all night.

But it's not long before Burrimummy starts complaining about Jaanaki. 'She eats loaves and loaves of bread, she steals.'

Things slowly begin to go missing from the house: a child's hairbrush, soap, cartons of milk. Beverly says she can't find a pot and a frying pan. I can't find a silver tray. An emerald ring goes missing, the only one left after the robbery. I tell Sadiq things are missing, that Burrimummy thinks Jaanaki is stealing. I'm still sorry for Jaanaki and would have carried on giving her the benefit of the doubt if Sadiq hadn't criticised me while defending her. He shouts that I am careless, untidy, and, like all bloody Indians, I am paranoid about the helpers. I treat them like slaves. He will not tolerate it.

I confront Jaanaki outside Burrimummy's bedroom, averting my gaze from her eyes squished inside the pink lids. 'Do you know where my ring is? How can a pot disappear? Can you look for the missing things?'

We can hear Burrimummy roaring, 'That woman is a thief.'

Jaanaki picks up her bag and leaves. I run behind her, but she keeps walking. I return to sit by Burrimummy's bed in my work clothes, wordless, wondering how to manage the situation. I call in sick.

'You created the problem,' Sadiq says, 'you solve it.'

But he goes off to look for Jaanaki.

I don't know what Sadiq says to her. He says that she's coming back on the condition that only he gives her instructions.

I am furious that Sadiq has taken Burrimummy's care out of my hands, but I can smell the faeces from Burrimummy's room and can't face it.

Jaanaki walks in and puts down her black handbag with greater confidence. 'Mr Sadiq offered me twice the money to come back, so I said okay.'

I say nothing. I am furious at this extravagance we can barely afford but grateful for the help. The missing things reappear, the ring by my bedside, the tray under a table, the pan under some lids.

A silver ashtray, a painting from India from Burrimummy's wall, umbrellas go missing. I complain to Sadiq. He does nothing.

'Like last time, you've misplaced it.'

'I don't think I'm removing paintings off the wall,' I reply.

He shrugs.

I go to Jaanaki. 'Tomorrow, when I get back from work, I hope to find everything.'

After Jaanaki leaves, I notice Burrimummy's sheets have not been changed.

In the morning I say to her, 'Well, have you found any of the missing things? The silver ashtray is worthless, you know.'

'Look at you,' she says. 'You have it all. I know fair-skin Indians like you from India feel you can rule us. You act nicey-nicey, but it's all show-off. TV, your rich husband, your big house. I used to be prettier than you. You still complaining. You will lose everything. Look how your grandmother stink. Excuse me please, I need to clean her up.'

I turn away, knowing I need her.

She complains to Sadiq.

'Who else could have taken everything?' I say to him.

His mouth set, he begins a hunt around the house. I follow him as he throws things around, looking in cupboards, in corners of the house, inside baskets and buckets, under beds.

'Jaanaki hasn't changed the bedsheets for days,' I say. 'Burrimummy smells.'

He tells Jaanaki to bathe Burrimummy. When they are both out of her bedroom, he looks under the bed. He finds everything there.

'Who hid these?' He's taut with rage.

I recoil at his anger, absorb shame that isn't mine and stammer, 'Burrimummy must have done it.'

'You said it was Jaanaki, and now you're saying it's Burrimummy?'

'You think I hid my OWN things to set up the nurse and Burrimummy? Why would I?'

Jaanaki brings Burrimummy back into the bedroom. She says she's sick of 'aspirations' being cast at her.

'You mean aspersions?' I say.

She throws me a hate-filled look.

Burrimummy lies back in bed and looks at us with interest.

Sadiq says, 'You can't treat Jaanaki like that. Look at her state. I credited you with more compassion, but I suppose this is how you treat servants in India.'

I sought Jaanaki out, heard her story, always took her side over Burrimummy's. I don't know if I said it or thought it.

Jaanaki has a half-smile on her face, the smile of a woman who thinks I have too much, who would like to bring me down a peg or two.

'Mr Sadiq, please don't fight with your missus because of little old me,' she says. 'But I must speak the truth. I believe your missus put these things in Mrs Baig suitcase to fire me. She don't like me. I believe she fevers one of the night nurses.'

'Favours,' I say, understanding what Jaanaki has done. She's hidden everything till it's convenient to steal at one shot.

Burrimummy says, 'Or she may have hidden everything to make it look like I did it or that Jaanaki did it. I don't know.'

Was Burrimummy accusing me of setting her up now?

I run upstairs to the bedroom and ring Angel. 'I can't do this alone any longer, Angel. It's Jaanaki and Burrimummy. They're warring. Sadiq is furious, blames me as usual. I'm exhausted.'

'I'll come as soon as I can.' Angel sounds reasonable and contained. I feel a surge of resentment against her. She had promised to return to Trinidad to help; she had returned, but she would not keep Burrimummy.

'I'm not staying here to be insulted,' I hear Jaanaki shouting.

I run downstairs to see Jaanaki holding her black handbag.

Burrimummy comes out of her bedroom, walking firmly, her back bent low. Her cheeks are rosy. 'My baba, what happened? What happened? Oh, God, did I do something?'

Sadiq says firmly, 'No, Burrimummy, you did not.'

'I hired Jaanaki,' I say. 'She was stealing. You take the side of a maid over me?'

Burrimummy watches with interest.

'Get out,' Sadiq shouts at me and turns away.

'You didn't hear your husband?' Jaanaki pushes me through the side door into the oil-stained garage, past our cars, towards the empty kennel. She hits me on my back, and I feel a shove and land on cardboard and concrete. Kneeling, my head grazes the roof of the kennel. I can't breathe. I smell illness, stale dog smells, smell our dog, Pushkin, who died of cancer some weeks before. Through the bars of the kennel, I see a kneeling figure, the white of her uniform, the flash of a curled pink hand waving at me, then vanishing.

I sit hugging my knees and close my eyes, unaware of the passage of time. I notice a rind of an orange and wonder about it. I get a flash of walking in a mall in Simla with Mummy, terrified of the monkeys that came suddenly at me, snatching the peanuts from my hand, Mummy's warm body as she pulled me close and said, 'Don't be scared my little quarter pint. They won't harm you.' And Daddy holding my arm at the skating rink in the fresh cold air. I hear voices and open my eyes.

Burrimummy and Sadiq are sitting on rattan chairs. I can see and hear them through the bars of the verandah. Sadiq with his feet stretched out, Burrimummy with crossed legs as if it was the cocktail hour. She is drinking something with ice, shaking the glass around. Sadiq is drinking, something clear, must be his usual gin and tonic.

He draws a cigarette from the silver box she'd presented to him, offers her one, lights hers, then his. I can hear her voice, snippets of a story I know well, at ease as if on the lawn of the Bangalore club in the evening, waiting for her silver service tea.

'Sadiq, darling, you know my mother put padlocks on everything, the store cupboard, the silver. She locked up clothes in steel trunks. She wore keys around her neck on a long thick chain that dangled at her stomach. One day that damned chain went missing, and she was convinced her ayah stole it. She called the ayah in, assembled all the servants, summoned the locksmith and made him lock up the ears of the ayah who cleaned her dressing room. The hole in the ayah's earlobe, already big from wearing cheap jewellery, tore wider under the heavy padlock. The next day Mumma found the chain in the drawing-room where she'd removed it after a party.

'Wow.' Sadiq says, passing his hand over his head. 'That's brutal.'

'I know,' Burrimummy says, 'absolutely savage.'

I hear the clink of ice.

Burrimummy appears the most normal I have seen since her return, like the grandmother I knew from 17 Rest House Road; Sadiq looks like Abbas, Burrimummy's young brother, filled with a casual privilege so huge he doesn't see it. She puts her head back and laughs. So does he. A flash of white teeth, a pointed white swollen ankle.

'Where is Poppet?' she asks.

Sadiq shrugs and lights another cigarette.

Of course, Jaanaki did this to me. She did it for Khaja, for every indentured labourer, for every badly treated Indian servant. She did it to avenge every battered woman, every poor woman without means or education. I am low hanging fruit. The wretched of the earth don't go to heaven. They bide their time and pass on the brutality like a stick on fire, as if it will stop burning if you give it to someone else.

I hear a click, the gate opens, and Angel pulls me up, brushes the dirt from my clothes. I have no idea how long I've been in the kennel. Too ashamed to look at my sister, I go to Burrimummy and Sadiq, shaking.

'Burrimummy, did you do this just to get rid of Jaanaki?'

Burrimummy looks at Sadiq. 'Did I do something?'

'Hide things. You must leave,' I tell her. 'It's either you or me in this house.'

Sadiq says, looking at Burrimummy, 'She stays. I can't let you put an old woman out of my house. You go.'

'Sadiq, darling,' Burrimummy says, 'does she want to leave because I'm here?'

'You are going nowhere while I am here. If anyone leaves, it will be her.'

I don't know if either of them knows I was shoved in the kennel, but I am furious with shame at them. I know what I must do. My hands shaking, I go upstairs and call Daddy. I tell him briefly what has happened. Then I go through the yellow pages and find a home for the elderly. I ask if they have space for one lady, a Mrs Baig, eighty-four-years-old, with diabetes and a failing heart. They do.

I tell them that I'll be there with her that evening.

By this time, Sadiq has left the house with Jaanaki. He must have paid

her off. I throw Burrimummy's things in an old suitcase and wait for
Daddy. When he arrives, I put them in the back of Daddy's car. Mummy
takes it all in with a sense of inevitability. Perhaps she, more than any of us,
saw it coming.

'Please, Aapa, keep her till I can make arrangements to have her,' Angel
says.

'Not for another second.' I understand I have let Angel down, but she
doesn't see my pain.

'What have I done, my darling?' Burrimummy begins quivering. 'What
have I done? I was calming Sadiq down for you. I've done nothing.'

I shove her into the back of the car. 'I'll bring the rest of your things
tomorrow.'

Burrimummy's departure changes little outwardly, except I clean out her
empty room and throw her smells away. I give away the piano I bought
for her and throw away all signs of her, including the cup and saucer by
her bedside.

TWENTY-ONE

St Lucia, 2016

Another night of insomnia. I lie awake to the grating chorus of cocricos and frogs, and wake, heart pounding, to a strip of sun slashing at my eyes. I walk out of the room to sit outside, waiting for the kettle to boil. The ocean is a flat blue, the sky flatter. There is a quiet here that should calm even the most disturbed mind, but my heart pounds as, showered and changed, I walk across to the house with a beach towel.

Derek is ready for the beach in shorts and a hat, like a boy prepared for an outing. He's holding my manuscript.

'That fear of violence in your marriage. How long ago was that?'

'Years ago.' It feels like yesterday.

'You stayed. Why?'

'Sadiq wasn't violent. It was an irrational fear, transference from my work. I saw snakes where there were ropes.'

I wonder at my slavish devotion to Walcott, to male, privileged writers who felt free to dump a family, a country even, to look after their own art. Some say we admire those we cannot be. I see writers like Walcott and Naipaul as being every bit as privileged, selfish, and as sexist as the great Romantic poets, from Byron, who put his child in an institution, to Percy Shelley, who discarded his first wife and, while with his second, slept with other women.

Derek writes of elation and the fermenting of continents and the sweetness of children in crisp ribbons and uniforms coming out of the churchyard into the brightness a hot St Lucian day. He writes of recreating identity leaf by leaf, banishing the residual hurt of slavery into something beatific, reflecting the landscape. He sees all that, but he doesn't seem to see Sigrid or anyone else, except concerning himself, his work. He gets to be the poet.

He is already thinking of something else.

'What happened to your grandmother after that incident?'

'I took her to a nursing home.' He looks frightened.

I think, 'Oh God. He has diabetes too.' Wounds that won't heal.

Sigrid arrives, beach bag in hand.

I notice Derek's hands, his eyes, like dried leaves, faded and blurred. He shouts, 'Sigrid, let's go.'

'We are going to look for the One Dollar Beach,' says Sigrid.

We set off, Derek in front, with Sigrid driving, me in the back.

We drive on roads bordered and overhung by a cathedral of thick trees, the monotony of green broken by the fluorescent houses and brightly painted roadside shacks and parlours. Every now and then, glimpses of sky and ocean.

It's all here, the stuff of his *Omeros* and his watercolours.

Sigrid says, 'I can't remember if it's called Five Dollar or One Dollar Beach.'

Derek says, 'Keep driving. We'll find it.'

In the backseat, I feel even more like a child – their child, just letting myself feel the breeze carrying the promise of rain, the sea, the smells of dense trees, wet earth, flowers. Derek turns around and gives me a darting look. I remember St Lucia was once known as 'Louanalao' by the Arawak Indians around 200 AD, meaning 'Island of the Iguanas'.

I practise the names of the island: Anse La Raye, Gros Islet, Soufriere; think of how a sixteenth century French privateer, Francis Le Clerc, put his stamp of centuries on this island, and how Derek's stamp will override that.

We wind slowly down towards Castries, past the Church of the Conception with its gingerbread balcony and gables, past the square named after Derek with its big bandstand, palms and a samaan tree and glimpse the ocean beyond the land. Finally, we come to a dead-end on a dirt road where we see a barebacked man with glistening skin walking with a cutlass.

Derek shouts, 'Is this One Dollar beach?'

'Nah,' says the man. 'Try the bumpy road from the petrol station.'

We follow that road to another beach.

'Nope, this isn't it either,' says Sigrid, driving on.

We stop again. Sigrid swerves off the main road and parks under a thicket of bamboo swaying and crackling with gusts of wind. The sun filters white light through the green cover onto what looks like the ruins of a Roman amphitheatre. Leaves blow about on its abandoned stage. I brush some leaves off what looks like a carved seat, one of many in semicircular rows facing the stage. Sigrid says the theatre was built to stage Derek's plays, set within the landscape he loved. The people never came to see them. The day begins to feel like a requiem to his old charged-up sense of possibility.

We don't find the beach, but eventually, Sigrid stops in Gros Islet, the fishing village where *Omeros* is mainly set. We sit in cabanas by the beach, watching boys take horses into the sea for a swim; the rain starts falling in thick drops, lashing at the tarp.

Derek says, 'Imagine the full moon rising out of the sea every month.' He recites his own lines. '*Where is your tribal memory? Sirs, in that grey vault. The sea. The sea has locked them up. The sea is History.*'

When the rain stops we move to the restaurant and order dinner. While waiting for soup, Derek says, 'Sigrid, the car. Move it. I want to see that sunset.'

Sigrid gets up. The rising tide has churned the beach into a tangle of stones, seaweed and flotsam. We watch as she moves the car. When she returns, her face is red. She is about to sit down when Derek says, 'I can still see it. I want it out of my sight. I want to see the sunset.'

She gets up again shifts the car about, creating imprints in the sand.

When she returns, he says, 'Sigrid, I can still see the damn car. I can't see the sunset.'

'Where, Derek? The sunset is lovely.'

'You see the sunset? I'm looking at metal. It belongs to a car. Not a sunset.'

Sigrid gets up again to do Derek's bidding as he picks at his food. I put my fork down in silent protest, unable to eat.

When Sigrid returns, I daren't look at her. It's the price of serving greatness, but she looks at Derek with a smile and asks brightly, 'Who's having dessert?'

Derek sits stony-faced. Dinner was fried fish and soursop juice, as pulpy as if we had just picked the fleshy fruit off a tree. The meal felt like detention, as if we are all supposed to digest his unhappiness.

The rain stops. Yellow light bores a hole through the pewter grey, turning us all, momentarily, into beatific, molten beings.

We drive home in silence in the thick tropical darkness. I go to my little room, change into my pyjamas, and circle like Burrimummy until it's almost light. I recall Derek's large mottled yellow hands and the roaring impotence of her large ageing body. You scrabble around the rubble of their lives – Burrimummy's, Derek's – looking for something from them; you turn away from ordinary people and realise by that you mean people who won't hurt you.

I sit outside and look across at his shaded veranda; empty chairs and tables throw ghostly shades from a single lightbulb.

'Write in the present,' he's said repeatedly. If we sit moping or writing morose poems and novels glorifying a nonexistent past, time passes us by.

I think he's had all his life to read and write and look at the light. Others, mostly women, do the stuff of the low fever of domesticity necessary to live. The male experience will never be the same as ours. Naipaul said the world was what it was, and we should stop whining and get on with things. He, too, walked away from the birth country he thought inferior – that, too, was an abandonment.

Much of what I remember of those years is in my work, among the nine hundred columns, the documentaries, the news reports. Reading them now, my life appears to have happened to someone else. I hadn't been paying attention to myself. Now Derek is forcing me to remember that time. But is it crucial to give brutality a face? Does naming it rob it of its power, and squeeze the life out of it? I had been in a cage. I looked for answers in the cage of all cages: in the prisons.

I went to the prison authorities and asked to interview those who had committed the worst crimes – the rape and murder of a minor, the killing of the elderly and women, the bludgeoning an entire family. I walked through security, saw my internet had been cut, handed in my phone and handbag, and went into a small dark room where six men sat surrounded by armed prison guards.

I told them, 'I don't want to know what crime you committed. Tell me about yourself, your parents, your childhood.'

A sixty-year-old inmate answered. He had lived in prison, six to a cell, let out for airing only for an hour a day and for meals since he was nineteen. They'd denied him contact with the outside world, so he spent all his time reading. He was in for the sexual abuse of a minor, a baby girl, and bludgeoning a man to death.

He spoke with moist, professor-like eyes. 'I was nine. My stepfather beat me regularly, broke belts on me, rained blows on me, and made me sit on a cheese grater for hours till my skin came off, and you saw blood and bone. Around then, I began collecting pigeons. I loved them, watched them grow, fly and return. One day my stepfather came home drunk and told me the pigeons were annoying him and sent me out to buy cigarettes. When I came back, he told me to go and clean them. He had slit their throats in the sink. When I cried, he made me kneel on the grater and whipped me and made me eat the meat.

'The happiest day of childhood was when my half-brother, just a baby of four, took a hammer and hit my stepfather on his head. As the blood poured down his head, I laughed and laughed and laughed.'

The inmate said thoughtfully, 'Just as my stepfather overpowered those pigeons, I raped a baby. I never thought I would be grateful for these years of endless hours simply to wonder why I am on earth. I know what it is. It is to see other people hurt just like me, to know they feel my hurt, and I feel theirs. It took incarceration and a terrible deed to make me see that.'

The inmate reminds me of the gems in the rubble of human mess, hard found human redemption. To cancel our dark sides is to live in a blank sanitised world, where no one has the permission to examine the debris of our souls, no one is granted redemption.

In my room, a reprieve comes that is as welcome as it is unexpected. Overcome with exhaustion, I sleep instantly.

TWENTY-TWO

Port of Spain, 1999

Under the noonday sun, I head through St James to Victoria's Nursing Home to Burrimummy, past the Chinese casinos, the Syrian cloth shops. The thump of calypso beats the air; a booming bass emanates from rum shops. I listen with Burrimummy's ears, jarred by the tunes set to nursery rhymes: 'Jump! Jump! Jump! Wave! Wave! Wave! I pass the Catholic Church on Long Circular Road and weave through Delhi, Calcutta and Mooniram streets – a patchwork of indentured labourers' memories from India – and slow down near James Temple, translucent white, lit lovingly by its keepers, a powerful symbol of the Hinduism that Burrimummy thinks has destroyed her life, and past the heavily guarded compound of the Jamaat Al Muslimeen, a refuge for the over one hundred men charged with murder, treason and an attempted coup.

Victoria's Senior Residence is a two-storey building, painted in beige and bearing a plaque that reads 'Inaugurated by the late Archbishop Anthony Pantin in 1990'. She is better off here. Only a mile away from our house, I can get to her in minutes. The home is inhabited by more than two dozen people in varying degrees of decay. Spotting an attendant through the burglar-proofed grille, I call out, 'Good day!'

'Good day,' the nurse calls back, rising to let me in. 'It lock,' she says. 'I go harra get de key.'

Several faces, crushed as stale tomatoes, peer out at me – bored, lonely, curious and resentful. Inside, I greet the nurse and, one by one, each of the old people. They sit enervated, febrile, or shivering in the torpor of the afternoon humidity in the television room. One emaciated man is slowly scratching himself as if drawing out the activity; a woman is standing in the middle of the room as if suspended in time and space; others are reclining, crossing and uncrossing their arms, spreading out the time. As I walk past them, they turn worn faces towards me as if in a slow underwater ballet. Burrimummy's quarters, the large room she shares with five other 'residents', are clinically clean and smell like a hospital ward. The room is laid out to maximise space with beds and cupboards with their names tagged on and, for those like Burrimummy who need them, commodes. Pine disinfectant rises from the terrazzo floors; a heavy floral air freshener mingles with stewed chicken and macaroni; beneath it lurks a foundation of human excrement, sweat and urine.

The woman in the bed next to Burrimummy's is beautifully dressed; the lace around her collar looks unnaturally white against her crepe-like neck. She has the wasted proportions of a supermodel; a beam of light hits a cheekbone, and I can imagine her at eighteen, elegant, proper. She nods politely at the nurse who asks her if she's finished her untouched meal. Old people get wafer-thin when they are dying slowly.

Burrimummy's bed is in the corner, close to the one window. She is illuminated by the afternoon light. The rest of the room is airless, dimly lit. With the light from the open window on her, she looks like the main act. She is curved into her usual C-shape, legs hanging to one side, one foot touching the floor, her torso on the bed – as if she is ready to get up and walk out. I can never visit without remembering her bitter smile, as if she expected this of me.

The blades of the fan that Angel bought her wheeze; a fly buzzes around a plate near her bed. I uncover it: stewed chicken, macaroni pie, some limp lettuce leaves. I take Burrimummy's soft face in my hands. 'Eid Mubarak, Burrimummy.'

She opens her mouth and eyes.

I sit at the edge of the bed.

'Poppet,' she says, 'where are the children?'

I am careful with my reply. 'They're at their grandparents.'

'Where is Sadiq?'

'Sadiq is still at the mosque.'

She has stopped asking to go to India. She has her locker key around her neck and her passport is in her cupboard by the bed.

'I waited for you this morning. You said you would come before going to the Masjid.'

'I came, but you were asleep. We all came.'

She twirls one hand slowly as if unscrewing a light bulb. It means she doesn't believe me.

'See what I brought for you.'

I empty the bag of nighties I've brought; they're of the softest muslin, in shades of olive and apple-green, cream, chocolate, lemon, rust-rimmed with silver. I'd walked for hours in the dead afternoon heat in downtown Port of Spain on streets smelling of anger and hustle, in and out of a dozen Lebanese cloth shops before I found them.

'What is it? Tablecloths? For the matron?'

'No, Burri, nighties, so soft. For you. Feel it.' I press one to her hand. 'Look, Burri, your colours.'

'Later. I can't see, I can't hear.'

I put them away in her cupboard marked BAIG in white chalk.

I feel pressure on my arm. Surprisingly firm. 'Burri?'

'Poppet, I need to send a letter to India to my bank manager.'

'Burri, there is nothing in the safe.'

'No, he's a friend. I want him to forward it to my lawyer. I need to get the money for the house. It's for you and Angel and Nur.'

'Give me the letter, Burrimummy.'

'No, I will give it to Sadiq.'

'Can I see it?'

'I'll show Sadiq.'

There is a rustle of silk.

'Eid Mubarak, My The.'

Mummy arrives, looking as if she had been transported from a brightly coloured world to this drab black and white one. She moves the air around her. She is dressed in a lace peach sari for Eid. Her face is luminescent, bare of make-up except for her plummy lipstick.

'Eid Mubarak, Nur. What did you bring to eat?' Burrimummy says.

'Faloodah and mangoes.'

Mummy wanders off to get a spoon.

The picnic basket is a version of the one Khaja carried containing our school lunches.

Mummy returns and spoons the sweet vermicelli sprinkled with ground pistachios, almonds and rosewater into a bowl. I give her my place on the bed. She feeds Burrimummy.

'It's a bit thick,' she says, spitting an almond. 'Nur, you can't cook, you know. Good thing you are good-looking.'

She reaches under her pillow and hands Mummy a sealed envelope addressed to her manager at the State Bank of India in Bangalore. 'Nur, will you post my letter?'

More Burrimummy drama.

'I'll send it by registered post, My The.' Mummy looks absurdly happy.

Burrimummy put her hands out, yellow, bloodless. 'My hands are bare. I can't live with bare hands.' Her distress is so real that I can't dismiss it as one of her dramas.

Mummy takes off all four gold bangles. She slips them on Burrimummy's swollen hands with some difficulty. 'Forgive me, My The, for all the times I've hurt you.'

Burrimummy's eyes are wet. 'Come here, Nur.' She pulls Mummy's face towards her and kisses her forehead.

'May Allah and his prophet bless you, my Nur. I've never stopped...'

She doesn't finish the sentence but says, 'Give.'

Mummy looks radiant, as a six-year-old child at birthday party spooning the vermicelli dessert into Burrimummy's mouth. White jelly slithers down her face in a rivulet to rest inside the cavity of her remaining breast.

I smell urine and Burrimummy's breath and taste my breakfast in my throat.

The attendant walks up to us and asks, 'Wappen? You wastin' your food again, Baig?'

'Can you please give me a towel to wipe her?' I ask.

'May I have bread 'n' butter, sister, may I?'

'Just now. I go see if I have time.'

Mummy takes a corner from her brocade sari, turns it to the soft side, and wipes Burrimummy.

'I'll go, Amma,' she says. 'Ved is waiting outside. Poppet will bring the basket for me.'

'Khuda Hafiz, my Nur, my Jaan. Please don't forget to post that letter. Rest House Road was always for you, Angel and Poppet. Please remember.'

Mummy leaves quickly, as if worried that Burrimummy will take back her benediction, the thing she's longed for all her married years.

An old woman shuffles back to her bed. She is preparing for her afternoon nap: creaming her hands, fixing her pillows in a mysterious order, putting on a thick sweater even though it is the dry season when the temperature rises to a steamy thirty-six degrees.

Burrimummy closes her eyes. I want her back.

I search for some memory to restore her power. I remember she'd seen Mrs Simpson during her honeymoon. I'd never known if they'd met.

'Burrimummy, tell me about your honeymoon. Did you meet Mrs Simpson? Was it at the opera?'

She shouts at me as if I had abused her. It was an error. I'd forgotten Burrimummy reserved grandeur only for herself, conferring it, refusing to let you share it by association.

'No, I did NOT meet MRS SIMPSON and THE KING OF ENGLAND. I saw them at the opera. That common bitch, that haramzaadi, that daughter of a pig, that COMMON woman, she MADE him abdicate. She FORCED him just so he could look at her ugly face all day.'

Noticing my stricken look, Burrimummy softens. 'But Nur's father, your Saied-uz-Zafar Khan, and I DID go to a party at the British embassy in Vienna at which they were present. I refused to curtsy to her. But I did have a nice conversation with Lord and Lady Willingdon. You know, darling' – her belly shakes, the way it used to in anticipation of laughter – 'when I was getting married in Bombay, I got fantastic presents. Mother kept a tab on everything, getting our secretary, Mastaan, to write them down and pack them carefully in various suitcases. The only thing missing when we set out on our train journey out of Hyderabad to Bombay was a solid-gold alarm clock encrusted with emeralds given by the Maharani of Jodhpur. We all hunted and hunted. Nobody could find that clock. You wouldn't believe how we found it.'

She's back. She's back.

'Please tell me, belovedest,' I say, overcome with happiness.

'We had almost the entire train to ourselves. I was asleep with our cousins, Ayesha and Mahbanoo. The ayahs were sleeping in the corridor. In the dead of night, we were awoken by a shrill noise. We thought we had arrived, but the train's wheels were thundering beneath us at a pace. Ayesha got up and hurried down the corridor. Mother was shouting, "Follow the noise! Follow the noise!" We all followed Ayesha to the end of the train till she sat down and covered her ears. Mother reached into Ayesha's blouse like a master detective and pulled out the whistling alarm clock from her nightdress. Mother said she would have liked to thrash Ayesha, but that would be like admitting to the world there was a thief in our family.'

I am laughing. Burrimummy is laughing. I lean over and clutch at her. She grips me tightly, shaking. There is a terrible smell. She is leaning on me with one hand and the other turns towards the commode next to the bed. Once on it, she slumps, her back curved.

'I want water on me,' she says, not looking up.

With the name BAIG branded on it, her nightie clings to her back; her silvery hair, with a few black strands, is stuck to her forehead, wet with perspiration.

I wave to the nurse. She comes to the bed.

'Can you please wash her hair?'

'There is no more shampoo.'

Burrimummy speaks as if she had been disturbed from a piano recital: 'I've been asking them to wash my hair for three days. They say they don't have shampoo. I know Angel has brought lots.'

'Shampoo done. Every day she wants her hair washed, and I wash it.'

Burrimummy says, looking down, speaking in Urdu now, 'She doesn't, you know. She doesn't.'

I look from one to the other.

'Please, bathe her; please, wash her hair.'

'I go see if I have time.'

'It's Eid. On this day, especially, she needs to be clean. So she can pray.'

'I go see.'

She walks off. I stand there, not knowing what to do. Burrimummy speaks in Urdu. 'That woman,' she says, pointing to the nurse, 'is always pushing and shoving me while cleaning me.'

'She pushes you, Burrimummy?'

'Yes.'

I change the subject, distraught. It's all my fault.

'Have you had lunch?' I ask her. I look at the untouched plate by the side of her bed.

'No, I'll have bread 'n' butter.'

I run to the kitchen, to the nurse sitting down with a cup of Ovaltine, her feet on another chair. They are swollen.

'I'm so sorry to bother you. Can my grandmother have some bread and butter?'

She looks at me as if I am mad.

'She have food by she bed.'

'Please.'

'I heard you the first time.'

'She will get sores if she's not clean. I brought shampoo. I brought soap.'

'I don't thief.'

'I'm so sorry. Please. Look, my grandmother doesn't know what she's saying. I believe you. I know you look after her as best as you can. I will bring more shampoo.'

I take out $100.

'This is for the shampoo.'

We both know that shampoo costs $20.

I go back to Burrimummy.

The nurse returns to the bed.

'What happen, Baig? Like you vex with me or what? Come, let we clean you up.' The nurse picks her up.

I take one side and the nurse the other. She shakes us off. 'I can walk, Poppet.'

I glimpse Burrimummy through the open door, her back hunched. The nurse goes in and out with baby wipes, clean panties, a towel and closes the door. I return to Burrimummy's bed. The dim light transforms Burrimummy's dorm into a theatre set.

'She okay,' the nurse says, bringing Burrimummy back, heaving her legs up on the bed. 'She clean now.' Burrimummy gives her a look of restrained rage.

The nurse leaves and returns with a sandwich with squares of processed cheese between two slices of white bread. Burrimummy starts chewing, knees in the air like old times.

'Burri,' I say. 'I'm going to India and then London for a few months.'

'I can't hear.'

'I'm GOING TO INDIA. Burri, I'm going to India with Mummy and Daddy and Winky.'

'To see your Nath uncles?'

'To Bhopal.'

'You are going to stay in the old palace?'

'No, Burri, that palace is in ruins now.'

'Then where, at the new Mahal?'

'No, Burri, that's a hotel.'

'Then, where?'

'At Shamla Kothi.'

Her face darkens. 'Why? There's nothing there. Mumma never wanted me to leave Bhopal. She always said Bhopal had a nineteen-gun salute; it came second only to Hyderabad's twenty-three-gun salute, and Puppa replied he didn't care if Savanur was the smallest of six hundred states, it was the oldest, dating to the sixteenth century and his ancestors had served every Mogul emperor since Aurangzeb. Bhopal only became a princely state in 1818.'

'Are you glad I'm going, Burri, to the same house where you lived when you got married?'

'I don't remember it. I don't know what you're talking about.'

'I'll miss you, Burri. I love you. I'll be home in six weeks.'

'Khuda Hafiz, my darling, I'll miss you.'

I feel unable to breathe in this airless room. I can't stay any longer.

While I watch a thin woman shuffling to the bathroom, Burrimummy says, 'Every morning, Nur's grandmother had her English secretary, a woman called Stella, bring me a formal embroidered Bhopali suit and whatever diamonds or emeralds she wanted me to wear. It means nothing, you know, when your husband is off with another woman. I preferred to spend my day in dressing gowns.'

I smell something. Very sweet rancid urine. She tugs at her adult diaper.

'Poppet, please take my Quran home. It's unclean here.'

I find it between nylon nighties, wrapped in the dark-purple velvet cover I remember from Rest House Road.

Suddenly, her eyes fill. A teardrop quivers on her nose.

'You know, darling. I never hid those things. I would never hurt you.'

I am filled with remorse and shame.

I close my eyes, unable to meet her watery ones.

'I know, Burrimummy.'

'May Allah and his Prophet be with you. Come home soon to your old bag.'

TWENTY-THREE

Bhopal, India, 1999

At the airport in Trinidad, as Winky, Mummy and I prepare to board a flight to London, Sadiq presses a credit card into my hand with a generous sum. 'Look after yourself.' Angel, occupied with her business and small children, adds, 'Have fun. I'll take care of Burrimummy.'

The invitation to attend a wedding in Mummy's ancestral home in Bhopal had come from Burrimummy's sister-in-law, Bia. Looking at photos of the two women when they were young, there was Burrimummy – tall, wilful, powerful, educated, a princess of Savanur – and Bia – smaller, delicate, a girl from a conservative family in Pakistan. They were married around the same time in the 1930s to two brothers, nephews of the Nawab of Bhopal. Both women were widowed when they were still young.

My grandfather, Saied-uz-Zafar Khan, died first, at a party, before he turned forty. Burrimummy had left by then, after a five-year marriage. Some years later, his younger brother, Rashid-u-Zafar Khan, died after having sired four children, leaving the entire estate to his wife and children. My grandfather was the elder brother, and by rights, if Burrimummy had stayed, she would be in Bia's position today. Mummy, characteristically unbothered by all this, was keen to attend the wedding, be among her people, and Winky and I agreed to accompany her.

On the flight, I whip through a book on my ancestors, *The Begums of Bhopal: A History of the Princely State of Bhopal*. It fills in some spaces in what I know. I learnt that in 1818, Bhopal became the second largest princely state in British India after the Anglo-Bhopal treaty between the East India Company and Nawab Nazar Muhammad (Nawab of Bhopal between 1816-1819); that my great-great-grandmother, Sultan Shahjahan Begum, whose mosque I visited in Woking, was Bhopal's begum for two periods (1844-60, with her mother acting as regent) and 1868-1901. She was the last in a line of four women who ruled Bhopal for over 111 years and built Shamla Kothi for the wedding of her elder grandson, Saied-uz-Zafar Khan, to my grandmother.

Burrimummy never met her father-in-law, Mummy's grandfather, General Obaidullah Khan, the brother of the Nawab of Bhopal, who died of colon cancer, but she spent a lot of time with his younger brother, her uncle-in-law, Hamidullah Khan, the then Nawab of Bhopal, who invited his nephew's abandoned bride to his wild, all-night hunting, swimming and dance parties at the farmhouse and palace, to make up for Saied-uz-Zafar Khan's defection from his husbandly duties.

Burrimummy knew the Nawab Hafiz Sir Hamidullah Khan had no sons, that her husband, the elder brother, was his favourite of his two nephews, but after Burrimummy left and Saied-uz-Zafar died, the younger brother, Rashid-uz-Zafar, gained complete control of his father, General Obaidullah's property. When Mummy, Saied's only daughter, married a Hindu, the stage had been set for her legal expulsion from a share in a property built for her father. At his death, the Nawab was succeeded by his daughter, Sajida Sultan. The Bollywood star, Saif Ali Khan, today holds this defunct title.

Winky, sitting next to me on the flight, tells me he 'knows' Mummy and Daddy met Rashid-uz-Zafar, Mummy's uncle, and Bia after their marriage at the Taj. Winky claims that he heard that Mummy's uncle was curt with them, didn't offer them anything more than lime juice, told them that his younger brother died heavily in debt and sent them on their way. Mummy, being young, filled with ideas of nobility from her grandfather, asked for nothing. Daddy also remained correct, chivalrous, with his soldier's pride, saying his wife wanted nothing and would accept whatever her uncle thought fair. Her uncle gave her a settlement of fewer than two lakhs. Later, Bia told Mummy that her uncle was unhappy with her for marrying a Hindu. Whatever the story, we were going to Mummy's ancestral home, and she had no part of it.

During a stopover in Delhi, Mummy and I go to an uptown mall and splurge on saris, tunics, silks, chiffons, and enjoy trying on luxuriant fabrics, embroidered shoes, sinking into the luxury of India.

At the Bhopal airport, Zoya, Bia's daughter-in-law, a tall woman in jeans, short hair and a wide-open smile, greets us warmly and garlands us with jasmine and roses. She is deferential to Mummy and playful and familiar with us. Winky declines her hand and hugs her, saying, 'Hello, Pretty.' Her intimate manner with us suggests a homecoming. When she is out of earshot, Winky says dryly of the effusive welcome: 'It was once your father's property. Your uncle kept it for himself. It's the least they can do.'

Mummy shrugs him off, says vaguely, 'Please don't speak of all that. It's in the past.'

In Zoya's jeep, we leave behind the din of the flat basin of the city. Zoya points out the Shamla palace on the hill, a façade of faded red brick, a shell where birds nest and weeds grow, now the almost abandoned crumbling property of the current Nawab of Bhopal, Saif Ali Khan, the Bollywood actor. While others are in awe, Mummy sees it as a stain on her family that the cricketer, 'Tiger' Pataudi married an actress, and it's a matter of shame to her that her cousin, their son, Saif Ali Khan, is an actor.

We stop and look at the palace. I know from Burrimummy's stories that this is where my grandfather dropped dead after drinking a cup of coffee early one morning after a wild party. Our grandfather died there, and they don't even know of our existence, I think. Remembered conversations between Burrimummy, Mummy and Daddy help me to put the pieces together.

Bhopal was the second largest state of the Raj, and at Shamla there was plenty of space to go around. Bia had coped with widowhood by filling up Shamla with her Pakistani relatives and, when it was time, marrying her sons to her nieces to consolidate her position as the sole owner of the entire property. Bia's sons, Asim and Asad, with Afghan physiques and the same face as Mummy, now run the whole show – the stud farms, the hotels, the lot. They are trading in the former exclusivity of these places for hard cash; they will not suffer like the maharanis hanging on in the crumbling wings of palaces with a single servant. Newly rich Indians are willing to pay for access to a world denied to their parents.

We stop for coffee in one of the hotels and see the centuries-old arched corridors, courtyards, vast ordered gardens. Stuffed tigers, photographs of the Begums at coronations, and trophies won at the races are on display. We suppose we are meant to assume they belong to the younger brother, as our grandfather is not mentioned. The only thing left of my grandfather are framed black and white photos of him at white and black-tie events, dancing at parties with European women, and close-up photographs with what could be any glamorous but forgotten movie star. He's purely decorative here, and when any of the family asks about him, he's laughed away, as if he was a recalcitrant child/man who loved horses, women, stud farms, and put the family into debt by giving everything away.

We rattle along a narrow road toward Shamla Kothi, with its many apartments, courtyards and wraparound balconies and stop under an ivy covered garage. Its entrance is guarded by two chowkidars.

Zoya, married to one of Mummy's cousins, lives in the grandest apartments, the ones Burrimummy lived in sixty years ago, as a new bride of eighteen. Glimpsing Zoya's garden, with its manicured sloping lawn and a graceful Venus pouring water, looking down towards the misty lake below, I think this must have been Burrimummy's view. We follow Zoya and a peon carrying our baggage from the garage to the circular veranda where lurid magenta and lilac bougainvillaea cover tall, circular white columns. I remember Burrimummy saying that her father-in-law, General Obaidullah Khan, couldn't decide what he wanted, so he invited all the architects he admired to design a palace that combined British Colonial, Italian Renaissance and Greek styles. Zoya stops by a door leading to a vast room with high ceilings, four-poster beds and old Persian carpets. This used to be my grandmother's bedroom. It is now Bia's bedroom. I picture Burrimummy sitting on the lawn as a young bride with Mohammed Ali Jinnah, my grandfather Saied, and the Nawab of Bhopal, speaking of partition and Bhopal's future, and now lying curled up like a C, in a home for the elderly in Trinidad, turning her face away from yam and cassava. I think of Burrimummy, a young woman filled with rage and passion, at Bia's desk, looking out over the landscaped gardens, writing letters to Savanur, waiting for her husband to come home, too sickened with heartache to touch the pianos in the house. What heaviness she must have felt; I wonder at how lightly she let it all go.

Winky and I are put in the nursery, where I imagine Mummy was put as a child, with space enough for a nursemaid to look after her. After we unpack, I wander around on the dimly lit veranda, looking for Mummy; I find her sleeping in Bia's four-poster bed.

Bia smiles at my surprise. She's too elegant to look like anyone's grandmother, slim, dignified, and commanding. She says, 'Your mother slept in this room as a child with your grandmother. After your grandfather died, they used to visit me here, and we all three slept in this room. It's okay; she's comfortable with me.' She puts elegant fingers on Mummy's head, and I leave, thinking about how we are all our ages at once.

Little has changed in the lives of the women of these erstwhile royal families. A manservant brings us tea with papaya. We breakfast on toast spread with fresh thick cream from the family farms. Over lunch, we meet the rest of the family, the children of my granduncle Rashid, and their children. Servants scuttle around us, serving up hot dishes and then dessert, coffee and fruit on china, with linen napkins in silver rings embossed with the Bhopal insignia. The conversation rolls around stud farms, the new nature resort, which recipe was passed down from which royal household, the bridal outfit.

They don't speak about Burrimummy; she is as taboo here as she is in my father's family – and no one mentions Saied either, except to say he shot the tiger stuffed in the lobby. Zoya, though, mentions them once.

That night, sipping lime juice, sitting on the roof, looking at the moon on the lake, Zoya tells us about ourselves, how on this spot our grandfather's youngest brother shot himself. The stories of brutality go back and back in Bhopal. Memories of my great grandfather, General Obaidullah Kahn, are still here. Winky and I hear stories we feel we have heard before, from Burrimummy. We know it was here, somewhere in these rooms, that General Obaidullah imprisoned his pregnant daughter-in-law for marrying his youngest son, Wahid, in secret, and somehow the girl and baby died. Zoya says, 'Wahid got out of bed one night, stood here and shot himself in the head. Over a woman whom he got pregnant.' The general also reportedly slapped another great-aunt so hard for not pronouncing a word in the Quran correctly that she died of a concussion, though it was put out that she died of diphtheria. We inherit not just the physical DNA from our ancestors but the emotional DNA. The begums were strong rulers, but the men they imported from Afghanistan for their strength and looks were cruel. And so, the most dramatic of stories are woven into everyday life, making the calamitous ordinary. This is how cruelty is normalised. I stay on the roof wanting to understand where Burrimummy came from, where Mummy was born and why she left. Before we go to bed, Zoya says, 'Your Burrimummy put a curse on us when she left, saying no daughter-in-law of this house would ever be happy.' From the sadness in her eyes, I wonder if she believes this to be true.

In less than twenty-four hours, we are absorbed into life at Kothi as the family prepares for the wedding of one of Mummy's cousins' daughters. The staff have created a set of *Heat and Dust*, with white tents on the vast lawn, stages, dance floors, cocktail bars. There are tall vases of freshly cut roses on every table. On the lawn every evening, people are stretched out on sofas with linen covers and silk cushions, while a live band softly plays Urdu Sufi music.

We mingle with the descendants of conquerors: privileged, moneyed people who have been marrying their own kind for generations, creating an entirely separate breed of Indians and Pakistanis. There are men in cravats reminiscing about Oxford days and languidly stretched-out groups of women, who look as if they've spent their lives in designer shops in the world's capitals, talking of marriages between their children. They are the elite of India and Pakistan, with tentacles in big business, politics, Bollywood, old aristocracy and titles, art, land, and flashy apartments in New York. Some descendants of these erstwhile rulers are impoverished, have lost everything but some jewels and a crumbling palace or two, but even they retain their sense of entitlement and contacts from the past.

They sit around waiting to be coaxed out of themselves by some delightful diversion, eyes hooded with smoke and alcohol, served by turbaned bearers in white, carrying silver trays. An army of staff manages everything so smoothly that one event goes on till the following day, then on to champagne breakfasts, then piling into jeeps to go to the stud farms for more poolside parties, picnics, and late-night drinking around open bonfires for the younger adults freshly returned from university in Europe.

No one speaks of the rise of tech India, one of the fastest-growing economies of the world, or of the prime minister, Modi, changing history books to erase the last traces of the Mughal influence in India. They don't speak of the Bhopal chemical disaster, the gas leak incident on the night of 3rd December 1984 at the pesticide plant at Union Carbide India Limited, that may have killed up to eight thousand people and maimed generations.

On that night, high in their mansions on the hills, these people locked up their doors and windows and remained safe.

Burrimummy did the same at Rest House Road – rubbed out all of India except the ditties the British brought, the potted meat she had for tea, and her horror of the ignorant Tamil servants whose biggest crime was to be unaware of manners, the English language and hygiene.

Winky and Mummy blend in seamlessly. It's as if their beauty gives them a similar privilege to the rest of the people here. Both are surrounded by admirers, needing to say little. Winky was born for this with his inbred languor and soporific, seductive eyes that accept all adulation. Tall, broad Winky, whom Burrimummy called Zafar, after her husband Saied-uz-Zafar, with his cheeky sexiness, boyishly handsome face, is a walking magnet for women of all shapes and sizes, colours and ages. In Bhopal, everybody pretends that he is just called Zafar, like his late grandfather. Our Hindu roots remain politely unacknowledged. Winky himself is increasingly obsessed with his resemblance to his grandfather, photographed with trophies he'd won at the races, dressed to the nines, surrounded by actresses – Parsee and white women. Of the trophies themselves, there is no sign.

'Really?' Winky asks, wide-eyed, as he listens to the old servant sitting on the floor chewing paan. 'Do you think I look like him? Really, did he have THAT many women? I have had nearly as many.'

Winky and I wonder how Mummy stands it, still managing to look more languidly entitled than the lot of them, how she could bear to see the initials of her mother and father everywhere, on the diamonds worn by her cousins and their children, on the entrance to the homes. After lunch, one of my uncles' grandchildren, my second cousin, shows Winky and me diamond buttons with an 'S' and emerald earrings. 'I'm going to wear this on my sherwani. It belonged to your grandfather.'

Winky lets them know he doesn't give a damn. He holds his rupees lightly, giving them away to the servants or anyone who makes a half-convincing plea. He's got what none of them has: his grandfather's looks.

Before the wedding, I see the women trooping towards the main drawing room where Mummy remembers a polished crystal chandelier and life-sized portraits of all the begums. We understand it's the viewing of the jewels before the wedding. It's the custom to show off what the bride has and what she's getting. I watch women pour into that room; it contains at least one of the four pianos my grandfather brought for his bride, my grandmother.

I follow the crowd to the viewing of the Bhopal jewels. I see the Pataudis being welcomed – the arm of the family that includes two famous actresses, Kareena Kapoor and her mother-in-law, Sharmila Tagore. The women are wearing obscenely expensive clothes, bags and diamonds that could feed the people who served them for years, holding drinks in soft, manicured hands.

I am about to enter the drawing-room when a member of the family –

so kind when I first arrived – bars my way: 'Please, don't pass through the drawing-room.'

The drawing-room, displaying jewels my grandmother has worn, belonging to my grandfather, is also shut to Mummy. She doesn't give a damn, she says, and she looks it, just as she doesn't give a damn that the late cricketer, the Nawab of Pataudi is an uncle, that Saif Ali Khan is a cousin. She is quietly contemptuous that they married actresses, and that's all she cares about – not their wealth or position but that they dance half-naked for a living. Her immutable sense of who she is, a Muslim princess of Savanur and Bhopal, who traces her genealogy to the sixteenth century, centres her. That and the love she had until she was six from her mother and grandfather.

'Never mind,' Mummy says, 'we have only a few more days here.'

Winky comes right out and asks her one evening, as she sits on the lawn with a Kashmiri shawl around her, looking as if she had lived nowhere else: 'Why don't you care, Mummy, that you lost everything?' She says, 'Oh, your father and I came here after getting married. They said there was nothing left, that my father had gambled it all away. They gave me a little bit, and I banked it.'

Winky responds sharply. 'But this is all worth millions, Mummy; their lawsuits are covered by *Time* magazine. You got nothing.'

'Leave it, Poppet and Winky. I have my family, and they are kind to me. That's plenty for me. No one gets everything. Life is a package. Your grandmother had plenty, but she wanted more. She chose to leave.'

I say wonderingly, 'Mummy, is it your looks or your childhood with your Savanur grandparents that makes you care so little?'

'I don't know about my looks, dear, but my mother loved me once. She gave me my faith, taught me the Quran, and I'm grateful to her for that. It's never failed me.'

'Would you do it again?'

'No. No. I would have listened to my mother. I would have, maybe, if she had spoken with kindness. Kindness is everything, you know. All this is nothing.'

I am introduced by another younger family member to various people. 'This is Poppet, our cousin from the West Indies.' The otherness I get in Trinidad follows me here.

As Mummy orders more tea in the garden, an old man who remembers Mummy as a child comes to her with trembling hands and tears in his eyes. Winky and I are with her, and his daughter asks us if we want to meet some locals who knew our grandfather. 'You both go,' says Mummy.

The daughter takes us down an alleyway leading to a courtyard shaded by a dense tamarind tree. An old woman in a darkened room tells us about our grandfather's generosity – so much like Winky's. How he never refused anyone anything. '*Chupa Valli*', they called him – hidden saint – for whom money was nothing more than the dirt of his hand. Then, suddenly, she is catching hold of my brother's feet, holding on to me, weeping, saying, 'All the pots and pans in Bhopal broke the day he died, all the food went sour for weeks.' It is the only real emotion we find linked to him.

We rush back to the Kothi. I sense we have committed some infractions, let down our hosts. Mummy's princely family on the hill rarely ventures down onto the streets of Bhopal. The daughter of the ancient man says, 'You know, a woman who once nursed your grandfather is still alive.' She gives us her number: a London number.

Winky says, 'Poppet, call now.'

We call, and a woman answers. Her voice rises when we tell her who we are and that we are in Shamla Kothi. She speaks eagerly, joyfully. Saied Nawab's grandchildren. She is clear. I can imagine her being vigorous when young.

'I met him in 1937, in Bombay when I worked at the St Georges Hospital as a private nurse. I was only twenty-three. He'd come to Bombay for the Royal Western India Turf Club races, run in the viceroys' races, and caught pneumonia there. He told me his horse, a bad-tempered stallion, won the gold cup. I nursed him at the Taj in Bombay for three weeks and for another three weeks in a flat in Malabar Hill. When he got better, he took me to Juhu beach for a picnic. I have a lovely picture of him that day. Your grandfather was big, tall – handsome in a rugged way. What he had was absolute charm. He could charm the ducks out of the water. He had a lovely smile, but, oddly, he was also a very modest man and could even come across as a bit shy. He had such smiley brown eyes.' We know what that means, another affair.

'After that, even when he was well, he sent for me every year, even after I got married. I was with his mother when he died, sleeping in Shamla. At about three in the morning, the servants from the palace arrived, and said, "You must wake up Begum Sahiba." I refused, saying, "I will wake her for her morning prayers." Then they told me Saied Nawab had died in the palace after a party. It gave me such a shock. He'd been to see his mother that night. He told us he was going to a party at the palace with the Nawab, his uncle. I took Begum Sahiba down to the palace across the lake and saw him flat out on a marble slab. Everybody said he'd had a massive heart attack. They said he had a cup of coffee and went to the bathroom and collapsed, but I don't believe he had a coronary. He checked himself out loads of times, and there was nothing wrong with his heart. Every morning he was up early, yachting or at the stables, riding. I daren't voice my opinion. It gave me such a shock. I'd nursed him for so long in Bombay that I'd gotten attached to him. His mother, Begum Sahiba, was so brave. Not a tear. She was so dignified – such a wonderful lady. For months after, every week, I used to go with her to his grave. She used to make me wear a dupatta to cover my head while she stood there. She was a very discreet lady; she never told me anything ever, and neither did his brother. He never had anything wrong with his heart. I never knew he had a daughter. I never knew he was married when I knew him.'

In her silence, I can see her calibrating her time with him. She's thinking, *he was married*. When people are too beautiful, they hurt everyone.

Winky and I look at one another. There are things we will never know, but we do know he was not a bastard, and why Burrimummy loved him.

The wedding over, Zoya takes me by the hand, as if to make amends for the insult of being banned from seeing the jewels. She says, 'Come. I want to show you something.'

We climb three flights of winding stairs and arrive in a tiny attic room with nothing in it except a bed and a steel trunk. Zoya unlocks the trunk and says, 'You might want to look at this. There are some old letters here that belonged to your grandfather.'

I find hundreds of letters. I whip through them, thinking that any minute Zoya could come in, stop me. There are thank-you notes from people my grandfather helped escape from Nazi hands, gratitude for money given, thousands of words of adoration. Dozens of photographs fall out of beautiful women in stylised poses from Bombay's Mehboob studios; there are photos of my grandfather on hunts and rides, dancing with European women, at the Delhi Durbar as a child, dressed as a prince. There are invitations to parties, the races, and descriptions of studs he might buy. I look at the photos of my grandfather in front of dead tiger after tiger and understand it was he and not his brother who shot them.

At the bottom of the trunk, I spot bundles of fine blue paper, neatly tied in black ribbons, written in a sloping, womanly hand. There are hundreds and hundreds of sheets, all with the Bhopal seal, written by a woman called Stella, Burrimummy's housekeeper, and, I think as I read them, quite possibly my grandfather's lover.

Shamla Palace, Bhopal

20.6.1938

My dear Saied Nawab,

Lady returned from Chiklod at 10:30 pm last night after having had dinner at Ahmedabad. It was at first thought, when her message arrived at 7:30 pm saying H.H. had left, that they would come here and have dinner, but they went straight to the palace.

She got back in a nasty temper, and no one knows why – she howled and yelled at her servants till dawn. Mrs Richardson tells me she kept grumbling about you being in Bombay so long. Saied, everyone wanted to know why she was not with you! (We would never tell them if they asked us!) And, if you intended to stay most of your time in Bombay, why shouldn't she stay there too!

She did take that black witch ayah this time and left the old man behind, so Miss

Wilson could not have accompanied her. Before going to Chiklod on Saturday evening, she had a padlock put on her bedroom door and locked up the whole place securely; I don't know who she thought would steal her things or what secrets she has hidden there.

She has been extolling the virtues of H.H. all day, what an utterly charming man he is, and so very kind, etc., etc.! There's one thing your mother and I have noticed: she is not going to the palace as often as before. When I returned from Bombay in April, she went there every evening, and if she did not go early enough, one of the girls came to fetch her, but now no one comes. Lady only goes there every second or third day. Perhaps her Highness and the girls are seeing through her, but they will never own up to it!

She has just ordered a whole lot of stuff to the value of Rs 4,500 or 5,000 from Asquith and Lord's – riding kit, trousers and shirts and another sporting kit. If you give her unlimited credit and not a fixed allowance, she will go on spending. Her own money she keeps shut up, will not even buy herself a packet of chocolates! If she does, she sends me the bill!

Did I tell you about the shoes she bought? Mrs Richardson came with a bill of Rs 10/ 8 for three pairs of shoes. I asked your mother and paid, and she then said that if she knew I was going to pay up so quickly, she could have gotten six pairs instead of three! Does she really think I control her expenditure, and can she not understand that I am given a small sum of money to keep only to spend it with Begum Sahiba's permission?

Begum Sahiba is so marvellous, behaves just magnificently, and never by word or deed lets anyone see how trying this girl is to her. She came in to see your mother at twelve o'clock today; she, looking like a sick cat, hardly spoke and just sat and played with the baby. She simply hates this daily visit, and you can see it in her face! Your mother treats her so kindly and with such remarkable dignity.

Begum Sahiba asked again when the old Savanur man was returning, and she was grumbling about it to Mrs Richardson, said he was her father's servant, and she was not going to send him back and was going to keep him here as he was very useful to her – of course, he is here as a watchdog, that's obvious.

Love, Stella.

Another letter. In Mumma's hand.

April 1938

My Saied Nawab,

I hope you are quite fit and strong again by the grace of God. You have always been so sweet, affectionate, and respectful to me, and I can never thank God enough for these noble qualities in my son.

I have wanted to write to you for some time, and I hope you will forgive the delay. You seem to be drifting so far from us, and this distance makes me feel so sad. I don't know where this letter will find you, but wherever you are, my love and thoughts are with you.

Dear Saied Nawab, many changes may take place, and fate may work strange things, but a mother can never change towards her child, and I love my child, Shahnur. I shall feel dreadfully sad if things go wrong and pray and trust Him, King and Master of this universe, to put them right. But if you think you cannot avoid the crisis and it is impossible to love my daughter again, let us do things in an amicable way instead of an ugly one.

I will try to make the girl understand that a small part of her life is over. After all, she is very young and that stands to her advantage. Besides, time is a wonderful cure for all heartaches. Thus, it can be settled quietly and sensibly. Life for a girl is very uncomfortable when companionship is dead, matrimony is dead. You have a heart of gold, and I know the girl is true and sincere, but loyalty and sincerity are not appreciated in this world. I am not writing this from a single point of view, but fairly and justly, like a person unconnected with either party. I always tell my children to ask God to open the door of their innocence and to give them the ability to realise a true friend from a sham one, as it breaks my heart to see them fall into false hands. No matter what you decide, act with kindness. My daughter may seem proud and robust but believe me when I say she loves you more than anyone. I wish I were clever enough to express myself better.

Always your True Friend and Mummy

Zoya said I could *look* at the contents in the trunk, the inference being they were the property of Shamla Kothi. On the last day, I walked around the property trying to absorb my grandparents. I looked at the tiger skins everyone claimed were shot by his brother Rashid. Histories had to be rewritten. The young widow had to survive and to do so, she had to obliterate my grandparents and mother. There were tears in Bia's eyes when she bade us farewell. I had taken as many papers as possible, shoved them under my shawl, and run to the guest room like a thief. Mummy says it's all rubbish. With the crumpled letters and the Wikipedia notes, I have plenty.

Almost as if I need proof of what I've witnessed, I look my family up on Wikipedia. I am startled to see my grandparents, the denouement of Empire, a bloody history of fractured lives, reduced to a tiny footnote on the Bhopal Royal Arc website.

Lieutenant-Colonel Fakhr ul-Mulk, Nawabazada Muhammad, Saied uz-Zafar Khan Bahadur. b. at Jahan Numa Palace, Bhopal, 17th January 1907, educ. privately. Cmsnd as 2nd-Lieut. Bhopal Sultania Infantry 10/9/1925, attached 1st Btn, The Black Watch 1931–1932, attached to the staff AHQ Mhow, 1932–1933, Military Sec to the Nawab 1934–1935, Maj and Cdt Bhopal Sultania Infantry 25/4/1935–1936. Rcvd: Silver Jubilee (1935) and Coron (1937) medals. mm. (second) at Bombay, 23rd May 1936 (div.), M Nawabzadi Shahnur Jahan Begum Sahiba [Begum Pasha] (b. 4th October 1914; m. second (div.), Colonel Mirza Sikander 'Ali' Baig, and d. from diabetic complications at a nursing home in Trinidad, 1997), eldest daughter of Major Meherban Nawab Abdu'l Majid Khan Sahib Bahadur, Dilair Jang, Nawab of Savanur, CBE, by his wife, Meherban

Nawab Khaliq un-Anisa Begum Sahiba, eldest daughter of Brigadier Mumtaz Yar ud-Daula, Nawab Mumtaz Ali Khan Bahadur, Mumtaz Yar Jang, sometime cdt the Nizam of Hyderabad's Sharf-i-Khas Troops.

i) Sahibzadi Anwar Zia Sultan Begum. b. April/May 1937 (d/o Shahanur Jahan). Settled in Trinidad. m. Delhi 22nd August 1960, Colonel Mahendra Nath (b. at Aligarh, 1932), Educ. DC Coll, Aligarh Muslim Univ, National Defence Acad, Dehra Dun, and Defence Services Staff Coll, Wellington, second son of Amar Nath, a zamindar from Aligarh, UP, by his wife, Kamla. She had issue, with one son and two daughters.

Two paragraphs for whole families. Even if this record is a watermark in the sand at high tide, it's a record that a vanished world existed, pouring its DNA into time, into us and the future. It's what all lives are reduced to. I wonder whether gathering up shards of the past will fill up the craters within me.

On my way to the airport for our evening flight to Delhi, my cousin tells me Burrimummy shot a tiger in the forests around Bhopal. I imagine her in a bathing suit with her white, white legs and all eyes on her, and the moonlight on her pale, lovely young face.

Burrimummy may have sat where I sat looking at the lake, deciding to pack up and leave when she was just twenty. I knew my playboy grandfather had women in his Bombay flat, but these photos, these letters are all tangible evidence of how spurned she must have felt after giving up her beloved piano for him. She was spied on, controlled and lonely. She rode out of Bhopal, the second richest state of India, to save her heart even if that intractability led her to loneliness and a second marriage where she was abused and used by her own cousin from the Pakistani military. She continued to love Saied-uz-Zafar but would not ask for anything from the wealthy family she left, either for herself or her daughter, proud of her lineage, founded in 1672 by Abdul Karim Khan, an Afghan from Kabul. She poured that excess love into Mummy, and when Mummy defected, she had nothing until Angel came along. I will show Burrimummy the letters. Let her know she was her Mumma and Puppa's beloved child.

TWENTY-FOUR

Kelly Village, Trinidad, 2000

She has been dead for less than twenty-four hours. On a hot day when the earth cracked, and leaves bristled, Burrimummy lay inside an open wooden box on the concrete floor of the shed, swaddled from head to foot in five separate lengths of white cotton. My grandmother's tiny band of mourners – Nur, Ved, Angel, Winky and I – stood under the shed watching the grave being dug with a mechanised excavator.

I feel Winky's hands heavy on my shoulders. We look at the box, at her face set as if in yellow marble. Burrimummy kicked him out of her house into a boarding school when he was a boy, after shooting a rubber band at a maid's breast. There was a rift for twenty years. She wouldn't forgive him for calling her a Pakistani spy or choosing Mummy over her. But when he unexpectedly turned up at the nursing home, his latest woman sitting in the dark outside in his car, with the engine still running, Burrimummy seemed to have forgotten all that and deftly took ownership of his looks.

'You are a very good-looking man – well-built, beautiful eyes, a typical Afghan Pathan, the kind imported by the Begums of Bhopal. You've taken after my brothers, who were both well over six feet.'

'Really, Burri?' He was longing for more. She gave it to him.

'Really, Winky.'

With a schoolboy's open vanity, he loved talking about his looks with a passion only rivalled by his obsession with women and theirs for him. 'It's a curse,' he said with unmistakable pride every time another woman punctured his tyres, flooded his house, and called him till he changed his number.

Grandmother and grandson happily spoke of his charms for the next thirty minutes, with Winky demanding to know what his grandfather looked like, whether he, Winky, was taller, and who was better looking. Then he overstepped. He never knew when to stop. Was it true that Zafar, his grandfather, liked Parsi women, Jewesses? 'In what way am I like my grandfather, Zafar? After all, you did name me after him, even though you think I'm a kafir.'

Burrimummy's face turned hard, 'No, you aren't a bloody shit like Nur's father. You don't go around with every randy whore in town.'

But that was just what Winky did, and she knew it. 'But I'm sure he loved your big white legs and round ass?' Winky reached for her bottom, fondling its sagging folds.

'What kind of talk is that Winky Baba – to your own grandmother?' she said, coyness in her crumpled face.

He pinched her. She screamed in a mock way the way she once did with her younger brother. They used filthy language like children in a colonial rose garden a long time ago, as if testing out forbidden words: behen-chot, sisterfucker; sewer ka baccha, son of a pig; motherfucker.

Burrimummy was more alive in that one short visit of his than she had been in all the hours Angel and I stole away from our lives to sit with her in the dark nursing home.

Mummy stands at the foot of the coffin, a still figure around whom a silvery grey sari billows, as if she is posing for an artist. At sixty, the childlike appeal of her perpetually startled, almond-shaped eyes give her the look of a brutalised calf, but I know her steely centre will hold her.

'She white like you,' the mortician says to Mummy. 'You is the daughter? You sure you don't want to touch her face?'

Mummy sinks, the folds of her sari blooming like Burrimummy's painted wood roses on the concrete. She holds her mother's unyielding feet swaddled in white cotton. 'Maafkaro, Amma. Forgive me.'

On her knees, her face contorted, she has the hungry, lonely expression of an abandoned child. I crouch by her, holding her, whispering, 'Remember, Mummy, she blessed you,' and support her weight as she slowly stands up.

The maulvi signals that it's time for the janazah – the prayer for the dead. Sadiq joins them. The men assemble, stand shoulder to shoulder – the undertaker, gravediggers and maulvi. In a dreamlike sequence, lips moving silently, saying the prayers in Arabic, the men kneel and rise in unison, their faces not registering the discomfort of repeatedly dropping to their knees on the rough floor.

Sadiq's dark face is ashen against his white shirt. He defended Burrimummy as if she was his blood as if he had more right over her than any of us. At times, he pitted me against her. It was to him and not Winky that she gave her father's gold cigarette holder, embossed with his name and title: 'Abdul Majid Khan, Nawab of Savanur'.

The grave is a coagulating wound ringed with red clay waiting to swallow her up. The excavator runs for a few seconds with the earth flying into the air like chocolate confetti, then cuts off. The gravediggers survey their work.

The janazah is over. The family, the maulvi, the attendants from the funeral home, and the machine operators scatter untidily. The men speak quietly for a moment, then close in on Burrimummy. A cock crows.

She would have liked the attention. She always had more respect for men. She would have fawned over the young visiting imam from Hyderabad speaking in Urdu. 'It's time. Pallbearers, please step forward.'

Daddy straightens up, hoisting his end. Sweat pours down his jawline and neck, but at sixty-eight, he still looks like a vigorous, straight-backed soldier.

The maulvi picks up a clod of clay, crumbles it and throws it in her grave, praying in Arabic. He says the kalma: 'La illah ha illall ah, Mohammed ur Rasool Allah.' God is one, and Mohammed is his Prophet.

As she is lowered into the grave feet first by the men, the maulvi translates Quranic verses.

Muttering prayers, the men throw in fistfuls of dirt one after the other. The gravediggers take over, shovelling blocks of clay, which make big thudding noises. A stiff breeze flattens the long blades of grass in the fields but I just have to close my eyes to go back.

Burrimummy sits at her piano with paan-stained mulberry lips, in her dressing gown, back straight as steel. Angel and I are in our cotton nighties on either side of her. Then she's bent over the keys, swaying in a circular motion, eyes shut, foot poised over the pedals playing her beloved Symphony No. 9. Her fingers turn feather-light, her low musical voice heavy with an old longing.

> Somewhere, my love, there will be songs to sing
> Although the snow covers the hope of Spring
> Somewhere a hill blossoms in green and gold
> And there are dreams, all that your heart can hold
>
> You'll come to me, out of the long-ago
> Warm as the wind, soft as the kiss of snow
> ………… think of me now and then
> Godspeed, my love, till you are mine again.

Angel and I linger, holding hands, remembering together, looking at the fresh mound before going to our cars.

TWENTY-FIVE

Burrimummy had been dead a year when Winky called a family meeting to tell us he had advanced colon cancer. We had been estranged since I married Sadiq, until our grandmother's death. He laughed wryly at our stricken faces, saying it was the same disease suffered by his late great-grandfather, Obaidullah. Daddy remarked that the Bhopal family had passed on something to him after all. I remembered how Winky had once written a letter to Burrimummy after she left Tobago. 'I love you, but I love Mummy more. If you want to continue to write to me, you must forgive my mother.'

But Burrimummy and her grandson, whom she called Zafar, after the only man she loved, never abandoned one another. Winky had made her funeral arrangements, not knowing indirectly that she would buy him time on earth.

After Burrimummy's death, I found among her things unsent letters to the lawyers and buyers in India about her 17 Rest House Road sale. The letter she asked Mummy to post to her lawyers on Eid day was enough to get matters started.

Daddy, who had power of attorney for 17 Rest House Road (which Burrimummy sold and reclaimed as a gift to Angel to prevent Mummy from getting her inheritance) had to appear in court in India on behalf of Angel and Mummy. When the money did come, a sum that could have bought a luxury home in Kensington, it allowed us to pay for advanced medical treatment for Winky, to try to give him more life. First, the money paid for the expensive chemo embolisation the doctors performed on him at the New York-Presbyterian Hospital, when they cut away the diseased liver and bought him six precious years before it took him.

Our visit to Johns Hopkins came after the fading of brief hope. Despite the hours of chemo he'd had, the cancer returned. His face, once the image of his Bhopal playboy grandfather's, grew huge with steroids, losing its shape, and then, three months before he died, became gaunt. He'd said firmly to the oncologist, 'No more chemo.'

We – Daddy, Mummy, Angel, Sadiq and I – rented an apartment in Baltimore near Johns Hopkins for Winky to have a drug that was still on trial, but his cancer had progressed too far. Even then, he flirted with a nurse. 'You're just like our grandfather,' I said, and that was the last time I heard him laugh.

In his final lucid moments, I asked him if he was afraid of death. He was not, he said with a wan smile. He'd had plenty of women, travel and work, made, lost and gave away enough money to last several lifetimes. No, he had no regrets but would I look after his two young daughters. I promised, but he need not have worried. The elder, Pixie, qualified as a lawyer and the younger, Adya, as a doctor. They did it on their own, as bravely as any Begum of Bhopal.

When Winky began shouting with pain, I knew it was time to take him to the hospital for morphine, and as Mummy and Daddy wouldn't make that decision, I had to do it. 'You're taking him to the hospital to die like a dog,' Mummy said about the morphine he needed to have. He was crying out as the ambulance staff carried him out.

When he died in Johns Hopkins, when I hoped the death rattle was just a deep restorative sleep, I felt a terrible betrayal, a cutting away of my own childhood. I understood, finally, what he felt when I got married, that I had broken our pact to be first for one another, before anyone else. I remembered how he picked me up from boarding school in England and took me to his university, where he locked me in his rooms to keep me safe from the other boys, cooked for me, helped me with maths, never allowed me out of his sight, took the train back from Plymouth to Beaconsfield with me, and the bus to my school, until I was safe there.

Even as his body lay there, still warm, waiting for the undertaker, I went to the basement of Johns Hopkins and placed the shoes the funeral director gave me next to my laptop – the only thing that hadn't gone into the incinerator – I wrote his obituary, which appeared in the *Trinidad Guardian*, published on January 14th 2007.

In a sunny flat overlooking a river in Baltimore near Johns Hopkins Hospital, our family spent this last month watching my handsome brother Winky die, his tall, powerful booming voice and body being ravaged by cancer.

We played a lot of scrabble and chess. We were all merciless when it came to the game. It was the way he liked it. No pity. No second chances. Checkmate was checkmate. Sometimes when he got too tired to play, I would hold my brother's hand and he mine. Together we would look at our interlocked fingers. His hands were twice my size, but the skin, the shape of the nails, and the shape of our palms were the same. Same hearts and bones. I would press my cheek next to his, feeling the warmth of our skin, not knowing where I ended and he began. The hollow inside me was an echo of his. There has to be a lesson in this, I thought, even though I didn't know what it would be.

After his cancer prognosis six years ago, through thirteen surgeries, the long chemo sessions that he described as a nuclear attack in his head, the light in his eyes dimmed even when he was in remission. I always thought of the human spirit as a concept, but I saw how empty eyes are without it.

We never acknowledge the bravery of living knowing you are dying. We don't realise how much of our zest for life comes with faith in the future. I talk of the law degree I've begun. It doesn't register. His niece buys him a calendar for Christmas, and he tells her quietly he won't need it.

Even with our arms around him physically, emotionally, we were sitting on separate boats, a man and his family drifting apart, us doubled over with the effort of stretching our hands out to him. But the tide pulled us apart, us to the living, and him towards the opaque mist.

In the end, with morphine, he was restored to his essential self, and it was as if we were children again, calling one another long-forgotten nicknames, from the times our parents loomed strong and protective.

He died six days after Christmas, and the lesson is dawning on me. Being with someone as they die is a miracle when there is no pain. As he took his last breath, he smiled. And afterwards, he looked as handsome as he was as a seventeen-year-old.

That's how Winky lived. He may have been afraid, but he never lived as if he was. From the time he was born in Calcutta in 1961, he lived vigorously. When we lived in Chandigarh, my mother was packing up her precious crockery to prepare for our shift to our father's new posting in Simla. Winky betted with me that he could jump over the lot. Before my mother could forbid him, he charged and landed in the middle of her precious crystal, and there was glass everywhere. The same fearless leaping made him headhunted in the construction industry, expertly turning around dying companies, quadrupling sales, and breaking into new markets. He defied my father's predictions that he would be a truck driver, walking away with an upper second degree in Construction Management from Reading University, England.

He was always leaping across glass. Sometimes he made it, sometimes he didn't, but he always jumped in and out again as if he knew his time was short. He had a vast life on three continents and spoke three languages. The world embraced his Bollywood charm and looks. His heart was in India; he loved the snowy mountains of Simla, leapt about army training grounds in Bangalore. He found love in a seaside town of England in Plymouth, in Costa Rica, and Trinidad. As the plane rocked on my way home after Winky died on December 31st, I forced myself to look at the dark clouds without fear.

TWENTY-SIX

St Lucia, 2016

On the morning of my departure, I sweep the room clean again and go down on my haunches with a damp cloth to pick up the remaining fragments of glass, pack, dress, and write a thank-you card, which turns into a lengthy apology for blowing up my hosts' stove, remove whatever US dollars I have from my wallet, stuff them in my jeans pockets and go straight to the kitchen where Sigrid is making breakfast, popping toast.

I blurt it out: 'I blew up your stove.' I hold out two one-hundred-dollar US bills. 'Please take this to replace it. It's all the US money I have, but I can send more to cover, you know, the inconvenience. I'm so sorry.'

She doesn't get a chance to respond. Over the monitor comes his voice, strong and loud. 'Sigrid, do not take money from that child.'

'I wasn't going to, Derek,' she shouts back. 'It's not a big deal. I was going to change the stove anyway.' Sigrid gives me a wide reassuring smile and offers me breakfast.

I am so relieved I don't know what to say. I have a cup of tea, and Sigrid wheels Derek to the porch and bustles away.

He gives me back my marked-up manuscript.

'You could be free.'

That's a thought.

'Your husband, do you love him?' Derek asks. He looks frail today.

My brain responds with images of Sadiq: tenderly standing in the shower with Winky, holding up his smashed body, washing all his soiled parts, shaving him, calling him 'son', even though Winky was older, sitting him down, dignifying him. Sadiq plunging through the crowd on the beach to give the drowning, frothing man mouth-to-mouth and walking away after the sputter of life. Sadiq weeping in my arms, saying, 'I'm sorry for all the wasted years and hurt. I didn't know better. I do now.'

I try to explain my experience of marriage.

'My father told me a story of how he landed a plane when he was a soldier. Impatient to take flight, he ignored the training. Midair, when it was time to land, he realised he didn't know what to do. So, he came down hard, with such a terrible force that the plane bounced up. He came back down very hard. By this time, he was sure he had broken some bones. I didn't have the words then when Sadiq and I were fighting. I didn't have the filter. But in the end, Sadiq and I found our way. We broke some bones, but we learnt and landed safely.

'You're taming the shrew.'

'You could call it that. Or he, me.' I laugh.

'You are happy with him.'

'I've got this amazing raw human. He is not mannered. He is brilliant, terrible. He is instinctual like your Caliban. I don't want to put labels on it. But I am finding a way of managing it and finding the elation of which you speak, in him, in his inchoate rage, in his loyalty.'

'So, if you see it in him, why not see it in Trinidad?'

I wonder if the taxi driver will be on time.

He keeps digging.

'You are frozen in a child's idea of India, of your grandmother, her gilded life. Why? Because you have not found your place here?'

'I am untethered,' I say, following his gaze so we are both looking out at the too bright ocean. 'I was temporary in Rest House Road; I feel temporary here.'

'Yes, but why did you write of your grandmother, a tortured relic of a lost gilded life? How can that comfort you?'

Liberated from the splintered stove, knowing I probably won't see him again, I speak, boldly.

'I acknowledge most of what you say, but I miss her. Whatever she was, she continues to comfort me even if she wasn't always kind; she runs like a thread through my days. I can't believe Burrimummy died.'

He says, 'You love people, and they die. My father died when he was thirty-one, in the most absurd way, of an ear infection. I was a year old and have no memory of him, except maybe I do. I thought I had a memory of him lying at the bottom of the stairs. That sparked the idea of memory as imagination.'

'So, you write for your father?' I knew it. Just as I write for Burrimummy.

'In a way, yes, I wrote to bring him alive – my mother must have sensed that, talked about him as if he had never gone. She didn't object to my decision to be a poet when I was nine.' He shuts his eyes, recites, '"Though they go mad they shall be sane; Though they sink through the sea they shall rise again; Though lovers be lost love shall not; And death shall have no dominion." You can't read Dante and Shakespeare and not see their work as elegiac. You are triumphing – coming out of tragedy. St Paul triumphs over death. Some great elegies write death in the present tense. There is only one tense in poetry, which is the present tense. What I'm saying is to write about the present.'

'I'll try that,' I say. 'And didn't Baldwin say, "Not everything that is faced can be changed, but nothing can be changed unless it's faced"?'

'So, you've faced it. You seem to have abandoned yourself, but Trinidad is porous, and you should let it in. People from every continent crammed into a tiny area like Port of Spain. Something is bound to ferment. Make something new. It is not Prospero who makes Caliban talk properly. No, tribal language is instinctual. Join that chorus now.'

I say, 'So you're saying, there is an advantage in forgetting old religions, old hatreds, old languages. Maybe in a few generations, after our children's children have finished with the gash of slavery and indentureship, we will have an identity we all yearn for as humans. Maybe when the people transplanted from old worlds – the Chinese, Syrian, Indian, European and African – are fully integrated and cross-fertilise, our small islands will represent a utopia to the world.'

'Now you're talking,' he says with a sly smile that gives me a flash of how devastating he must have been when he was in his prime to women. A smile that makes me think he led me here all along. I am not aware of the look I gave him, but the question came.

'Do you love me?'

'Yes,' I say, though he reminds me of my grandmother, though he already belongs in the past. 'Yes,' I repeat.

His face crumples like a brown paper bag. He knows what I have to offer isn't much. The best thing is a witness to his dying light. He'll take that.

The sun has shifted the lines on his face, softening his eyes, clearing his brow, like a Gauguin painting.

In his face, simultaneously, I see the one-year-old child who lost his father, the schoolboy, and the young man's vigour, the wolfish charm of a celebrated poet.

Burrimummy also lived many ages in an instant. You could see the eighteen-year-old in her, the chubby child rejected by her mother, the lover – as if her thoughts conducted all her expressions.

'Derek, what do you get from the sea?'

'Have you read my poem, "Love after Love?"'

I say, 'I haven't, but I will. I always think of you as I first met you, drumming. Thank you, Derek.'

Sigrid's voice, cheerful, relieved. 'Dear, your taxi is here.'

He's not done with me. He holds my hand as if we are at the end of a church service. 'You've read Milton. The loss of innocence. You had that. It can be regained. Through the writing.'

I think of Freud. Love and work. Work and love. Of Diana Athill, Naipaul's editor, who never got over her first love jilting her, an RAF pilot she'd loved since she was fifteen, until she published her first short story to great acclaim. It took that for the heartache to go.

'Don't forget, crimson and khaki,' he says.

Meeting Derek has made me want to push past wanting to live in a dark

room forever and ever. I, too, can see the shifting light in this new world.
I need to somehow land safely in this life.

'I see you, Derek.'

'I know,' he says. 'Now see yourself.'

I know what he means, what he has intended in that love poem. He
would be horrified to learn it's the same as what new-age, self-help people
propagate.

Give bread. Sit here. Eat. Love again the stranger who was your self.

I wait while he wheels himself back to his room – then drag my suitcase
down the two steps from the cottage, across the lawn, to the front of the
house, and climb into the waiting taxi.

TWENTY-SEVEN

Trinidad, 2016

Back in Trinidad, the sleeping pills don't work. I keep waking through the night exasperatingly alert. Driving, I freeze at a traffic light, forgetting where I am or how to get to where I want to go. I'm desperate for a cigarette. I hunt for the dollars I keep in the car for the boys who accost drivers at traffic lights and clean their windshields. I call through the car window to a young man. 'Can you get me two single cigarettes from the bar? Keep the change.' I thrust dollar bills at him without counting. He brings me two cigarettes, grinning, showing his gold teeth.

'Don't fight up,' he says, lighting my cigarette.

I must have looked terrible.

I circle the Savannah, dry leaves and withered pink blossoms rushing at my windshield, stop, and get out of the car to sit on a bench opposite Whitehall, with its white coral from Barbados glowing like a ghost of the past. Boys are walking home, faces shiny after a football game; the flowers around the cannonball treelike rubbery painted roses under the lamplight where I met Derek all those years ago.

I don't know how long I sit on the park bench and smoke, taking a light from a coconut vendor. The night breeze feels like the dawn, like Burrimummy's minty breath after she prays. Over the cicadas and frogs, I hear the roar of lions from the zoo, caged and drugged. I get into the car, look at the key, ignition and brakes and am unsure what to do with it all. I understand I've forgotten how to drive. I call Sadiq, who comes for me.

I must have learnt circling from Burrimummy. I wheel now, from the bedroom to balcony to guest room... In Rest House Road, she would shout out to Mummy from the bedroom, 'Nur, I loved you. I took care of you', and then she would move to sit at the piano with her head bent, wondering what happened to her.

Restive, despite the sleeping pill, I circle towards the kitchen and hear Sadiq calming Pia, calming Tej. Soft, low voices, the three of them sorting things out between themselves. It began a long time ago, this thing they have: Groups of Three. It's a joke that Tej started in a museum in London after Tej, Pia and Sadiq wanted to see one thing, and I another. 'Groups of three, Ma,' he said, the three of them laughing, and I stood there suddenly not sure of what I wanted to see.

Now, of the two of us, Sadiq, the man on whom I've pinned every failure, every broken night, is the calm one – he of the formerly explosive temper saying, calm down, calm down, to us all.

My son, Tej, is saying, 'Mummy is this amazing person who gets pulled down by wanting to sort everyone out, which makes her resentful.' When did he turn so insightful?

'Mummy is highly strung, wanting things to look right,' says Pia. 'Thank God Aunty Angel calls and calms me every day.'

What about me, I want to say. I'm your mother. I was tough, but I know the world is full of bastards.

Angel has told me nothing of calling Pia. She holds every card close. She raised her daughter as gently as a rose petal, and I'd brought up mine to brave storms. 'I want you to be able to land in Timbuktu in a parachute and survive,' I used to say to Pia.

What I want to say to Pia now is: I'm your mother, and you are your own person, but I would die for you (I hear her saying, *Ma, don't be so dramatic*). You can't survive if you're tender.

I try not to think of our estrangement, her keeping me at arm's length for the years she's been at boarding school, saying that she couldn't risk another of my outbursts. I thought I had spent my time shielding them, helping them grow to be their best selves and soar. Pia once said, 'Mummy, you will move a truck with your hands if you think it's in our way.' I wonder if she still thinks that. Tej wrote to me, thanking me for loving him, for understanding him in his wordless spaces.

I hear Tej say, 'Maybe Mummy needs more structure. Working all night, sleeping funny hours.'

Now they are adults, I don't seem to know them.

The doorbell rings. Sounds of welcome, laughter, glasses, music. Whatever damage I did, it hasn't been insuperable. But it could be.

I slide back upstairs, quietly. I think that nobody in this family sees things in the same way. They don't consider my working from home, my writing is a real job. They don't know me. When I felt unloved or left out by my parents, I didn't stop loving them. I stopped loving myself. I hope I've not done this to them.

Later, I wander into the guest room where Sadiq is lying in bed, reading. His calm infuriates me. As I approach, he raises one shoulder, a gesture I'm familiar with, but something infinitely tired in his eyes strikes me. He's expecting me to rage.

'I'm sorry,' I say, sitting down.

'I don't know what to do about us,' he says.

Those were my lines. What was Sadiq saying?

'What do you mean, my Sadu?' My hands are on his face. I am kissing his eyes, his nose, his lips. 'No, my Sadiq, I love you.'

'The children are fed up. I am fed up.'

'What do you mean?'

'Look, Poppet, for the hundredth time, I know I had a bad temper, but that was long ago when the children were babies. You never forgive, never forget. I'm sorry for hurting your feelings. I've tried and tried. Now you're hurting us all. You're relentless.'

'What do you mean?'

'I mean,' he says, 'I can't live like this, and I can't leave since I love you, so this has to stop. I've paid and paid and paid. No more. You're punishing us. You don't see your blind spots.'

My blind spots. This shouting. The children speaking of my rage.

What did he mean? I had thought that Pia, with her beauty and her brilliance, had to be prepared for the world. My mother taught me tough love, and that's what got me through life.

I ask Sadiq, 'What do you want? You want out?'

He nods. 'Yes. I'll do whatever you want. We'll do that. If you want to stay, you must. If you want to leave, I'll help you. Everything remains ours. You won't want for anything.'

Wow, he's willing to pay a high price to get rid of me.

'Except for your company?'

He looks directly at me. When did his eyes get so hurt looking?

'We all love you, you know, but do you think you can stop being angry? Don't push your daughter away.'

I shake Sadiq off.

'I need to sleep,' I say, feeling the rage of the caged.

As I try to sleep, Baptist voices spin around the neighbourhood, buzzing like mosquitoes in the rainy season; it's impossible to identify which nearby house, garage or yard they come from or if they are in my head.

The humming of 'Onward, Christian Soldiers' sounds as smooth as cocoa butter, but the accompanying voices, speaking in tongues and catching the spirit, are punctuated by the gunshot sounds of bamboo being split by a cutlass as decorative stands for the upcoming Hindu festival of lights.

I hear Burrimummy's voice, saying, 'No, no, that's wrong, not Christian soldiers, Mohammedan soldiers, surely.' I feel my eyes get heavy as I read an old school copy of *The Tempest*, by my bedside since my return from St Lucia.

Be not afeard; the isle is full of noises
Sounds, and sweet airs, that give delight and hurt not.
Sometimes a thousand twangling instruments
Will hum about mine ears; and sometime voices,

That, if I then had waked after long sleep,
Will make me sleep again…

I dream Angel is five years old, crying, refusing to believe Burrimummy has died, saying in warbling baby language, in Urdu, 'Nei, nei, nei. No, no, no.'

The phone by my bedside rings shrilly. The voice on the line is distinct. It's an English voice, Stella, Burrimummy's spying English housekeeper, calling long distance from a long time ago, from the palace in Bhopal, saying, 'I can't tell you – I can't tell you. It's your grandmother. She's gone.'

I am saying, 'Speak up; I can't hear you.' It doesn't feel strange that Stella and I are both stricken by this loss, although she was Burrimummy's enemy so many years back and is dead, and I am her living granddaughter.

I dream of Winky, with giant eagle wings, flying into the sun, his face cheeky, unfallen; and Angel and me in the sea, she screaming joyfully, 'Look, I can jump deep', her head near mine, us holding hands, going in velvety warm water, coming up for air. I dream of the trellis of wood roses on Burrimummy's garage, colours shifting from gold, to silver, to dark wood until the wall crumbles. A man is thrusting roses at me outside a flower show in London, saying, 'Go on, take them, they will die anyway', and Burrimummy is putting them in Angel's bath.

In between the dreams, I wake, sweating. I feel the rough irritation of the foam on my face where the cotton pillowcase has slipped off; tangled sheets are at my feet. It takes me a few long seconds to realise that the phone hasn't rung. I must call Angel, make it okay with her.

Then I dream of the rainbow in the puddle, the nearby dead puppy. I wake with a start, my heart pounding, feeling cold water on my face. I am lying on the bathroom floor, near a bucket.

*

I wake to blankness, a white fog. I'm in a hospital bed with levers on the side and call out for Sadiq. A nurse holds my hand. I stay in bed obediently, take my pills when the nurse gives them to me at three or four hourly intervals.

The Pill Lady, with a pad and pen in her hands, crossed legs under a floral skirt and sensible shoes, says Sadiq brought me here. It was nothing alarming, she says, quick to reassure me. I'd be out soon. First, I needed to learn to do things I'd forgotten to do on my own: eat, sleep and live. *Drive.* Exhaustion, she said. *You can break down or break through.*

I wonder how anyone could feel hope in a room like this – neon lights, ghosts of other people's nightmares, smells of disinfectant.

It's difficult to know where to begin. She's swallowed me whole. I am in a cage, and she's smoking a cigarette. I don't know where Burrimummy begins and I end. Now I am her.

But you're not her.

No, no, that's not it at all. Why do we continually turn on people we love. I don't know why everything ends with betrayal.

You won't understand love until it's you who you love. Come back to yourself.

How?

Write down what love is; how its failure led you here.

After she has left, I look at the white table beside my bed where the pen and pad sit. I write the heading. 'You won't understand love until it's you who you love.' I scratch it out. So awkwardly written. I've forgotten how to write too. 'It's you who you love.' What the hell is that? When I shut my eyes, memory comes at me. I am ten, in Simla. The snow has been falling. The telephone rings. Daddy is holding it away from himself and announcing that Brigadier X, with whom he played bridge last night, had shot himself. Mummy says, 'Oh, my God!' Later, I eavesdrop as Daddy, who was sent to investigate, tells Mummy about finding blood on the snow and a bald, dead servant girl, bloodied eyes staring into space, frozen tears on her face, her lips blue. The brigadier's wife had discovered her husband in bed with the young servant, had cut and shaved the girl's long hair, stripped her naked and made her carry buckets of hot water into the snow. She'd poured the water on the servant, jabbed her eyes with knitting needles and left her to freeze. The brigadier had found the girl and shot himself in his study.

'It was either shoot himself or face being court-martialled. He had no choice,' Daddy said.

I wonder how much of this I truly remember, how much is imagination, but I reflect how all of them, the brigadier, his wife, the servant, loved others more than they loved themselves; they – except no doubt the girl – were willing to die for how others made them feel. I must sort out the difference between desire and love before I can deal with love.

The nurse hands me some more pills, which I swallow with metallic tasting canned pineapple juice by my bedside. I close my eyes, remember, and afterwards obediently write it down for the Pill Lady.

I'm with Mummy and Daddy at the officers' club. It's Holi, the festival of colour, a time of abandonment. Large tubs of coloured water are spread out on the vast grounds under old, gnarled trees. My friends' mothers and officers' wives are in white chiffon saris and thin Kashmiri cotton kurtas, drinking, laughing coquettishly and staring frankly at officers who aren't their husbands. They are sinking their white-clad bodies into the tubs of dyed water and rising shaking off the water like dogs, their white clothing wetly coiled about them and now unevenly spattered with colours whose names Burrimummy taught us: aureolin, yellow like haldi; amaranth, a reddish rose; cerulean, blue but deeper like the setting sky on a clear day. They are brought cannabis-infused milk on silver trays by liveried waiters, drink it in one shot, wiping their mouths, competing, performing for the men. Mummy stands apart, as if to say this exhibition will not give you the love you're after. Her slim form, wrapped in six yards of chiffon and silk, is like a statue waiting for offerings. I see the hungry stares of the officers and the darker orderlies shifting from the women whose breasts show through wet chiffon and coming to rest on Mummy. They want the unavailable prize, not the attainable ones. What had I been learning? That women are empty vessels until they are admired? Or that pursuing unattainable beauty is even more treacherous than quenching available desire? I knew Mummy was regularly attacked, sometimes viciously, by other women for her beauty, for the admiration she got without trying.

They didn't know this desire meant nothing to her, not if it didn't mutate into a love that looked after her. And when my father does that (even now, in his 80s, he says, 'Look at the sunlight on your mother's face, it's the most beautiful face I've seen), her beauty has done its work. But I don't think she ever had a chance to love herself until Burrimummy left Tobago, her children had left home, and Daddy was preoccupied with other things. She turned to nuns for comfort, to the Quran, turned Sufi, and survived.

The Pill Lady says, 'People who have been hurt go numb or go porous. They can also turn into perpetrators or saviours. Some of us hover between the two. Darkness serves to connect us even as it can destroy us. The trick is to allow our many selves to exist democratically. Don't let either side eclipse the other.' That's all too much for me.

Jaanaki had pushed an unoccupied person into a cage. It was as if all the abused servant girls of Rest House Road had returned through Jaanaki to punish people who believed they deserved better, because they were born more fortunate. Jaanaki had punished me for her own pain and for what I took for granted, the sense of entitlement she saw. She had been able to occupy me as a person because I had come into the world like a monkey, according to Burrimummy, emptied out of human love. I had thought, too, that if you're empty, unending approbation could fill you up – the kind the women in the officers' club were seeking with their exhibitionism. You discover that's not true; you could be the most desired woman in the world, and you could still feel bereft. That's what Mummy has been trying to say. Don't depend on people. Bow like a mendicant to that God, to that sky, whatever you believe in. I hope I'm ready to do that.

The nurse opens the curtains to reveal sun-washed milky skies, an ocean like shattered glass. There are white lilies in the vase next to my bed. It smells like Rest House Road. My head is clearer.

Today, the Pill Lady wears bright geometrical prints. I wonder how she can bear that sizzle of colour. She looks at me, pen poised over her notebook.

I say, 'As much as I tried, I couldn't get Burrimummy to love me. She had Angel for that.'

'It was your sister who was abandoned, not you. You see that, don't you? Your parents gave her away. She was doubly abandoned, first by her mother and then by your grandmother.'

I am surprised. Is the Pill Lady saying Angel had the worse deal?

'But Angel was treated like a princess. Remember the rose petals, and no one raising a hand to her.'

'Angel was made a princess, given a false sense of privilege, but not allowed to voice her loss. When she was abandoned again by your grand-mother, I'm surprised she didn't shut herself down without connection to anyone in the family. She was not allowed to know herself.'

I have lived many ages with Angel. She and I mourn two different Burrimummy's. The accordion of our relationship goes back and forth very slowly and sometimes freezes in time, so she is still my baby and I her aapa. We will make our way back to one another.

I trawl through the past, hovering between sleep, and dull wakefulness, looking out at the car park and the distant blue of the ocean.

I hadn't expected the Pill Lady's probing of my dreams, her excavation of things I never wanted to see again. She asks me about my first memory. It's an absence; I can't pin it down.

What else?

Well, there was the puppy tortured by my older, now dead brother. The way he encouraged boys to prod at my four-year-old self. But that's nothing compared to what he gave me, that's still part of me. I'm still seeing the world through his eyes. Perhaps I mixed up love and torture from the start. The way the rainbow was reflected in the puddle with the dying puppy.

Between sessions with the Pill Lady, I ask myself stern questions in her voice.

I think of Winky in a way I haven't been able to for years, remembering how the only time Angel and I were allowed in a disco in Tobago, he forbade boys from dancing with us, grabbing Angel closer when a boy asked her to dance, saying 'She's with me', grabbing me and saying, 'She's with me, too', when the same boy approached me. With him, there was belonging and possessive control.

'Do you think you deserved that, being prodded by your brother with a stick?' The Pill Lady is back.

No, I didn't, but he was just six or seven to my four. He did what he thought was expected of him, as a boy, around other bullying boys, among the army types we grew up with. He grew up with the idea of killing Pakistani soldiers and learning to swim by being flung into the deep end of the army swimming pool by an orderly. I understand why Winky let them bully me; it took away his pain.

After the Pill Lady leaves and the lights dim, the night floats back in. I remember when Winky went missing, ten days before he died. I found him, in his wheelchair, in the lift, pointing at his distorted, bloated stomach and his gaunt face. He held onto me, saying, 'I'm so ugly, I don't want anyone to see me, but he seemed to feel relief when Sadiq bathed and lathered him, with the warm water flowing over him, crooned to him, hugging him as if he were the most precious thing in life.

I call my parents after a night of deep, drug-induced sleep, still heavy-headed. Their voices come at me, anxious, loving. Desperation makes you wily: I say I've gone to Tobago to do an interview for the television station.

My voice sounds heavy even to me. 'Mummy, that time I was bleeding in the head after boys threw stones at me in the park, who took me to the hospital?'

'Why bring that up now? It was years ago. If you must know, that was Burrimummy, dear. She went crazy. She stopped a man going to work and just hopped in the back of his car, holding you in her arms. After that, she tried taking you back to Bangalore.'

'Where was Angel?'

'She wasn't born, darling. Why are you digging at the past, dear? I know it was hard for you, but you must remember, you can't have it all, all the time. Life comes in a package for everyone. Are you there, my Dainty?'

'When you were three months old, we were in her flat in Bombay. Daddy and I, Winky and you. The Marathi ayah bathed and oiled you and put you in the sun on the balcony. It was near the Parsee temple, where vultures circle to consume their dead. Burrimummy came up to the roof just in time to grab you while a vulture hovered over you. She begged me to let her take you home, hung on to you until your father went to Rest House Road and got you back. Mumma said it was wrong to separate a child from her mother.' She pauses. 'Why are you asking all this?'

'Why did you let Angel go when she was just five days old?' Five days after my own son was born, I'd held him and wondered how any mother could let her child go.

'After giving birth to Angel, I was exhausted from labour and had a terrible migraine. I couldn't bear the sound of crying or light. Burri-mummy stayed with me. After five days, she said, "I'll keep Angel and give her back when you are stronger." Daddy was furious, but he had his orders to go to Assam to command four engineer regiments for the seventeen-day war against Pakistan.'

'Why didn't you take Angel back? I could never have done that to Pia or Tej.'

'Your grandmother said she was alone, had no one to love, nothing to live for; I'd ruined her life. What was I to do?'

Perhaps Mummy was careless when she was young, but since then, she had comforted me countless times, holding my hand while I wept, never needing to be told anything. She had supported me silently in India through the saga of the unsuitable suitors, stoutly loving me through my unloved moments. I saw how damaged she had been by Burrimummy, the blows to her head and marvelled at her capacity to be so little touched by her own mother's rage. Beauty punished her with her mother's envy but also gifted her with grace. A hundred others gave her love: the builder with ten gold chains who sat and ate her food and somehow ended up ironing her curtains instead of fixing the roof; the taxi driver in London who screeched to a stop for her; the woman cleaning the toilet at the Taj wanting to embrace her. She has been loved through her dark days.

I understand Mummy's Sufism. She brought me up tough as I'd brought up Pia. She said Allah was refining me, like a diamond, chipping away at the edges so the light would be brighter. I want to tell Pia all this but don't have the words, tell her that the anger was misguided anxiety, unending love.

'Poppet, are you there? No point rehashing the past, dear; you must stop that. Your father wants to speak to you.'

'Hello, my Poppet Polly. Why don't you visit us?'

'Daddy, I wanted to ask you. What could my first memory be?'

'You were a tiny baby when I took you to a battlefield in Punjab. You were in the arms of a young major who became a general.'

'What did I see?'

'A field, tanks, and a few Pakistani dead bodies. But I'm sure you didn't see the bodies and can't possibly remember it.'

'Baba, do you still scream at night about the war?'

'Yes, I do.'

Daddy had often woke shouting, dreaming of being bombed by Pakistani aircraft and carrying dead soldiers across a river. He quieted only after Mummy sat up, put his head in her lap, the nightlight on, and read Quran suras to him.

'I love you, my Daddy.'

'I love you, my Poppet Polly.'

Perhaps some people compensate for their carelessness with you by their beauty and ability to give you a strange, big life. My parents are those people. We all have our own way of doing the accounts.

Later, after the pills gave me the regular and peaceful sleep that had evaded me for weeks, the nurse accompanies me for a walk to the gazebo in the car park, where I sit with a cigarette and read from my ancient copy of

The Tempest, filled with my childhood annotations. It makes me comfortable with the noises of this island, the voices within me.

> *The clouds me thought would open and show riches*
> *Ready to drop upon me, that when I waked*
> *I cried to dream again.'*

Watching the sea break frothy white against black rocks, I recall what happiness felt like. The ocean. It was everywhere when we landed in Tobago from India. It was there as we walked home from school, along the beach, sea pearly with the sun's light. It was there when, at twelve, I first fell in love, at a moonlight picnic, water swirling around my legs dangling off the jetty, while I stared at the outline of a boy with dimples. I willed him to turn around to wave at me. It was there when Burrimummy came with us to the beach. She waded like a warrior into the sea until her sari, six yards of blanched cotton, ballooned around her as if she was being baptised, her hair loosened, shining silver as the sun beat down on her.

Everything seems to have begun with Burrimummy, and now everything has ended there. Burrimummy wrote a will saying everything was shared between Angel and me. She, Shahnur, the queen among kings, a Muslim without compromise, had battled for Rest House Road from Victoria's Nursing home for us all, her children.

The nurse says, 'Your daughter left this.' I must have looked uncomprehending. 'A pretty, pretty girl, slim with plenty dark curly hair and a face like yours.'

'Yes,' I say, 'that's my girl.'

I read the note.

Dear Momma,

I wish I could see you today, but they wouldn't let me. I just wanted to say thank you for everything, for being the first person I would call on for any of my trivial whims, my happiest moments, saddest moments, and everything in between. I hope that I can follow in your footsteps one day. I love you best, Mom. Don't ever forget.

Your Seraphina

I see Sadiq walking towards me, imagine myself wrapped around him tonight and all the nights. I am going nowhere. I will merge my books with his.

Behind him, Pia and Tej come towards me. I breathe in Pia's curls, grip Tej's hand. She whispers, 'Mummy, remember what I wrote about loving you best.'

'I want to go home,' I say.

TWENTY-SEVEN

For every poet it is always morning in the world; history a forgotten, insomniac night. The fate of poetry is to fall in love with the world in spite of history.
— Derek Walcott

March 17th 2017

Derek is dead. I watch his state funeral on television. I wonder what he would have thought of the flag-draped casket, the cortege that made its way to the Cathedral Basilica of the Immaculate Conception, led by the Royal St Lucia Police Force band. He is beyond us all now, fully restored to his old glory with each reading, recital and hymn – a requiem for one of the greatest poets of our century. He is entirely and in perpetuity restored to the pinnacle of his life: Sir Derek Alton Walcott KCSL OBE OCC (January 23rd 1930 – March 17th 2017) St Lucian poet and playwright, recipient of the 1992 Nobel Prize in Literature. That's how he will remain. He found his place in the world.

He had called me after I was back in Trinidad. Each time he asked me if I loved him. Each time I said yes. He came to Trinidad in between. Sigrid dropped him off at my apartment once. I took him up to the twenty-third floor and wheeled him to the balcony with a view of the Savannah, the Northern Range, the ocean, the cemetery.

'Take me back. Take me back. There is no landscape here.'

Oh God, he was afraid of heights. I took him to my library.

He looked at his books on my shelves.

I asked him to recite something to me.

'"Take down the love letters from the bookshelf, the photographs, the desperate notes. Sit. Feast on your life."'

Derek's face was deeply lined, his eyes faded like pewter shades of the ocean, as helpless as a child in a wheelchair. How could I not feel love? Perhaps he only wanted another final witness. I was willing to give him that. He was too close to the earth to play any games.

He was curious, wanted to extract a nugget from me for his new world. There is no single narrative, he had said, for these islands. Indian, African, Chinese, Syrian, European. People from old continents washed up into a small city like Port of Spain, with fading memories of native languages and landscapes. Naturally, there is percolation. There could be five continents in a single face and there was a perpetual, fevered creativity, churning, surging and exploding like the ocean. He was right. How else do we produce two Nobel Laureates (we'll claim Derek) and a disproportionate number of athletes, writers, scholars and artists?

With the view of Port of Spain he loved, Derek was looking at me with the eyes of a dying man, wanting not conquest but to be told that he was worthy of love. I assured him he was. A few months later, he was dead.

It was privilege enough to have witnessed a former gatekeeper crumbling, yet dedicated to his exacting craft till the end, still crazy about the sunsets and, in a touching humility, giving of himself.

I dare not say he loved me in any sense, but it felt close to it, knowing that I could do nothing for him. I also knew that the more you do for people, the more you love them, though sometimes you have to face the recipient's resentment over what they fear is a debt they can't repay. He'd given me a lot. Work and love. Love and work. I reread the poem he'd recited, 'Love after Love', understanding that it told me to inhabit the self I had ignored all these years, while knowing that loving others can also be a bullet to the skull.

While others honour him in a state funeral, I try to remember him at his temple, the sea. I sit on the shore where we poured Winky's ashes, grey dust flying towards the water from our outstretched palms.

The sea took Winky; the earth swallowed my grandparents. My grandfather, Nawabazada Saied-uz-Zafar Khan, prince of Bhopal, lies in an unmarked grave in the family cemetery in Bhopal; Burrimummy Nawabzadi Shahnur Jehan Begum has sunk deep into the earth in a village in Trinidad, making way for fresh burials. Derek is beneath the earth in his beloved St Lucia, the unending sound of the ocean nearby.

Crimson and khaki, he had said. I look up at the sky, a lurid red from the Saharan dust, and down along the smooth brown beach.

I fancy the motes of dust swirling ashen and scaly between the ocean and the sky are disintegrated brocade curtains from that room in Savanur, or fragments of gold from Mumma's charred chiffon saris. Somehow it all glints in the night when you think nothing is left.

I allow myself one last memory. His voice.

"Though they go mad, they shall be sane, Though they sink through the sea they shall rise again; Though lovers be lost love shall not; And death shall have no dominion."

As I get up to go home, I like to imagine there were snowy egrets flying at the dying sun, like a benediction.

March 17, 2017
Trinidad

FROM THE FAMILY ALBUM

Puppa, the author's great grandfather, the last ruling Nawab of Savanur,
Abdul Majid Khan (1890-1954), at his installation in 1911, with the
British Resident, Sir Evan McConachie

The Nawab and Begum of Savanur with their children in the 1950s.
The seated child is the author's mother.

The author's great-great-maternal Grandmother, Sadrunissa Khanum Begum Mumtaz (1870-1951) presented to Queen Victoria in London 1898

To wish you not great grandeur,

Nor store of worldly wealth

But only a mind contented,

Peace, Happiness and Health.

From

The Nawab and Begum of Savanur.

The Palace,
Savanur.

Christmas, 1915.

SAVANUR

Christmas card, 1915 and the author's great-grandmother, 'Mumma', Begum of Savanur, Khaliq un-Anisa (1898-1971)

Author's grandmother as a child with her parents, the Nawab and Begum of Savanur, circa 1920

Baby Zia, the author's mother, in the arms of her English nurse, surrounded by Indian and English staff (standing), including the family's tutor. Burrimummy has her back to the camera. Late 1940s

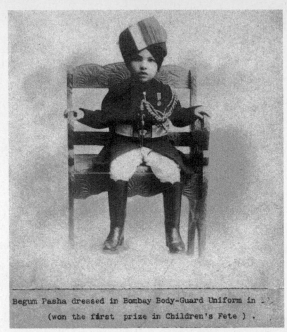

Begum Pasha dressed in Bombay Body-Guard Uniform in 19
(won the first prize in Children's Fete).

The author's grandmother wins a fancy dress prize as a colonial Bombay guard, circa 1920

Portrait of the author's grandmother, Shahnur Jehan Begum (Burrimummy) before her marriage circa 1935

The author's paternal grandparents, Mr Amar Nath Mathur (1900-1981) and Mrs Kamla Mathur (1911-1964)

The author's maternal grandparents, Sultan Shahnur Jehan Begum and Nawab Saied uz-Zafar Khan, on their honeymoon in Austria, late 1930s

The author's parents at their wedding circa 1960

My parents dancing

The author with her mother, great-grandmother, Mumma and her grandmother, Burrimummy, circa 1970s

The author, her parents and brother, late 1970s

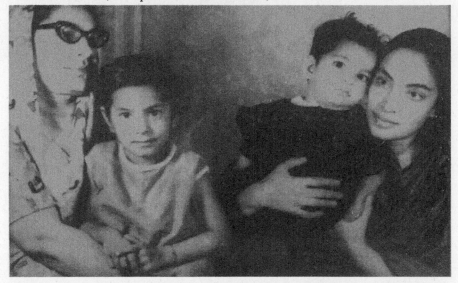

My grandmother, the author, my sister and my mother, 1970s

ACKNOWLEDGEMENTS

I've been lugging the idea of this book since 2001, when the *Guardian* editor, Libby Brooks, gave me a column to write about my family, and a former agent from Little, Brown, Jane Bradish Ellames, picked it up. Jane has long left the business, but hers was the seed. I am hugely grateful to the Leather Lane workshops, where Kit de Waal, Justin David, Annie Murray, Jake Jones, Sophie Morgan looked at another incarnation of this work as fiction.

Meeting Monique Roffey in 2013 made me a writer. Her workshops and guidance pushed me to attend the Guardian UEA workshops with Gillian Slovo, James Scudamore, tutorials with Maggie Gee.

I am especially grateful to Amanda Smyth, who held my hand when I wanted to put this MS into a drawer and introduced me to Alan Mahar, Maria Alvarez and Mez Packer, who gave me valuable advice.

Unending thanks to Marina Salandy Brown, who flooded these islands with literature and gives Caribbean writers their place in the sun.

(Faber) and Jill Dawson helped me to develop my craft. My darling friends, Marcella Marx and BB, were the first to cheer me on, to imagine an actual book. Lezanne Clannachan and Robin Hemley evaluated early drafts; Donna Hillyer, Katie Zdybel, Jay Sivell and David Haviland read later ones.

To our Caribbean greats who've tutored, guided and inspired me – Sir Derek Walcott, Jacob Ross, Vahni (Anthony Ezekiel) Capildeo, Marlon James, Earl Lovelace, Shivanee Ramlochan, I will never be able to thank you enough. A special thanks to Sigrid Nama for hosting me in St Lucia and to Anna and Elizabeth Walcott for facilitating interviews with their father, Derek Walcott.

To the brilliant Trinidad writer friends, love and thanks for inspiring and teaching me: Trailblazers Ayanna Lloyd Banwo, Ingrid Persaud, Claire Adam, Judy Raymond, Nicholas Laughlin, Joan Dayal, Desiree Seebaran, Debbie Jacob, Lisa Allen-Agostini, Haddassah Williams, Kanisha Dolsingh, Gilbert O'Sullivan, Teresa White, Francesca Hawkins, you each carried me here.

Thank you to Jeremy Poynting and Jacob Ross, the best editors in England; Hannah Bannister, the very foundation of Peepal Tree Press; Katie Read; and Laura Duffy, a consummate artist, for bringing it all together. Thank you to my cousin, Farah Edwards Khan, who has generously helped me with so much background on Bhopal.

Thank you to Donna Hillyer, Katie Zydbel, and Denise Mohammed for your sharp eyes on this.

The following books were invaluable when researching my family history: Shaharyar M. Khan, *The Begums of Bhopal – A Dynasty of Women Rulers in Raj India*, and Krishnaji Nageshrao Chitnis, *The Nawabs of Savanur*.

Finally, thank you to my family, without whom this book wouldn't exist.

ABOUT THE AUTHOR

Ira Mathur is an Indian-born Trinidadian multimedia journalist and a *Sunday Guardian* columnist (www.irasroom.org) with degrees in literature, law and journalism. She was longlisted for the 2021 Bath Novel Award for *Touching Dr Simone*, due out in 2023.

Mathur studied creative writing in London with diplomas from The University of East Anglia/Guardian & the Faber Academy. Her creative writing tutors include Maggie Gee, James Scudamore, and Gillian Slovo, and Monique Roffey.

In 2019 Mathur was longlisted for the Johnson and Amoy Achong Caribbean Writers Prize. An Arvon award-winning excerpt of her memoir is anthologized in *Thicker Than Water* (Peekash Press, 2018). In 2018 she was shortlisted for the Bridport Short Story Prize, the Lorian Hemmingway and Small Axe Literary Competition.